THE MIRROR
OF DECEPTION

THE MIRROR
OF DECEPTION

How Britain turned the Nazi spy
machine against itself

Günter
Peis

Weidenfeld and Nicolson
London

© Econ Verlag GmbH 1976
Published in Germany under the title
So ging Deutschland in die Falle

Translated by William Steedman

English translation © 1977
Weidenfeld and Nicolson

First published in Great Britain by
Weidenfeld and Nicolson
11 St John's Hill London SW11

ISBN 0 297 77343 7

Printed and bound in Great Britain by
Morrison & Gibb Ltd, London and Edinburgh

Contents

Illustrations

Introduction

When in 1959 I boarded a Lufthansa plane in Hamburg to fly to England for an interview, I never dreamed how much of my time that job would consume. In London I had discovered probably the greatest spy ever to have worked for the Germans, and if anyone had told me at the time that my meeting would still be keeping me busy fifteen years later, this book would never have been written.

Looking back it was probably a good thing that the man I was to interview in London at first refused to reveal any details of his past. That forced me to look up and question his former companions, going from one to another, trying to find my way through the thickets of the European espionage jungle. And it also swept away the aura of bogus heroism, for bit by bit the story I had proposed to tell about the 'super agent' developed into a reconstruction of the deadly game of chess played during the war by the British Secret Intelligence Service and its German counterpart, the Abwehr.

In order to throw some light on apparently illogical moves and counter-moves by the two warring parties I have not restricted my story to the central figure of that German top agent in London. In the fifteen years of research I have spoken to many others, spies and saboteurs, with many outstanding – and many incompetent – intelligence strategists in both camps. I even succeeded in interviewing two 'dead men', former Abwehr officers, one of whom was reported – in books published after the war – to have died in 1956, while the other had allegedly been hanged in 1944.

It would take far too much space to try and list all those who have helped me in my worldwide researches and so have played a part in clearing up some of the nebulous intelligence operations I have tried to describe. My thanks are also due to those who refused to help or even tried to prevent my prying into those events. By their resistance these men, the former double agents, many of them living under assumed names, spurred me on to a thorough investigation. It is quite possible, of course, that in my reconstruction of the secret war their lies have again proved an effective weapon and I have occasionally been a victim of deception myself.

Documents such as Embassy dispatches, agents' reports and lecture notes were useful to me only because they enabled me to check various dates, names or places. Otherwise these reports seemed suitable only as comedy scripts, with their biased efforts to gloss over any unfavourable truths.

Another category that afforded me a lot of amusement were the memoirs of a number of super agents and super strategists, all of which seemed to have in common the claim that the writer had been the greatest of all wartime agents. All these men have exaggerated their own importance, then as now. For in fact they were no more than tiny cogs in the vast machinery of war, unpredictable adventurers whose actions were often dictated by an urge to appear important, by love, by some odd complex or simply by greed. Some of the dramatis personae whose privacy I respect are referred to by cover names. But the others, some of whom regard themselves as historic figures, are described under their proper names and as they appeared to me.

Günter Peis
Munich 1976

1 On the trail of a German masterspy

Shortly before midnight on 5 November 1969, on the winding mountain road from Igls down to Innsbruck, a mysterious accident occurred. It did not reach the columns of the local Tyrolean press, and for various reasons it does not appear in any police records, so it has remained unexplained to this day. And as well as my life, something else narrowly escaped with me: the reputation of the quietest and safest car since the war, the image of the German 'NSU RO 80' with the new Wankel engine.

I am a journalist and was testing this car as an ordinary driver, intending to write a piece called '100,000 kilometres in the German dream car'. The article was never written: after only 26,761 kilometres, with a sharp report which burst like a grenade somewhere on my left my dream car was suddenly transformed into a three-wheeler which ploughed up sparks from the asphalt and then smashed into the crash barrier overlooking a sheer drop into the gorge of the Sill. By the lights of an approaching car I saw my left front wheel racing away on its own down the valley. Fortunately I was only doing 40 kph by the clock when the front wheel and hub parted company from the axle – much faster, and this book would never have been written.

By daybreak the car had already been towed away and was in the workshop of the Innsbruck NSU depot, awaiting the experts from Neckarsulm who appeared a few hours later. The man sent by NSU to the site of the accident fished the sheared-off parts of the vehicle out of the Sill Gorge and packed away the split pins, nuts, wheel and axle for expert examination at the main factory at Neckarsulm.

Less than twenty-four hours later Herr Helm, the travelling engineer from the factory, was back in Innsbruck with the results of the investigations. The NSU experts had only one explanation: sabotage! Yet when Herr Helm asked me whether I had any enemies, I could only say that I had no idea who might want to harm me.

Although I tried to laugh off the NSU expert's verdict, my nonchalance was a sham. I was closing my ears to his talk of sabotage so as to banish my own suspicions. Yet it was like trying to shoo away the wasps from a pot of honey – the more I tried to stifle my own thoughts, the more starkly I remembered the matter-of-fact threats made long before the accident by three different men. I had never taken them seriously until then, although they were made by tough professionals: spies and saboteurs, blackmailers and kidnappers, in hiding in remote corners of Europe. These men had assured me that they would stop at nothing if I revealed their names and their true stories. They had all been mixed up in a secret affair which happened during the war, and in which I had become more and more involved in my turn.

Something happened in the Tower of London 10 December 1942 which is directly related to the complex secret events which I tried for years to unravel. How far some people still living have that scene on their conscience I did not discover until I had researched all the factors connected with it.

None of the men who took part in that execution will ever be able to forget what took place that day, even though the execution squad was to dispatch several more Germans during the course of the war. On the scaffold the hangman pushed the knot higher to widen the noose. Judging by what was going on at the entrance it was going to be difficult to execute the German who was fighting for his life, like a tiger, with four English prison warders. At last they threw him to the ground, where he lay hitting out and screaming for help.

The hangman now became impatient with his assistants' failure to cope with the young German. 'Tie him to that chair over there,' he ordered. One of the men fetched a chair from the corner. Then they took hold of the condemned man more forcefully and set about roping him to the chair.

'Let me go, please, I'm not a spy! I'm not a spy,' the German kept screaming, louder and louder.

'I'm not a spy!' That was exactly what he protested over and over again to his judge, Lord Jowitt, 'I only parachuted over England for love. I wanted to go back to America as quickly as possible. I wanted to see my wife and children again.'

But the journey of Karl Richter, a German from the Sudetenland and a sailor on the Hamburg-America Line, would end here, in the Tower. Now they bound him fast to the chair and carried him the last twenty yards of his life.

It was learned later that on that same day the condemned man's mother, Martha Richter, was sitting at home in Graslitz writing a Christmas letter to her only son, whom she imagined to be somewhere in North Germany. 'The dear Lord will always protect you, Karl. You must believe firmly in Him.' The same 'God bless you' came from the English prison chaplain, but Richter no longer heard the words. He continued to struggle the whole time until, with the noose round his neck, and still sitting on the chair, he dropped through the trapdoor. The 'Artiste' – Richter's code name in the German Secret Service – was dead and written off. 'The man was exceptionally well cut out for the job,' recalled the Hamburg Abwehr officer who sent him into the fire with a false passport, a pistol, English pound notes and some hard German sausage. 'He was a daredevil and an optimist, always up to some prank.'

Apart from Richter, seven other German parachute agents ended up on the gallows during the war. They were all recruited as spies and saboteurs by officers of the Abwehr, the German Military Secret Service, which trained them and dropped them over England. There they were to destroy key installations of the British armaments industry, sabotage public transport and spy out military secrets. For this purpose they all parachuted out of the 'spy taxi' – a night-flying Heinkel 111 – with the same optimism as Karl Richter, their faces grim with the determination to fulfil their missions.

But every one of them failed. Seized by British police dogs, or with their parachute harness caught in a tree, they had waited in vain for help from the German contact who was in charge of the 'bank' – twenty thousand pounds supposedly at the disposal of the men from Hamburg once they had landed.

Where was this man who was to finance the missions of the comrades coming after him, the top German agent registered in the Abwehr Department I in Berlin under the symbol 'thirty-seven-twenty-five'? 3725 had been one of the first to jump out over England and avoid capture. He was at liberty, somewhere in London.

With every additional German imprisoned or executed after landing, agent 3725 became more precious to the German High Command. Karl Richter and his other companions would have to stay put wherever they got caught in the police net. The few 'write-offs', as captured spies were called in Abwehr slang, were insignificant compared with the single secret radio contact through which, night after night, the Wehrmacht High Command received 'high-grade' information from the very heart of the enemy. Agent 3725 was contributing to the 'great cause' of final German victory. He could not be put at risk by getting involved in hopeless rescue operations.

For Hitler, 3725 had become a prize that he could boast about. He told the then Italian Foreign Minister, Count Ciano: 'We have an agent in London who sends us up to twenty-nine reports a day!' In the evaluation sections of the army, the airforce and the navy, the reports were repeatedly marked 'of value', and the controlling officers in the Abwehr post in Hamburg rated their 3725 'a reliable and hard-working agent'.

His radio officer, Leutnant Richard Wein, who was familiar with the agent's career from over a thousand radio messages, recalled: '3725 got more and more reckless. Time and again we warned him to be careful, but he seemed to take little notice of our warnings. He penetrated direct into British ministries for top-secret information. Later he even blackmailed some intelligence officer, who betrayed some of the enemy's important military plans.'

Wein had developed heart trouble after the war, and he became breathless telling me about 3725 in his little garden in Hamburg-Ohlstedt. During the day his wife worked as a cleaning woman in a Hamburg tobacconist's, a thing her husband found degrading, but the hours he spent talking about the war made him forget about the wounds that kept him house-bound. He said it was just as well his wife was not there, since he had kept the 3725 affair secret even from her. She had no idea that for four of the decisive years of his life Richard Wein had handled Germany's most successful spy. He had trained him in radio here, in the little garden hut where we were now sitting discussing the past. He told me:

Although he came to us here at home every day for weeks – I had to teach him how to transmit – we never discussed private matters. When I addressed 3725 I always referred to him as 'lad'. You may not believe this, but I never discovered who he really was, his name, nor where he came from. All I knew was that our Abwehr post had put him up at the Phoenix Hotel, across the road from Hamburg Central Station, together with some other agents.

As a result of his friendship with 3725, Wein had been his long-range guide for four years: 'The cause [by which he meant the war] might have turned out differently if those fatheads in Berlin had made better use of our reports at the time. Just imagine' – Wein was getting excited now, but he still spoke in a subdued voice, as if afraid that someone in the garden might be listening to our conversation through the thin walls of the garden shed – 'to build up his cover he even managed to marry an English girl. It was fantastic. And he was the man who directed our V-weapons. You know of course that those things could not be controlled with complete accuracy, so 3725 had to radio where the actual point of impact was. Those rockets cost us millions . . . But the most crucial message was sent by 3725 when we were really up against it. I received it myself: "Date of invasion finally settled. Operation starts early June." '

That was the beginning of the end of the Thousand-Year Reich. Barely a year later, when the British were at the gates of Hamburg – the Abwehr post in the Knochenhauerstrasse had already been evacuated to the Restaurant Randel in Wellingsbüttel, and the heads of sections were busy burning their secret files – the German star agent reported for the last time from his London hideout. In the confusion of the imminent capitulation he received his last order from the radio station in Hamburg–Wohldorf: 'Stay qrv . . .', which means: 'Stay tuned . . . we will be back!' That was the end of the radio link between London and Hamburg, the last call-sign of probably the greatest spy who ever worked for Germany.

I wanted to know what had happened to 3725 afterwards, after the war – had he ever contacted any of his friends in Hamburg? Wein shrugged his shoulders: 'I don't think so; if he had, he would certainly have come to me first. Perhaps the lad dumped his transmitter or buried it – I don't know. He most likely disappeared without trace, in the days of the German collapse, in the flush of Allied victory. All I know is what happened to me.'

Richard Wein recalled: 'After the war, when they had me locked up in Neuengamme, the British interrogation officers tried to find out all they could about 3725. But I kept my mouth shut. They kept calling me names because they couldn't get anything out of me. Otherwise I could have been well paid if I had betrayed 3725.'

For years Richard Wein was the silent guardian of one of the greatest secrets of the Third Reich. Although Germany was forced to surrender in 1945, Herr Wein took his victory home with him after the war, like a trump card, although the game was long since over. His victory was 'thirty-seven-twenty-five', whom the British never caught. This satisfaction had consoled him in many an adversity.

'Do you think 3725 is still alive?' I asked. 'I am sure of it.' Wein replied, and worked out that at the time the affair started in 1940 he was twenty-eight. '3725 was certainly younger than I. It was difficult to estimate his age. At the time he might have been just over twenty. A thin little fellow, small and tough.'

I had purposely not taken any notes, so as not to distract Herr Wein or to make him suspicious.

'The success of thirty-seven-twenty-five' – Herr Wein always articulated the number with special emphasis – 'lay in the fact that he was inconspicuous.' Wein recalled that his opposite number in London was short-sighted, although it was his duty to see everything and yet never himself be noticed; also that 3725 never talked much though he spoke five languages fluently. 'His face was nondescript, the kind you see every day in the tram.' So Wein described the man they never caught, as I started my personal hunt, thirteen years after the war.

'There are people who open the door for you, politely and helpfully,' Herr Wein remarked, as if he had lost the thread of the story. 'They let you go ahead, and when you turn round to thank them for their kind gesture they have disappeared as if the earth had swallowed them up. That is the sort of man 3725 is.'

Although I had been unable to discover either the name or the origin of 3725, nevertheless, during my long discussions with Herr Wein I had at least been able to attach a face to the number, and a figure began to emerge, one that my imagination brought to life in a distinct way. It was a man hiding in the dark, whom I wanted to bring to the light in order to see whether he was identical with the picture I had drawn in my imagination.

'If you manage to find 3725, you will have got hold of a sensational story,' the man facing me said encouragingly. 'It will prove to you that the German Abwehr did not just deal in flops, as many people believe. We had our successes too, and 3725 was the greatest. I can guarantee that.'

It was not just that I wanted to prove Sir Winston Churchill wrong when he said in his memoirs that during the war no German agent succeeded in staying at large for more than forty-eight hours. I simply wanted to find this mysterious man who – as Herr Wein and subsequently other Abwehr officers assured me – had done more for Germany than an entire army.

It was no accident that the Phoenix Hotel was hit during the RAF raid on Hamburg on 21 June 1944. One of the many bombs that exploded near the station was intended to destroy the lair which housed – apart from members of the German women's forces and men on leave from the front – eight German spies due for dispatch to Britain even in the last year of the war. Four other 'guests' who were lodging there but who, for reasons of security, had not been registered, were intended for sabotage missions behind the Allied lines in Northern France.

Fortunately only the upper floors of the hotel were gutted, with the result that the proprietor survived the RAF attack. I tried to find Herr Harbeck, with the naive idea that before leaving for England, 3725 might have left a suitcase behind. When I finally located Herr Harbeck he did not hand me an old cardboard suitcase belonging to 3725, as I had hoped, but he did provide a clue which took me a little closer to the elusive spy. At the same time it drew me even further into the labyrinth of international secret service links that went on being forged far beyond the end of the war. The ex-proprietor of the Phoenix Hotel was able to identify 3725 on the strength of the personal description that Herr Wein had given me.

'The short, thin man with glasses and the timid appearance can only have been Herr Schmidt,' he told me. 'He was the first of twelve secret agents who arrived at my hotel unannounced after the beginning of the war. I had to observe these people unobtrusively, and report anything I noticed to the Abwehr.

'Schmidt,' Herr Harbeck continued, 'lived in room 101 on the second floor, where exactly eleven years earlier Adolf Hitler had lodged. At that time the original entries for Hitler, Hess and Goering were still on display in the hotel lobby. Schmidt stayed with us a long time. He often sat at table with my family and was touchingly attentive to my children. He had no girl friends. He was heart and soul for the cause of Greater Germany – ready for anything. He originally came from North Schleswig, somewhere in the border country, where the people are particularly aware of being German.'

This last casual remark took me on to Flensburg, Ratzeburg and then to Denmark. After many false trails and talks with border people and old agent recruiters I eventually landed up in Apenrade. There I was directed further along the trail of one of the best-kept secrets of the war by an old Dane who helped out at weekends at the petrol station opposite the hotel where Herr Wein and I had stayed for three days. He ran his screwdriver over the local map of 'Apenrade and Environs' to show me the shortest way to the remote farm of Georg Bruhn. He had known the

German-born farmer from his youth, and thought the old man must be the uncle of the Schmidt I was looking for.

'Schmidt's father was a highly respected lawyer in this area,' said the old man. 'His wife was a Bruhn, and Georg Bruhn is her brother, so he should be Schmidt's uncle.' Before I let in the clutch, he dampened my optimism again: 'You won't get much out of Bruhn. Here in North Schleswig none of the farmers talk much.'

Richard Wein, who was accompanying me on this trip – he had had to ask his doctor for permission – spluttered with excitement. 'I'd think I was seeing things if we found Schmidt here. Still, in his place I should have left England as fast as I could after the war and gone to ground somewhere where nothing could happen to me.' I was prepared for anything and secretly hoped that Schmidt was sitting on the tractor that was coming towards us along the field track. All the signs were that he had withdrawn to the seclusion of this farm not far from the German frontier. But it was Herr Bruhn who sat on the tractor that was now standing beside my car. I did not tell him what I had come for till later, when we were sitting face to face in his large living room.

'I'm looking for your nephew.'

'Do you mean Wulf or Kai?'

For a moment I was at a loss. Then I said: 'I mean the one who was in England.'

'Wulf, then.'

'Yes,' I replied, 'Wulf Schmidt.' At the same time I sensed that Herr Bruhn knew something about his nephew that he was not prepared to reveal. The next few words would show whether I was on the track of the spy from London or not.

'I don't know whether you are aware what Wulf was up to in England,' I went on cautiously. Herr Bruhn came back like a shot:

'Why? What do *you* know about it?'

'Everything,' I replied confidently. 'His story is written and ready. I only wanted to show it to Herr Schmidt to make quite sure we do not publish anything that might harm him. I have been sent by the editor of my magazine, just to be on the safe side.'

For a moment Herr Bruhn was baffled, then:

'Surely you could give me the story, and I could send it on to Wulf?'

So Wulf was not living there!

'Sorry, I can't let anyone have the manuscript. It's an editorial secret.'

'In that case I shall have to write to Wulf and tell him to get in touch with you . . . Let me have your address!'

Now it was essential to get hold of Wulf's whereabouts. Obviously I must not chance Herr Bruhn getting in touch with his nephew either by letter or by telephone. If I did, 3725 would have been warned and I would probably never find him. So I curbed my curiosity so as not to betray too great an interest in Wulf Schmidt. Trying to sound detached about his nephew, I said:

'There's no time to write, I'm afraid. I thought I might find your nephew here and discuss the matter with him personally. In any case I have no idea what your relations are with your nephew. For all I know you may be at daggers drawn. Also the story is due to appear in the next issue. That's why I drove straight up here from Hamburg . . .'

'In that case it is probably best if I put you in direct touch with Wulf . . . excuse me for a moment.'

Herr Bruhn left the room. Before taking things any further he wanted to talk to his wife. Wein and I remained behind in the living room, with its antique chests and cupboards. While Bruhn and his wife were conferring out in the passage, we were too tense to exchange even one word with one another.

After a few minutes the Bruhns came back into the living room and remained standing for a moment in front of the table where Herr Wein and I were sitting. Then Herr Bruhn handed me a light-blue airmail envelope:

'If the matter is as you say, you should perhaps best talk to Wulf himself. His address is on here – and his new name. Wulf now actually calls himself Harry – Harry Johnson.* Last year, when he suddenly turned up again in the company of an Englishman, he begged me not to ask any questions. It was all very mysterious . . . After all, he hadn't shown up here for ten years . . . Then suddenly he was back. On account of some matter of inheritance.'

I should mention that when he gave me the envelope, Herr Bruhn also showed me a family photograph of Schmidt with his wife and child. This photograph was to be of great assistance to me only three days later, when at last I stood face to face with 'Mr Johnson' in a London suburb. Herr Wein looked at the picture too and grinned at me. Then he relaxed the tension which had momentarily come over us all

*In deference to the British Official Secrets Act I have invented the name Johnson to conceal his identity.

9

with the spontaneous remark: 'That's our thirty-seven-twenty-five as large as life. He hasn't changed a bit.'

Georg Bruhn could not make much sense out of all this. All he knew was that as a boy Wulf had often spent his holidays here on the farm. Then he disappeared for many years, before turning up again as 'Mr Johnson'. And now here was Richard Wein referring to the mysterious number under which his nephew was registered somewhere or other. To the taciturn farmer from Schleswig-Holstein it was all very odd. Perhaps that was the reason why he asked no more questions.

It is not explained in the second chapter of the Hague Regulations on Land Warfare whether or not there are circumstances in which a spy who goes to ground in enemy territory can subsequently still be condemned to death. Before flying to London I had studied this chapter very carefully, in order to be quite clear about the possible legal implications of meeting a former spy in former enemy territory. The consequence of the possible discovery of Mr Johnson, alias Wulf Dietrich Schmidt, was a question-mark in my plans. Nor had I given a thought to what would happen to me if the English police caught me at a secret meeting with the German spy in the heart of London. The possibility of that acutally happening was as good as nil, for no one knew what I intended to do.

The situation could only have arisen if the telephone call I made to Mr Johnson from the Savoy Hotel in London had been tapped by British Intelligence. When I called the spy at the accumulator factory where he worked in the publicity department, I merely mentioned my name and asked if we could meet. I passed on greetings from his uncle in Denmark and suggested that we should not continue the conversation over the telephone.

At the other end of the line a soft friendly voice said: 'But I haven't got an uncle in Denmark. And why should we not talk on the telephone?'

I pressed Mr Johnson to agree to a meeting, and he finally agreed, though not before remarking that he could not think how he could be of assistance to me.

'Come at eight tonight. Do you know where I live?'

'Yes.'

Before getting in the tube train at Charing Cross that evening, I already knew the way. The day before I had reconnoitred the street and the house. Now, as I arrived for our meeting and stepped into the small front garden of the terraced house, I looked down the street once more. I wanted to be quite sure that no one was following me.

After a moment's hesitation I rang the doorbell and heard steps descending wooden stairs. It was shortly after eight on a hot July evening, and dusk was beginning to fall. The man I had been looking for for years opened the door just a crack and remained standing in the half-light. Beyond doubt he was Mr Johnson, alias Wulf Dietrich Schmidt, whose photograph Herr Bruhn had shown me in the family album.

I spoke my name. Mr Johnson said: 'How do you do?' and opened the door a little wider. Inside he offered me a seat on a worn leather chair. He remained standing in front of me and said: 'My name is Harry Johnson.'

Then he sat down opposite me, with his back to the window, so that he remained in the dark. I was looking at a gaunt, bespectacled face with a slight nervous twitch. Probably he was not always so tense, but just now I was about to rediscover the Herr Schmidt who had passed himself off as an Englishman for nineteen years and had felt fairly secure in his role.

The room we sat in was the living quarters of a bachelor who came home only to sleep. The house lacked comfort. Mr Johnson acted like a man in the early days after a divorce.

'What can I do for you?' he finally asked in a controlled voice.

I told him in English that I had been looking for him for a long time – many years in fact – but that did not seem to impress him. Rather, he asked me to come straight to the point.

'What brings you here anyway?' he wanted to know. So I told him that his uncle in Denmark had given me his address. At this he forced a smile and repeated what he had already told me on the telephone: that he had no uncle in Denmark.

'I think you've got the wrong man!'

But I was sure that I had found the right one: 'You sent your uncle some photographs. What's more, Leutnant Wein recognized you on them and asked to be remembered to you.'

Johnson did not react at all to Wein's greetings and the conversation went on haltingly. My questions were brief and his answers were even shorter. He just kept shaking his head and swore he was not the man I was looking for. He could not speak a word of German. He had no friends in Hamburg. He couldn't for the life of him think what I had come about. His answers sounded so convincing that I began to wonder whether this was a case of twin brothers, or of a double. After all there are about a hundred thousand Schmidts in the world, and even more men who look as nondescript as the man sitting facing me.

Still, we went on sounding one another out, and Mr Johnson began to find my story interesting.

'Carry on. Your story sounds fascinating!'

At this first encounter I was at a disadvantage. I was in a strange house and did not know whether there were other people sitting next door or upstairs, listening in to our conversation. Also, since I was asking the questions, Johnson could stay back, as in a tennis match, to see which corner I was aiming the ball at. In fact, most of the balls bounced back as if I had served them against a stone wall. Although Mr Johnson 'spoke five languages fluently', he was sparing in his answers. He said 'Yes' or 'No' or, when he was really being talkative: 'I just can't see what you mean.'

I mentioned several names he must recognize if he were the man I was looking for. No response. Then after much beating about the bush I suddenly asked him whether the name Gartenfeld meant anything to him (this was the pilot who had flown Schmidt over the Channel and dropped him north-west of London in 1940). Again no reply. Instead Johnson jumped up suddenly and asked me whether I would like a cup of tea. I nodded and he left the room.

Earlier, when I had appealed to him to speak quite frankly, I had told him that he need not worry about his safety – I had not told a soul where I was going. Perhaps that was a mistake. Now, when he handed me a cup of tea, I waited for him to take the first sip. Richard Wein, who would dearly have liked to be at this reunion with his thirty-seven-twenty-five (though his doctor forbade it), had told me that before leaving for England Schmidt had been given a cyanide capsule, just in case. At this moment I had to remember that. Johnson was facing the possibility that his life as a stolid, middle-class Englishman was on the point of collapse. My discovery of the most successful German spy of all time could make headlines all over the world.

Perhaps it was because this was going through his mind that he made the slip that opened up his guard. Johnson had still not answered my question about Gartenfeld, and I purposely did not mention that name again. I wanted him to ask the questions, reasoning that the things that interested him most would be the ones he found it most difficult to talk about. Now he put his cup down on the table between us:

12

'What is Captain Gartenfeld doing these days?'

He had lost.

I paused for a few moments before replying: 'How did you know that Gartenfeld was a captain, Herr Schmidt?'

There was a tense moment. Then Wulf Dietrich Schmidt said, with a North German accent: 'Hell, I never thought anyone would ever call me by my old name again!'

With these first words in German, suddenly the reserved Mr Johnson had again become Wulf Schmidt, whose past welled up as if some flood gates had been opened. For twenty years he had not been able to tell anyone who he really was.

'None of my English friends know how I came to this country. They all believe I have always been here. Ask any policeman, or the editor of our local paper, or any of the lads in our football club. They will all tell you: "Mr Johnson has always been here. He's a local man." '

'And what does your wife know about your past?'

'No more than anyone else . . . incidentally, I am separated from her and she has custody of the child . . . but that's another story.'

When the conversation came round to his wife, Wulf Schmidt, in his dark lounge suit and inconspicuous tie, had got up and crossed the room to some low shelves full of old newspapers and faded documents. He knelt down, and from the bottom shelf he took an old certificate and a battered notebook bound in brown leather. First he showed me the certificate awarding the Iron Cross, First Class, and under it the signature: 'The Führer and Commander in Chief of the German Wehrmacht, Adolf Hitler'.

'This is fantastic!' I could not think of anything else to say. As a journalist I was thinking not so much of the story that only we two now knew about as of the effect it would have. In my mind's eye I could see the newspaper boys swarming out from Fleet Street with the banner headlines 'Hitler's Master Spy Unearthed in London'!

Schmidt said, as if he had guessed my thoughts, 'My story is one of the great sensations of all time. Maybe you can't quite grasp it, but . . .'

'I quite believe you,' I interrupted him.

'How can you, when you still don't know the real truth? For that, you would have to have a look at this notebook. That is where I have it all written down. In code of course. There it is, just as it really happened!' When he said 'have a look', Schmidt tightened his grip on the leather-bound secret diary.

Now, in just a few sentences, he ranged over his memorable years. He mentioned events whose details I was not to learn until much later, headings that would make a table of contents for a fat book.

'Did you know that I worked as a journalist and photographer, myself?'

'Fantastic,' I said again, thinking of Fleet Street.

'Then there's a lot you don't know. That was my cover. With that I was able to move about fairly freely here . . . Did you know that I was received by the King and Churchill?'

'Fantastic!'

'I even have photographs of it.'

I knew that Schmidt's Abwehr bosses in Berlin had supplied him with enough cash to set up a comfortable home for himself and his English wife.

'So this is the house you spent the war in – and bought with the Reich's money that Canaris sent over.'

'And on top of that, remember that at one time during the war the British had four policemen billeted here in this house, with me of all people!'

I said 'Fantastic' for one last time, and begged Schmidt not to go on just now, but to tell me the story in detail later on.

'Telling stories – and especially listening to them – is like eating,' I said. 'It's best done on an empty stomach.'

'I'm not going to say more in any case,' Schmidt suddenly broke off. For a moment I was afraid I might have hurt his feelings, now of all times, just when the sensitive little man was about to tell me about his exploits. The floodgates that I had had the luck to open only half an hour ago, Schmidt now firmly closed again.

'I can never tell my story. I am not allowed to,' he stressed again. 'I am sure the papers would pay a lot of money for it. We could both afford better houses than this. But I should never be able to live in my house, because I'd never be able to relax in it . . . Have you ever had really good friends?'

'Yes, of course.'

'I mean friends you can rely on. People you owe your life to.'

At the time I did not know how literally Schmidt meant those words. It was only much later in my researches that I found out why Schmidt owed some of his friends a debt of gratitude for saving his life.

'I cannot speak about my past, because in doing so I should inevitably betray friends who gave me important items of information during the war. These friends still occupy positions of trust in British ministries.

I don't suppose much could happen to me now, but my friends – they could still be convicted.'

'But surely we need not mention your friends?' I tried to object.

'At the time we were all in it together,' Schmidt went on, 'and today we stick together. My informants of those days are still in the same boat with me. They can never get out, and please try to understand that I can't either. If I were exposed now my informants would automatically be caught also. I don't think you could really answer for that. It just wouldn't be worth it to ruin all those lives for the sake of some sensational story. I mentioned the two houses we could buy with the royalties: you would never be happy in yours either. Your conscience would not let you sleep if you had to tell yourself that for the price of a house you destroyed a German soldier who had risked life and limb for his country, and who did his duty – no more than that!'

'It is not my fault that Germany lost the war. The idiots in the High Command should have read my reports on the invasion a bit more carefully . . . But they seem to have thrown my radio messages into the waste paper basket. Too bad!'

'But what are we going to do about your story now? I mean, where do we go from here?'

'Forget that you ever met me – and what I have told you!' Schmidt suggested in a slightly peremptory tone.

After years of research, just when I thought I had netted the biggest catch of my career, I was supposed to let the fish get clean away.

'You are putting me in an awkward situation, Herr Schmidt.' And I went on to give him an explanation that would keep the door open for further discussion: 'My editor doesn't know that I'm sitting here with you at this moment, but he has financed my researches, including flying to England to find the spy who did more for Germany than an entire army! This is the kind of unwritten history that the public is really interested in reading.'

'Just tell them that you didn't find me!'

I feigned disappointment: 'That is asking too much!'

Before we parted Schmidt told me emphatically that he no longer had much to lose in life, and that he had means of stopping any further disclosures about his past at any time, 'both through London or through Bonn'! There was a lot at stake, he said cryptically, 'particularly as far as the Russians are concerned!'

I sat with the editor-in-chief of the magazine in his large fourth-floor office in Hamburg, working out how to turn the secret Wulf Schmidt project into a world headline story. He wanted the Schmidt story to do better than his famous magazine feature 'The One That Got Away'. The same ambition also dictated the tone of the campaign we were going to start before the publication of the series. The blare of publicity was to reach its climax with an international press conference in Bonn, where we envisaged Wulf Schmidt thanking the British Ambassador for the unwitting hospitality which Her Majesty's Government had granted him, the German spy, for more than twenty years. Then, with the flashbulbs popping and the cameras whirring, Schmidt would hand over his British passport and the press card which identified him as Harry Johnson, and which had gained him entry everywhere during the war – particularly into the Ministry of Defence.

While we were sitting in Hamburg working out the programme for a grand homecoming, the hero of our story was sitting unsuspecting in the publicity department of the company he worked for, with no intention of giving up his English disguise.

'Surely it must be possible to solve this problem,' said the editor-in-chief. 'How much does a man like that earn over there?'

'No idea. Schmidt runs an old Morris. He is decently dressed and not too badly off . . . I reckon he gets about fifteen hundred Marks.'

'In that case we'll employ him in our research department – for life. If he has managed to survive the war as an Abwehr agent I won't need any references . . .' He was getting quite enthusiastic at the idea of installing Germany's most successful spy in his office.

With the offer of a six-figure royalty and adequate compensation for giving up his residency in England, I thought I might be able to induce Schmidt to come back to Germany. Instead I got the cold shoulder, and 'Mr Johnson' was offended by the idea that one could uproot a man with money and a new house.

'You can't replace the friends I've lived with for twenty years,' he protested, 'even though they were all my enemies. In any case, talk is cheap.'

From this last remark I thought I could detect a faint chance of bringing Schmidt round.

A week later I sat in the same worn leather chair and handed the former spy a written offer from the magazine. He was well aware of his importance, and reacted like an oyster on the point of losing its precious pearl: 'Keep your money, and leave me in peace.'

Next morning, I was back in the office on the fourth floor of the

Hamburg office reporting the sorry outcome of my negotiations ('Schmidt doesn't want anything ... Schmidt won't say anything ... Schmidt isn't coming'). I was asked, 'Does this man really exist, or are you just imagining things?'

Next morning, before boarding the plane for London at Hamburg-Fuhlsbüttel, I made the editor of the magazine promise that he would not tell anyone the name or the address of the man we were going to see together. With this understanding he accompanied me to London, to the grey terraced house. There Schmidt greeted the uninvited guest from Hamburg with the words: 'You could have saved yourself the journey!'

Despite this discouraging reception we talked to Wulf Schmidt for more than an hour, till both sides had exhausted all their arguments. Yet what we left behind in the dreary house after taking our leave was a man who had become unsure of himself, still clutching his brown notebook, and with the fear that we might drop our bombshell at any time.

When we got into the tube train to Charing Cross, we were both clear about our next step. The editor-in-chief only wanted to know one thing: 'How long will it take you to wear down this man?'

'Perhaps ten years,' I said, 'but it might be very much sooner!'

With these last two words I was really relying more on intuition than anything else, for I had noted one tiny clue: a golden pin which Schmidt wore on his right lapel, and which bore two small wheels connected with a cross. I knew this badge and wondered what Schmidt had got to do with Mainz.

In the carnival city on the Rhine there was no reason to make guesses about the past of a foreign guest whom everyone I asked described as 'typically English'. His background was well known to the city fathers of Mainz, and he was above suspicion. So it was an unsuspecting Mayor Stein who on 10 May 1959 had welcomed the English guest of honour, Harry Johnson, here as the emissary of their twin town in England to attend the twinning exhibition in the Palace of the former Electors.

When Johnson, surrounded by the Mainz accordion ensemble, thanked them in English for the invitation (the head of the City Library had to translate his speech into German!), none of the dignitaries present had any idea that the amiable Englishman in the dark double-breasted suit had once been called Schmidt. No one listening to his speech would have believed that 'Mr Johnson' – who had done much, after the war, to help restore Anglo-German relations – was the same secret agent thirty-seven-twenty-five who had been decorated by Hitler for bravery. While he spoke about 'healing the wounds of war', the Iron Cross, First Class, lay in a drawer at home as a perpetual secret reminder of those wounds.

In Mainz no one knows to this day who Mr Johnson really was. During my inquiries I have never said a word about the past of the guest of honour from England. On the contrary, my main interest as a journalist now centred on the many links between the twin towns, a plausible cover as I worked to unearth the secret that Wulf Schmidt did not want to divulge at any price.

With the help of a letter from the town clerk to the Mayor of Mainz ('It was a pleasant surprise when Mr Johnson handed me your present of two records of Beethoven's Ninth Symphony . . .'), and with the aid of an English colleague who was also very interested in the efforts of the twinning society to promote friendship between the two countries, I finally got in touch with Mr Johnson's immediate circle, and obtained a description from the pen of his best friend.

During the war Mr Johnson worked for a photographic agency in town. At that time our paper did not have a full-time photographer, so Harry was sent off to record various events. He was an excellent photographer and very accurate in his work.

After the war he worked full-time for our local paper. He was an interesting person, but there must have been something in his past, because he was very reticent about his background. He told me once that he was Danish, born in Schleswig-Holstein, in the border region between Denmark and Germany. He had served in the Danish army and had subsequently been sent by Unilever as a planter to the German Cameroons. Then he even worked on a ranch in Argentina.

Once I went on holiday to Germany with him. There I got to know some of his relatives, who were very well off and influential.

Something odd happened on these visits, something I could not explain: Mr Johnson was never addressed by the first name I knew, namely Harry. His relatives used another, German name, which I have forgotten.

Johnson travelled on a British passport. He spoke fluent German, as well as Dutch, Spanish, Swedish, French and Italian.

On our journey he was constantly troubled by stomach pain. He told me how, during his stay in Argentina, he had his appendix removed with only a local anaesthetic. I was very struck by this, as I had never heard of this mode of operating before.

Johnson is very gregarious and has a lot of friends, particularly among the police. Two of them even used to live in his house. He is a crossword fanatic.

During the war he lived for a while in accommodation on the edge of town. Now I remember something else he told me: before he started working for our paper as a freelance photographer in 1943, he must have been employed in some curious government outfit on the northern outskirts of London. There, he told me, he had to interpret aerial photographs from Germany . . .

What was the connection between Schmidt, the German spy in London, and the highly decorated Luftwaffe officer of the same name who according to the employment index of the German High Command was 'temporarily seconded in 1943 to the Central Photographic Section of the Reich Air Ministry', and who was employed there on the same kind of evaluation of aerial photographs as his namesake in England?

The connection was startling, and set me another conundrum: the Luftwaffe Captain Kai Schmidt in the Central Photographic Section in Berlin was the brother of Wulf Schmidt in London, who had apparently succeeded in infiltrating the very nerve centre of the RAF.

For six months I rummaged among military archives and reference indexes. I flew back and forth between Hamburg and London a dozen times, until the ring around Wulf Schmidt slowly began to tighten. One further chapter of his past I discovered in a letter filed in the accounts department of the African Fruit Company at 1 Trostbrücke in Hamburg. In this letter, dated 2 December 1959, Schmidt had dropped his disguise for the first time. Apparently he needed money and had remembered that he had 800 Reichsmarks to his credit with the African Fruit Company, dating from his employment by them before the war, and deposited in a trustee account in the Hamburg Volksbank. Without any further explanation he wrote: '. . . Please note that in the meantime I have changed my name.' The signature read: 'Harry Johnson, formerly Wulf Schmidt'.

It was only a short journey from the firm's accounts department to visit Georg Storm, the retired business manager of the AFC in Cameroon. He told me:

The African Fruit Company owned an enormous banana plantation at the foot of the Cameroon Mountain, which was divided up into smaller holdings. On one of them, 'Sun Farm', lived Wulf Schmidt, earning a salary of twenty pounds a month. A houseboy, personal cook, board and lodgings were part of the salary. Because of the vermin Schmidt, like the other farm managers, lived in a house on stilts, standing some six feet above ground. In those days our vermin were lizards, geckos and snakes . . .

The houses were a considerable distance apart, and linked by telephone. If you could not find anything to do in the evenings you took to booze. Wulf Schmidt did a lot of reading – and I still remember his collection of HMV records.

The farms were also connected by a narrow-gauge railway that took the bananas down to the harbour. We had radio on the plantation too, and even in the middle of Africa we could hear Hitler's speeches, which were awfully aggressive before the Czech crisis. There was a smell of war in the air, but then it passed again. We and the British held a joint thanksgiving service in the church. Wulf Schmidt was there too. And when we saw him going back to his farm and getting smaller and smaller in the distance we used to say: 'I wonder where that sun helmet is taking Schmidt?'

In my researches I had not yet managed to penetrate to the hidden core of his past. Still, I had a few traces; as many as a man does leave behind when he disappears from this world or when – like Wulf Schmidt – he goes to ground in the spy labyrinth.

Every piece of information I obtained was like a door opening and letting me into an unknown room. I thought of this image when I was sitting facing the sister of the ex-spy, who is married to a doctor and lives in a small town in North Germany. She told me:

The rest of us children were tall, fair-haired and strong. Wulf was small and thin; so father sent him to work on the farms. The idea was to make him strong. He had to learn to ride in Eutin. He accompanied horse transports to Argentina and even managed to get his school certificate in Berlin. He did everything to live up to his father's ideas of how he should be. But Wulf simply did not get stronger.

After a while her husband joined us, a man who viewed his work as a doctor in the same ethical and moral light that he had tried to maintain as an officer during the war, and the rest of the conversation was conducted in a tone of admiration for the brother-in-law who had gone to ground in England. In his eyes Wulf was a great, unknown hero. And his wife added: 'Of course he was for the German cause, heart and soul.'

The last time brother and sister had seen one another was Christmas 1939, before his mission to England. On that occasion the sister accompanied her brother the short distance from the Phoenix Hotel to the Central Station:

Wulf was going to Berlin to see father again. Earlier he had stuffed some ration cards into my pocket – 'You can have as many of those as you like.' I can still see him as he left. He was standing at the open window of the compartment and said: 'We shan't see each other again until after the war!' Then the train drew slowly out of the station – and I am quite certain of this: if he had a choice in the matter, he would have jumped straight off again!'

2 'Agents wanted for fast-selling export commodity'

The code name was Sealion, the target was England, the aim was the conquest of Britain. 'The British Isles will become the Western corner-stone of the new Europe under German leadership,' Hitler had said in 1940 in an order to the High Command of the Army. The successful conclusion of Operation Sealion, with the military occupation and political subjugation of Britain, was to be the last chapter in the story of the Blitzkrieg. The preparations for Operation Sealion fell into two parts: one consisted in assembling 300,000 German soldiers equipped with 10,000 guns along the continental Channel coast, the other consisted in the preparations for the invasion by the Abwehr under its chief, Admiral Wilhelm Canaris. This, the German Secret Service's part of the battle against the Western Allies, started quietly and unobtrusively in two newly decorated offices belonging to a firm of importers and exporters called Stegemann, in the Grosse Burstah, behind the Hamburg Rathausmarkt.

The two rooms were equipped with only the barest essentials. The file cases on the shelves had writing on the labels on the spine but in fact they were empty and Fräulein Kammer, the secretary who sat in the front office, was just as much a blind as the well-sharpened pencils. As a rule she sat in the Hamburg Abwehr office in the Knochenhauerstrasse typing out agents' reports. And the well-known watchmaker who did business in the same house as the firm of Stegemann never dreamed that on the floor above him a war was being waged between German spies and Britain and America. When it all started Hamburg was still at peace, though there was a whiff of gunpowder in the air. The big ships were still entering and leaving the port, and this was of particular importance for Stegemann & Co.

Almost every agent who went aboard one of those ships carrying a forged passport and a secret camera, or who was flown into enemy territory in Captain Gartenfeld's blacked out 'spy taxi' after war had broken out, had at some time come to the Grosse Burstah hoping to get a job and had climbed the stairs to the first floor and knocked at the door with the simple nameplate: 'R. Stegemann, Export/Import'. Wulf Schmidt had been one of the first.

The firm of Stegemann was a one-man business with insignificant contacts abroad, but, as any curious secret service could discover, it had been entered in the Hamburg commercial register for many years. And it was this that had persuaded Hauptmann Dr Praetorius, the head of the economic intelligence section of the Hamburg Abwehr station, to take over the firm as a cover for the German Secret Service.

Herr Stegemann himself was in his late fifties, and in appearance the perfect caricature of the portly manager: large, bald and powerful. He cared little what his new 'sleeping partners' wanted to export – after all they were paying him a fixed salary. He was quite content to pay the rent and the electricity bills in his own name and to go to the newspaper offices to collect the letters that had been sent to a box number in reply to an advertisement for potential agents for a 'fast-selling export commodity'. But he was never allowed to open those letters, nor to talk to the applicants when they arrived, apart from exchanging the usual greetings.

The task of making the initial contact and summing the applicants up – of 'talent spotting' – fell to Dr Scholz, alias Leutnant Huckriede. In the opinion of his superior officer Dr Praetorius he was practically pre-destined for the job. He had been to school in Wisconsin, USA, and after World War One he had spent years in the United States working as a journalist. He had been to England as a member of a Düsseldorf choral society and was as much at home in London or Southampton as he was in Fréjus on the Mediterranean, where his first espionage mission, a recce on behalf of the Hamburg Abwehr station in preparation for the coming war, had taken him.

Before joining the German Secret Service he had often been useful to Dr Praetorius. As editor-in-chief of a Hamburg shipping periodical he had supplied him with aerial photographs of foreign ports and the like, photographs which were sent first to the HQ in the Knochenhauerstrasse and then to the 'fox's lair' – the Abwehr HQ in the Tirpitzufer in Berlin.

Dr Scholz was a native of Berlin and he took his job very seriously. He was a key figure because he had to be able to spot whether any of the applicants who had answered the advertisement in the Hamburg

Fremdenblatt 'Situations Vacant' columns were what the Abwehr called 'listeners' – enemy agents whose job it is to discover the Abwehr under-cover offices so that they could photograph future callers from a convenient hiding place. After this it was his job to sort out from the many applicants the dozen or so who were suitable for the Intelligence Service: go-getters with their heads screwed on, unhappy women without followers, romantically inclined girls who nevertheless had their wits about them, 'versatile ladies and gentlemen who, as holders of neutral passports, are particularly suited to represent our firm abroad'!

When Fräulein Kammer opened the door to the boss's office a hat sailed through the air through both rooms and landed on the hat rack behind Dr Scholz's desk. As the hat spun to a stop, a tall, thin, red-haired sailor strode in with a springy step and laughingly introduced himself: 'Karl Richter'.

This man, bringing the atmosphere of a night on the tiles on the Reeperbahn into the sedate offices of the export firm, was the first Dr Scholz ever chose as suitable material for espionage against England. Moreover his sphere of action was settled almost the moment he put in an appearance: Richter would use the London underworld as a base for his espionage activities!

As proof of his identity Richter produced his seaman's book and, without waiting to be asked, started on his family history:

'I've just come from the United States and have been paid off here in Hamburg. I'm married, and my wife and child are still over there, living on the West Coast. For the last four weeks I have been trying to find a ship to take me back . . . But now I've seen this funny offer . . .' Richter laughed – 'of course I would be very interested.'

He was asked what he thought so funny about the advertisement and answered, quite unabashed: 'I'll do anything, climb a drainpipe if you want me to!'

'In that case I'd try to get into show business if I were you,' Dr Scholz suggested. But Richter said he would not want to appear in public: 'At least not here in Hamburg where I am known!'

Dr Scholz was beginning to feel uncomfortable. And while he was trying to think whether there had been some clue in the *Fremdenblatt* advertisement, the sailor went on offering his services: 'I would be quite prepared to do anything you like in Intelligence . . .'

Dr Scholz swallowed hard before asking: 'And what do you mean by that, Herr Richter?'

'Whatever you say ... burglary or getting rid of someone ... I mean by force!'

Scholz and Richter carried on their cat-and-mouse game for three more meetings, and although Richter knew very well what it was all about, Dr Scholz carefully avoided any direct reference to what he was after. But at any rate he now felt sure enough of Richter's capabilities to feel he could introduce him to the real head of the firm.

It was at their next meeting in the Hotel Reichshof that Richter met his new employer, Dr Praetorius. He was the epitome of the elderly German schoolmaster: a thin neck rose out of a high, stiff collar and above it was a face with a permanently offended look and wearing steel-rimmed spectacles. Praetorius, who was also a member of the Nazi Party, was ever conscious of the most important rule of the Intelligence Service: always remember your cover. As a result this very correct gentleman, who had worked himself up from unemployment after the first war to the position of legal adviser to a brewery association, always looked very ill at ease.

As Praetorius stepped up to take a closer look at him, Richter, by way of introduction, repeated his party piece with the hat and, quite unabashed, used the headgear of his future chief for the purpose. All Praetorius could do was to look round rather helplessly and not a little annoyed.

But next morning as he signed the documents approving the 'employment' of Karl Richter as agent No. 3526, cover name Artiste, he remarked: 'This man could certainly go far!' Dr Praetorius had hit on the cover name Artiste himself. Now, he said, he felt like a circus director and began to think about ways and means of utilizing his artiste's acrobatic accomplishments in the battle against Britain.

While Richter was still being kept in the dark concerning his future, the men in the Knochenhauerstrasse were busy planning his great trapeze act across the Channel, destined to become a suicide mission. The man who could not believe his luck was being grappled to the German Secret Service with an invisible chain: first he was paid minor expenses by the firm of 'Stegemann', then there were larger advance payments – for which Richter could offer no surety but his life.

In order to play down their intentions with regard to Richter, Dr Scholz now spoke his piece about the Reich Ministry of Economics: 'They expect our representatives to supply a certain amount of information about reaction abroad!'

Richter said 'Naturally!' and laughed.

The talk about 'orange purchases in Spain' and the harmless 'information for the Ministry of Economics' was considered by all concerned to be a kind of routine camouflage of their actual intentions.

When at last Dr Praetorius initiated him into his real mission, Richter laughed, just as he had done when they first met: 'I smelt that rat from the very start!'

Now Richter was sent off on secret reconnaissance missions around Hamburg, but on the same conditions as he might find in enemy territory: 'If the works security guards catch you and hand you over to the Gestapo that's just your bad luck!'

In fact Richter was convinced that his employers would get him out of trouble. As a result he carried out his first espionage briefs with verve and self-confidence: in spite of the strict guard systems he managed to enter a number of industrial sites in Hamburg and Harburg, mostly at night and without being detected. He made detailed drawings of safe access routes and vulnerable points in the machine rooms, power plants and production sheds, where explosives and incendiary devices could best be planted.

The experts of the Abwehr station were very impressed with Richter's thoroughness when they went to check his reports on the important installations he had managed to penetrate undetected and Dr Praetorius gave him top marks for his efforts. (The same sense of satisfaction was felt, though not expressed, thirteen months later by the MI5 interrogators to whom Richter also disclosed the more vulnerable spots in those Hamburg establishments that he had so efficiently penetrated on behalf of the Abwehr.)

The Abwehr had put everything they had into Richter's training: he had the best radio instructors and the latest in secret inks, he was given genuine pound notes and a British ration book that had been obtained via Portugal. He was to be built up into the star of the Hamburg Abwehr station and Dr Praetorius was already beginning to savour the praise from his chiefs in Berlin.

In order to avoid the risks involved in a parachute landing (said Dr Scholz: 'At that time Richter would have dropped straight on to the pitchforks of the Home Guard, who were scanning the sky every night for the German airborne invaders!'), the German occupation forces simply requisitioned a fast private motorboat that was tied up in Imuiden harbour. It was in this boat, which was not only fast but quiet as well, that Karl Richter was to go to England as the secret advance guard. He was to be followed by the troops already standing ready on the Channel coast to carry out Hitler's wish that Britain should become the Western cornerstone of the new Europe.

To be on the safe side, in case he did not return, Richter had signed a contract with the Abwehr and had insisted on formulating the clauses he considered most important:

> ... and in the event of my being killed while carrying out my mission, the Abwehr will pay to my mother, Martha Richter, resident in Graslitz/Sudeten-gan, the sum of 20,000 Reichsmarks. They also agree that in the event of my death I shall be posthumously awarded the Iron Cross, First Class, and the decoration shall also be handed over to my mother.

Wulf Schmidt, who had read the advertisement in the Hamburg *Fremdenblatt* and applied to the firm of Stegemann for a job as a salesman, went through the same routine as Richter. But in his case Dr Scholz, alias Huckriede, was inclined to dismiss the application of 'this insignificant little man in the threadbare suit' after their first serious conversation. These sentiments were shared by Dr Praetorius after he had briefly cast a disparaging eye over Schmidt in the Hotel Reichshof: 'What on earth could we do with that little man? The first puff of wind would blow him over!'

It was in the course of the long conversations I had with Dr Scholz at his holiday home on the Island of Sylt that I learned about the next chapter in the story of 3725. And it was this very chapter that Harry Johnson, as he told me on one of my visits to London, wanted 'buried for ever'!

Scholz might have forgotten his agent long ago, had it not been for the fact that having practically decided to have nothing more to do with Schmidt, he suddenly changed his mind about 'the little man from Apenrade'. In his talks he had discovered that Schmidt was riddled with complexes. Could they not be turned to advantage, might not Wulf Schmidt's weaknesses be exploited?

In the next few years, when Schmidt had fought his way to the top as 'the most successful German agent operating against the British', Dr Scholz's part in this metamorphosis was not forgotten. In 1943 the Führer awarded him the Cross for Meritorious Service in recognition of his outstanding performance in running agent 3725.

Dr Scholz could still clearly remember the decisive conversation with Wulf Schmidt and the words he threw down as a challenge. It was in the room in the Phoenix Hotel that the Abwehr had reserved for meetings with their agents. Schmidt sat on the sofa while Dr Scholz stood facing him, leaning against the window.

'Now you can see, Herr Schmidt, why it took so long for us to get acquainted. After all, I could hardly give you a visiting card with "Abwehr" on it! For all I knew, you might have been an agent of the British . . .'

Schmidt smiled. He sat, hunched up, patiently listening to Dr Scholz's explanation as if grateful to him for all the trouble he had taken.

'I am not sure whether you quite understand what "Abwehr" means. It all sounds rather novelettish. Whoever belongs to the Abwehr is a soldier, but with duties far more onerous than those of any other member of the forces. He wears no uniform. He has no comrade at his side. He is quite alone . . .'

'That is just what I like,' Schmidt interrupted him.

'Being on your own is all very nice, Schmidt, but being all on your own when it is a matter of life and death is not quite the same. If you get caught there is nothing we can do for you, nor will you be treated as a prisoner of war. You will be hanged. I just want to make that quite clear!'

'The risk is the same as for any other soldier,' Schmidt replied. 'Only the method is different. But why should I not see it through?'

Dr Scholz remembered those words as if they had been spoken the day before.

'See it through! That is what matters, and it is just that which worries me about you. Please don't misunderstand me, but you do not strike me as being the toughest of men. Just imagine: you drop by parachute and land in a river. It is winter and you have no change of clothes. You may even break something. There you are, miserable and alone. No stretcher bearers come if you call for help. There is no dressing station, no doctor, nothing. I am not sure that you are the sort of man to stand up to that kind of situation!'

'How often I've heard that sort of remark! All those big strong men who say they can handle anything, but when it comes to the test they just fold up!'

Dr Scholz gazed out of the window, apparently deep in thought. Then he turned, sat down at the table with Schmidt and pulled a printed form out of his pocket for Schmidt to read.

'You can still pull back, Schmidt. You only need to sign this paper and forget that we ever met. Then you go back to your job . . . I think that would be best. Don't you agree?'

Schmidt did not answer. He folded the form and gave it back to Dr Scholz, unread. From that moment on he was irrevocably tied to the 'Abwehr shop'. The contracts, binding him to secrecy and regulating his status were not signed until later. In any case it was assumed from the start that his espionage mission would be over in a few months' time:

'By then,' said the confident Dr Scholz, 'we shall all be over there!' It was agreed that they should spend Christmas 1940 together in London.

The operational plans for the German invasion of England were briefly as follows: Army Groups A and B were to provide three attacking formations in the Calais, Le Havre and Cherbourg areas, namely the 16th, 9th and 6th armies. The invasion was to take place along a broad front, with the 16th and 9th armies landing between Portsmouth and Ramsgate and the 6th army attacking in the area of Lyme Regis. After destroying the enemy forces, a line was to be established from Maldon to the mouth of the Severn. Depending on the situation, the Germans were to occupy the more important coastal towns and industrial centres and to cut off London from the rest of the country.

In Berlin even more care was lavished on the 'second wave' than on the actual battle, for this concerned the administrative reorganization of the British Isles. Within the framework of these plans Kapitän zur See Herbert Wichmann, who had recently become head of the Abwehr station in Hamburg, was to be transferred to London as the Abwehr chief in Britain. With the practical experience he would have gained by then, Wulf Schmidt would inevitably be his most important helper. His father, the Berlin notary public and lawyer William Schmidt, would be proud of him. At last Wulf would have managed to get a steady job!

Wulf Schmidt, who had learned how to handle subordinates when he was in Cameroon, would at last emerge from the shadow cast over him by his brother Kai, who was forever being held up to him as a model. Shortly after Hitler's accession to power Kai had joined the Magdeburg aerosports club and in 1935 he obtained a civil pilot's licence at the flying school in Cottbus, from where he went to the training school for fighter pilots at Schleissheim near Munich. Then he successively worked for Lufthansa, became a flying instructor employed by the Air Ministry, and finally, when war broke out, was posted to the secret 'Gartenfeld Squadron' whose task it was to drop agents like brother Wulf behind enemy lines.

Unlike Karl Richter, on whom so many Abwehr hopes were pinned,

Wulf Schmidt was not going to travel to England in a smart motor-boat. He was going, as someone put it 'second class, single'. But as Dr Praetorius had predicted that he would be blown over by the first puff of wind they were prepared to accept the risk implicit in any parachute drop in the dark.

The danger of a crash landing was all the more serious as it might also destroy the radio strapped to the agent's chest – in those days the sets were heavy clumsy boxes. In the following months Wulf's was to act as a kind of umbilical cord, tying him to mother Germany. At that time no one could predict that it might also serve to transmit some poisons back into the mother . . .

The next 'Stegemann travellers' were two young attractive women whose names have so far never figured in any book on espionage. Their adventures would fill two fat books, with absolutely no need for embroidery.

Ursula Bayuomi was twenty-two, and apart from a very seductive figure (her radio instructor Richard Wein remembered her 'long, slender legs I would love to have wrapped round me') she had three other assets that made her seem predestined to become a successful spy. For one thing she had a perfectly genuine background. At some time, when she was still a schoolgirl called Ursula Wolf, she had travelled to England on a trip organized by her school and there she had met an Egyptian fruit importer whom she had subsequently married shortly before the outbreak of war. The marriage had not lasted very long but she still had a very useful Egyptian passport. Secondly, her husband was living in Cairo at the time, and this lent plausibility to her cover story, which was to the effect that she was trying to escape from the Nazis in order to join him. In fact her job was to obtain information which might be useful in the event of it becoming necessary to occupy Turkey. She was to report on the state of the roads, locate petrol and food dumps and try to discover whether there was any drilling for oil going on. But her main target was the jugular vein of the British war machine: to reconnoitre the oil pipelines in the Middle East and, if possible the refineries at Abadan. Dr Praetorius had to curb her enthusiasm: 'No sabotage, you understand, Mrs Bayuomi. That is a man's job!'

The third asset which the 'Stegemann bosses' thought would not only ensure Ursula's reliability but also greatly reduce any danger of her trying to go over to the enemy was her two-year-old child, who was placed in a children's home in Bad Harzburg at Abwehr expense. The idea was that the children's home should be the letterbox for reports from the Middle East – the addressee was to be the little girl who was just learning to walk.

The woman in charge of the home had strict instructions that any letters asking about the child's welfare (and, incidentally containing messages in secret ink written between the lines) were to be forwarded at once to the Abwehr station in Hamburg. She was also to leave it to them to answer any such letters.

Before Ursula Bayuomi set off on her travels the Abwehr gave her a farewell champagne luncheon at the Hotel Reichshof, which was remembered, among other things, for the fact that some careless smoker managed to set light to Ursula Bayuomi's veil and the flames might have spread had it not been for the prompt action of other guests, of whom none was more gallant than a certain Egyptian prince living in exile and whom Ursula had met somewhere in Hamburg. Everyone thought him a very charming fellow, and the Abwehr were delighted when he offered to accompany Mrs Bayuomi on her travels. He was a sensitive man, interested in the arts and something of an amateur painter who, Dr Scholz recalled, 'was so madly in love with Ursula Bayuomi that he never left her alone for one moment!'

After the party, with its unforseen fireworks, Ursula and her mother, accompanied by a large number of gentlemen, all in civilian clothes, walked across to the Hamburg Central Station and boarded the Vienna-Budapest express with her Egyptian prince. The Abwehr deputation stayed on the platform until the train had vanished from sight. The mood was a happy one. Dr Scholz secretly envied the prince, and Dr Praetorius simply said: 'I can hardly wait for the results!'

If any of them could have had any idea of what was to happen in the next few weeks, they would have had the train stopped at the next signal. Ursula's sensitive companion was not only a competent painter; thanks to his thorough training by the British Secret Service he was also an expert photographer. Most important of all, the charming prince knew of a fast safe means of getting his films to London.

Waltraut Oertel, the second female spy recruited by the firm of Stegemann, started her career in the room next to Wulf Schmidt's in the Phoenix Hotel and did not formally end it until ten years after the war in Sydney, where she was employed as a shorthand typist in the German Embassy. It was there that I discovered her.

When she started working for 'Stegemann', Frau Oertel, née Kuschel, was divorced from her husband, a Hamburg export agent. Towards the end of her career she was Mrs Clapham, and was very anxious to marry an American with whom she had fallen in love. And that was the reason for the ex-spy's efforts to get her papers in order once and for all. For fifteen years she had passed as Mrs Clapham. The British passport which had been obtained for her in Budapest in 1941 had never been queried by any authority, a fact which filled the old Abwehr Captain with pride.

The much-travelled lady's sudden decision after many years to give up her game of hide-and-seek might have had unfortunate consequences for the reputation of the Federal German Republic after the war. The disclosure that the Embassy secretary Mrs Clapham had once been the spy Oertel would have caused the German Foreign Ministry serious embarrassment, and in order to prevent it some whitewashing was done behind the scenes.

Dr Scholz, who at the beginning of the war had transformed her into a legitimate bearer of an English passport, now had to attend the rebirth of Waltraut Oertel, testifying that 'she (Waltraut Oertel alias Clapham) is a German patriot who proved herself willing to risk her life unreservedly for her fatherland'.

In 1939 that sacrifice had involved Dr Praetorius eyeing the knees of the twenty-six-year-old applicant with the disapproving look of a priest and telling Dr Scholz: 'Tell that young woman to sit properly and pull her dress down!'

Dr Scholz suppressed a laugh, as Waltraut Oertel, who was sitting on a hard office chair, pulled the light summer skirt down over her knees and hid the offending parts of her anatomy behind Dr Scholz's writing desk.

If Dr Praetorius' reception made her feel unsure of herself (he had turned up quite by chance at the Stegemann office) the feeling did not last long. As she passed through the various stages of her training one by one, from radio training in the Abwehr safe house in Hamburg (over a well-known tobacconist's shop at the corner of the Jungfernstieg and the Colonnaden) to parachute training on Lüneburg Heath, the stocky, newly hatched Abwehr agent was as jolly as ever.

But the smile rapidly wore off when she was given her marching orders for her first mission as an agent, to travel to Yugoslavia via Munich and Graz, dressed like a peasant woman, barefoot and with a scarf round her head. Apart from this 'perfect camouflage', Dr

Praetorius had provided his agent with a fat bundle of US dollar bills. Waltraut Oertel was to reconnoitre the industrial strength and military installations in the Balkans, which the German troops were to occupy at some later date.

In addition to English, Waltraut Oertel spoke fluent Serbo-Croat, which helped in getting overnight accommodation in barns and sheds until she finally managed to get herself smuggled into the barracks of a Serbian officer. Simple curiosity on the one hand and her Yugoslav lover's blind passion on the other hand very quickly led to the arrest of the German spy, who was deported to Austria with all possible speed. As she crossed the frontier into Styria, Waltraut Oertel was seized by the Gestapo, and as a gesture of gratitude and punishment for her spying activities in Yugoslavia she was beaten almost beyond recognition by mistake.

But the blows rained down upon her by the Gestapo officers did not kill the East Prussian; on the contrary, they strengthened her resolve for her real mission, the fight against the British, which she was now to carry on without mercy, but with considerable finesse. Her first blow was struck at a seventy-year-old British mining engineer, Mr Maxwell C. B. Clapham, whom Dr Scholz introduced to Waltraut in the Budapest Gellert Hotel, when she had fully recovered from her Balkan trip. The ageing reprobate from London was flattered by the attention paid him by his 'lovely girl'.

In a moment of mental aberration old Mr Clapham fell for everything that the German Secret Service planned. Since he had gone through a form of marriage with an Englishwoman living in Hungary only two weeks ago, he could unfortunately no longer marry his new idol, who described herself as Sophie Kukralova, a refugee from the Nazis. So Waltraut Oertel simply marched her Englishman off to a Registry Office where he happily said yes to every question he was asked. That was how the German spy became Clapham's daughter by adoption, entitled to hold a genuine British passport. As a token of appreciation for his cooperation Maxwell C. B. Clapham was allowed to spend a few more happy and harmless hours in the Hotel Gellert with his adopted daughter Sophie. Then the Gestapo sent him to a concentration camp to prevent him becoming a nuisance to his beloved daughter as she went about her business obtaining information on the oil refineries in the Middle East.

On her journey through Turkey the German spy was given commendable assistance by the British Ambassador Sir Hugh Knatchbull-

Hugessen, who was later to become famous through the Cicero affair. In blissful ignorance he made a contribution to Waltraut Oertel's expenses for travel and accommodation out of Embassy funds, and with that help the emissary from the export firm of Stegemann in Hamburg was able to continue on her journey to Cairo.

The Supreme Commanders of all three arms of the services were present on 2 July 1940 when Generaloberst Wilhelm Keitel presided over a meeting. Apart from the General Staff officers, the head of the Abwehr, Admiral Canaris, and his departmental commanders, Hans Piekenbrock and Erwin von Lahousen, were also present.

Keitel informed the officers present officially of Hitler's decision that 'given certain conditions' the invasion of Britain would take place shortly. The various arms of the services were to submit as soon as possible their ideas on the possible occupation of the British Isles. Then Keitel turned to Admiral Canaris and outlined the duties of the Abwehr within the general plans for the invasion. They were to report immediately on the enemy's troop strength, defence measures, lines of retreat, plans for the evacuation of the civilian population etc.

Canaris listened to Keitel's instructions in silence. Although he carefully tried to conceal his views, his features showed all too clearly the scepticism with which he viewed this over-hasty undertaking.

The conference was over. Most of the officers remained in the conference room in small groups, excitedly discussing the plans. Canaris, Piekenbrock and Lahousen were the first to leave. As they walked through the long hall towards the staircase, Canaris clasped his hands behind his back as he always did when he was nervous. The white-haired admiral looked up at the tall figure of Lahousen who was walking at his side with a glance that said: this is madness.

'You know, when it comes to crossing the Channel I suddenly develop hydrophobia . . .'

'We certainly are in a fix,' replied the Viennese aristocrat who had transferred to the Abwehr from Austrian Intelligence only two years earlier.

'We would need to land entire companies of agents in England!' Canaris sighed. 'Where on earth are we going to get hold of that many would-be suicides?'

Nobody could remember the exact date, but Dr Scholz, who had accompanied Karl Richter and a Dutch captain whom he had never met before the short distance from the seaman's mission in Esbjerg to the harbour, remembered that the journey of the German agent Artiste began on a stormy night in August 1940. The men who slipped silently with their heavy loads down to the quay must have been optimists, otherwise with a storm brewing they would have postponed their dangerous voyage for a few days. If they had it might have saved the captain, who was destined never to return.

Although the boat was fairly large, there was little room for Richter and his companion, but this only became clear when they had got the food and fuel on board, as well as all the spare lights and replacement parts for the engine which the captain insisted on taking along – 'Otherwise you can all go to hell!'

Dr Scholz recalled that these were the only words of farewell spoken that night. Even Richter, who was trying to squeeze himself in between all the junk, was subdued, still smarting under Scholz's rebuke for his behaviour at the farewell party the previous night in the Esbjerg Abwehr offices.

Dr Scholz, the controller, was worried that the beefy Richter who had been under considerable physical and mental strain for the last few weeks might become violent on the journey. Only a few hours earlier he had tried to release some of his pent-up emotions when he grabbed the Dutch captain from Ijmuiden by the lapels and shouted: 'We'll land where I tell you to!' Then he had tried to calm himself down by taking about ten Aquavits.

If it had been entirely up to him, Dr Scholz would have cancelled the whole operation and returned to Hamburg to sort things out, but after two false starts (caused by violent storms) the weather forecast seemed reasonable at last, even if everything else had not worked out exactly as they had planned it in Hamburg.

The boat bore no markings. As a result it had almost been fired at and sunk by a German high-speed launch which found it next day off the English coast and towed it back to Hamburg.

The red-haired sailor who claimed to be Karl Richter, on a secret Abwehr mission which he was not allowed to discuss, sat wrapped in blankets in one of the cabins of the launch, completely exhausted. He had managed to save his life by signalling with his torch and shouting 'Don't shoot!'

At that point he had already survived the worst: the Dutchman had gone mad and Richter had been obliged to tie him to the wheel to prevent him jumping overboard. His screams had been drowned by the roar of the waves, but then he had torn himself loose and was washed over board and there were no more cries as the tall waves crashed over him and swallowed him up.

For a whole day and night, Richter was alone in the boat, drifting helplessly in the storm. He even shouted across to his enemies for help, but the British coastguards, whom he thought he saw now and again, seemed not to notice him – in any case, it would hardly have occurred to them that the first German to land would arrive in their island in that sort of weather.

3 Spies galore: Major Ritter

Some three months after the Germans had occupied Belgium a black two-litre BMW saloon car with Hamburg numberplates turned off the Cologne-Aaachen road a short distance from the Belgian frontier and came to a halt in a narrow cutting in the forest.

The car papers were in the name of Reinhold & Co, of Spalding-strasse 4, Hamburg, and the driver, Karl Schnurre, in grey chauffeur's uniform and peak cap, was one of the most capable members of his profession. 'He drove with the aplomb with which he fathered nine children' was the admiring comment of his boss, Major Nikolaus Ritter, Head of I/Luft, the air intelligence section of the Hamburg Abwehr station.

That morning between five and half past, Schnurre had picked up the three passengers, all in civilian clothes, at different addresses in Hamburg: first Ritter, then his assistant Leutnant Georg Sessler and finally Wulf Schmidt, who had climbed into the car at the Phoenix Hotel.

Now before taking off for England the time had come for Schmidt to make his last practice radio contact with Hamburg-Wohldorf, where Leutnant Richard Wein would be waiting to receive him. Silently the three passengers got out of the car and went a little deeper into the forest, leaving Schnurre behind.

No one could remember exactly when agent 3725 made that last contact with the Abwehr radio station in Hamburg. Major Ritter, whom I met in Hamburg, thought it must have been in July 1940, but Leutnant Sessler, whom I ran to earth in the South of France, living in a country house surrounded by dogs and guarded by an armed Tunisian, said it must have been in August.

And when I spoke to him in London Wulf Schmidt alias Harry

Johnson, who surely must have known when his espionage career started, refused to tell me anything about his past and especially about that secret trip to England.

'Don't waste your time,' he said. 'You won't get anything out of me!'

So in the absence of any concrete information about the exact dates I was forced to rely even more on the memories of Ritter and Sessler, Schmidt's companions on that part of the trip. At least they were able to recall certain events that had occurred before that trip to Brussels.

Only recently Karl Richter's first attempt to land on the south coast of England had ended in failure. At the same time the operation designed to get Ursula Bayuomi to Abadan had come to grief in Budapest. Having extracted every item of information from her and photographed her from every angle, the exiled Egyptian prince had completed his task on behalf of the British Secret Service and passed her on to an Hungarian officer with whom she hoped to continue her adventures. When Dr Praetorius heard of this surprisingly sudden change of lovers he reacted sharply: 'That damned British Secret Service is at the bottom of this!' So to prevent Wulf Schmidt's mission being endangered by a loose tongue, Ursula Bayuomi was forcibly removed from Budapest and brought back to Hamburg, whence she was dispatched to the one place where her inside knowledge was not likely to do any damage – the concentration camp at Ravensbrück.

Richter had stayed behind in the Phoenix Hotel, trying to get rid of his cold by pouring quantities of hot grog down his throat, and while Schmidt, having finished his practice contact with Hamburg, was dismantling his set and stowing it away in the boot of the car, Ritter was being coddled by his Abwehr masters like a boxer preparing for a championship fight. Dr Praetorius, who had only reluctantly given his approval for 'little Schmidt's' departure, was more than ever convinced that only his Artiste, Karl Richter, could pull off a coup for the German Abwehr: 'That storm off the English coast has made that lad even tougher . . . and more *experienced*!'

The 'circus director' set great store by experience, though it was difficult to say what that amounted to before any Germans had actually landed in England, let alone those spies who – like Wulf Schmidt – were about to jump into the unknown, or like Karl Richter, Günther Schütz, Goesta Caroli, Joseph Jakobs or Hans Reysen, were soon to follow agent 3725.

Just before Wulf Schmidt had set off on his adventures, Dr Praetorius had been slowly edged out of the Hamburg 'circus' and a new man stepped into the limelight, anxious to serve Hitler with the same loyalty with which he had formerly served the German Kaiser. He was Major Nikolaus Ritter, alias Dr Rantzau, alias Dr Roland, alias Dr Reimer, alias Dr Reinhold, alias Dr Renken, alias Dr Ranken ... The choice of his cover names alone, all of which had to begin with the letter R, typified the imaginative qualities of this jack-in-the-box whose knowledge of espionage had largely been acquired out of books. The jovial forty-year-old textile engineer from the Rhineland satisfied his desire to impress by having his fictitious doctorate entered in the Berlin University records; he made up for lack of experience in intelligence work by a blind faith in the Führer and by inexhaustible self-confidence.

It was this Major Ritter who now instructed the chauffeur: 'Step on it Schnurre, we have to get moving.'

Even at the beginning of the war Nikolaus Ritter, who had climbed the Abwehr ladder in double quick time, had been at the top of his military career as Major and Head of I/Luft, the air intelligence section of the Hamburg Abwehr station. (Ritter: 'I came directly under Canaris ... he was the only man who could give me orders.') To some extent he owed this success to his two 'watchdogs' Dr Kahler (a cover name), a former collaborator of the Nazi Gauleiter of Hamburg, Karl Kaufmann, and the man who was now sitting in the back of the car with Wulf Schmidt, Leutnant Georg Sessler of the St Pauli Boxing Club which had also produced the world champion, Max Schmeling.

Kahler was useful to his boss when level-headed thinking was required; Sessler was the man who translated Ritter's more adventurous schemes into action ('without batting an eyelid'). By its complementary nature the 'Ritter Trio' gained a reputation as the most successful team serving the ageing Abwehr chief, Admiral Wilhelm Canaris.

It was after one of his long morning rides in the Berlin Tiergarten in July 1937 that Canaris sent a teleprint order to Major Ritter in Hamburg: 'In view of your long-standing connections with America you will, with immediate effect, take over responsibility for intelligence work against the US airforce and aircraft industry!'

With this general authority Ritter could now move in with his secretary in the Knochenhauerstrasse (he was living in a furnished room 'with use of bathroom' on the first floor of the Alsterchaussee No. 17, in Hamburg). His love for his secretary, whom he married on 17 March 1939, was perhaps the driving force of the Abwehr Major (whose first wife had been an American) towards his 'outstanding successes'.

When I interviewed him in Munich in 1953, Ritter's resounding self-esteem enabled him to inform me: 'I got a note from Canaris telling me that I was one of his best officers – in fact, all he could say was that I was better than excellent!'

When Canaris allegedly made this statement Ritter, who thought himself a 'keen judge of people', was working day and night. He was the man with the 'golden touch' because the five most successful agents who had ever worked for the Germans in America were depending on him like so many puppets.

Ritter insisted on taking a personal and 'comradely' interest in the welfare of each one of these agents, just as he was now taking little Schmidt under his fatherly wing on the journey to Brussels. But the first man with whom the senior air intelligence officer established 'a close human relationship' was Frederic Joubert Duquesne, a well-known saboteur and spy, who had been the subject of intensive study by the American and British Secret Services as far back as 1916. With a device in a crate full of films he had shipped from Brazil to New York, he had set fire to the steamer *Tennyson*, which subsequently sank. He had managed to avoid charges for murder, fraud and participation in the destruction of the *Tennyson* by feigning an incurable nervous disease.

Duquesne sawed through the bars of his windows in the Bellevue Hospital and escaped. In 1925 he bumped into the then textile engineer Nikolaus Ritter, and that was when the friendship started which was now to be exploited to further the German 'conquest of the world'. During the Boer War Duquesne, a South African soldier of fortune, claimed to have been one of the guards of a young English captive who was later to become British Prime Minister. It was his boast that 'I kicked Churchill's backside!' The Boer's insatiable hatred of Britain was Ritter's best guarantee in recruiting Duquesne on Canaris' behalf for work for the Abwehr in 1938.

The second puppet whose strings Ritter grasped in the course of his secret visit to America was Else Woistenfeld, secretary in the legal department of the German Consulate General in New York, White Hall, St Patrick's Place. She was to pass on messages and pay the agents' salaries.

The third puppet was Lilly Barbara Stein, a Viennese Jew. She was sent to America via Hamburg with instructions from Ritter to set up a fashion salon – 'Women usually talk about their husbands' work!'

Incidentally, Ritter's secret recruiting drive in America had been undertaken in spite of strong reservations on the part of his 'Admiral', who argued: 'It would be very awkward if you showed yourself in America. We should not risk your being arrested as an Abwehr officer!' But Ritter brushed his chief's doubts aside. He was convinced that only he could successfully carry out this 'delicate mission' in America. It may have been his painfully straight parting, drawn as if with a ruler, that convinced Canaris that nothing could go wrong. (Ritter on the subject of himself: 'When I dressed as a civilian I behaved like one, though of course I am one hundred per cent a soldier!').

He didn't know (nor did he recognize) fear or danger, and was able to calm the fears of the Abwehr chief: 'None of the agents know my real name, Herr Admiral. I know exactly how to behave and I am quite sure that I can carry out my mission without mishap!' However, even on the ship to New York a reporter whom he knew and who was working for the *Staatszeitung*, a German-language paper published in New York tapped him on the shoulder exclaiming: 'Good heavens Ritter! what are you doing here? I thought you had been called up to the Luftwaffe!' And Ritter, in his uncontrollable desire to be up front, allowed himself to be photographed repeatedly, not only with the journalist, but also at various wreath-laying ceremonies with the Military Attaché, Boetticher.

It was in this careless manner that he completed his boy-scout act in the United States, while in the Knochenhauerstrasse in Hamburg his wife arranged the transfer of financial support through the 'Chamber of Commerce' and also through a secret mail drop, an artist. (Ritter in a statement to the press: 'I cannot tell you his name. The artist, who is still alive, is a descendant of the Polish king Sobiesky.')

The biggest catch that Ritter brought back from the USA was Hermann Lang. He had been employed since 1929 by the armaments firm Carl L. Norden Inc, manufacturers of the famous Norden bomb-sight. Lang had sold the plans of that bombsight to the Germans and Georg Sessler, disguised as a steward on North German Lloyd, had brought them to Berlin from New York concealed in a hollow walking stick.

And now that the proven operator was sitting next to Wulf Schmidt, like a well-trained watchdog, he was responsible for the security of agent 3725 until the moment he climbed into Captain Gartenfeld's plane.

In order to ensure one hundred per cent security for Wulf Schmidt's journey to London, the Abwehr stations involved and Gartenfeld's special squadron had carefully tried to anticipate every conceivable betrayal of the secret mission. France, Belgium and Holland, countries occupied by the Germans, were saturated with Allied agents who promptly radioed their observations to London. For this reason it had been decided that those taking part in this secret manoeuvre should not meet again until the last minute before take-off.

Until then no one was to catch sight of Wulf Schmidt, for whom Ritter had found a room in a second-rate boarding house. In order to mislead any possible enemy agents, the crew of the plane were not billeted in Brussels but in Amsterdam. The men had been separated like the segments of an orange, so that none of them should even guess what was afoot. Ritter, Sessler and Schnurre had booked in at the Metropole Hotel in Brussels. The crew of the aircraft in Amsterdam were even more cautious: Hauptmann Gartenfeld, the head of the team, stayed at the Hotel Suisse in the Kalverstraat; the navigator, Oberleutnant Nebel, in the Krasnopolski; while the dispatching officer, Corporal Achtelik from Upper Silesia, the observer, Karl-Heinz Sussmann, and the radio operator, Wagner, had separate rooms in the Roode Leeuw. They all wore civilian clothes and addressed one another by cover names, including Major Ritter, who had chosen the alias 'Dr Renken' for this operation.

For Wulf Schmidt the Abwehr station in Brussels had discovered a particularly inconspicuous hideout, a boarding house near the old Northern railway station which was under German surveillance and in which the Swede Goesta Caroli was also accommodated. He too had been trained by the Hamburg Abwehr station and was to be dropped over England together with Wulf Schmidt. Here in the easily supervised rooms of the boarding house the two spies no longer needed to be guarded: Schmidt and Caroli, who had been carefully brought to Brussels by different routes, had been tested long enough to ensure their political and personal reliability. Now that the two were standing at the edge of the volcano, waiting to jump into the flames, their impresario Major Ritter felt he could rely on his two agents' instinct of self-preservation: 'Danger binds men together . . . each one will make sure he does not lose sight of the other!'

The fact that Ritter was right at least on this point was demonstrated within the first few days of their stay in Brussels. The group had already been waiting for a week for favourable flying weather and for a moon-lit night, when Gartenfeld could approach his target visually in order to make sure of the right dropping zone. In this nerve-racking situation, something happened that none of the participants had expected – least of all Wulf Schmidt, to whom it never occurred that his friend Goesta Caroli would fall head over heels in love with the chambermaid at the boarding house.

Although the two agents had been strictly forbidden to enter the Hotel Metropole, Wulf Schmidt nevertheless knocked at Ritter's door one evening to report the incident: '. . . And I am sure the girl knows of our plans.'

Even if she did not know it then she got to know next evening when she and her father were arrested by two Gestapo agents. The old Belgian was told that his daughter had pried into German affairs and that they would both be shot if they ever mentioned a single word about their arrest. After this threat the frightened Belgian was allowed to take his daughter off again, though with another proviso: on no account was the girl to leave her room during the next fourteen days. After that, Ritter calculated, her lover Caroli was bound to have left Brussels without a trace.

Carrots and whips are just as much the tools of an agent runner's trade as blind obedience; an iron concept that Ritter allowed to lead him – more blind than obedient – through the Hitler era. It was to his skilful distribution of praise and threats that he owed the espionage successes envied by colleagues both above and below him in rank. And it was this technique that had brought him one of his greatest coups: the recruitment of the German-born American electrical engineer Harry Sebold, alias Harry Sawyer, as Abwehr head agent in the United States.

Sebold had returned to Germany in September 1939 to visit his aged mother in Muelheim/Ruhr. When his ship docked in Hamburg a hand descended on his shoulder.

'Gestapo! Welcome to Germany, Herr Sebold!'

Now the former German soldier, who had emigrated to the United States after World War One and had made a career for himself there was not to be left in peace.

'Is it true, Herr Sebold, that your grandfather was a Jew?'

After that there was no escape for him.

Nikolaus Ritter, who had chosen the clean-shaven, forty-year-old electrical engineer as the head of the German network in America, remembered his first meeting with Sebold in a cafe in Münster in September 1939:

I introduced myself as Dr Renken – and naturally I was quite frank with him from the very start. Sebold said of course he was prepared to work for us against the Americans, but when I asked him to come back to Hamburg with me he said it might look suspicious if he stayed away for so long without sufficient money. 'We can arrange that quite easily through contacts in the various consulates,' I said. But Sebold wanted to arrange matters himself. He went off to Cologne and when he got back he told me that he had been able to arrange matters direct with the American Consul. Sebold made a very reliable impression, so I had no doubts about his integrity.

In fact, Ritter's faith in the engineer from the Ruhr knew no bounds. Sebold was instructed in espionage techniques on the Pension Klopstock in Hamburg (Ritter had made the acquaintance of the owner's daughter on his Atlantic crossing), was given all the latest gadgets that the German Abwehr had to offer at the beginning of 1940 and sent back to America. The newly appointed spy boss was the first Abwehr agent to be given the secret 'microdots', the size of a pinhead, carefully concealed in his wrist watch, and containing his standing instructions:

Coordinate the activities of the following Abwehr agents in North America and form them into a disciplined agent network. The names and addresses of the agents already working in the USA are: Col. (retd) Duquesne, 17 East 42nd Street, New York; Lilly Stein, 17 East 54th Street, New York; Everett Roeder, 210 Smith Street, Long Island; Hermann Lang, Glendale, Long Island.

Then Ritter supplied his confidant with the names and cover addresses of some thirty other German secret agents in other parts of the United States, Brazil, Portugal and even China. Sebold alias Harry Sawyer was to use these cover addresses to send his reports to Germany, particularly if his radio link with Hamburg should break down. The unsuspecting Ritter had handed over the entire pre-war German intelligence network to a man who as recently as 1936 had become a naturalized American citizen.

Shortly after his return to New York on 8 February 1940, Harry Sawyer moved into his office in 42nd Street West as instructed. The nameplate on the door bore the words 'Harry Sawyer, Electrical Engineer'. Two days later, on 10 February, an overseas cable arrived in Hamburg from New York saying: 'Arrived safely stop had pleasant journey stop.' Decoded, this meant: 'No trouble on arrival, am not under surveillance, am beginning work as instructed!'

In the period that followed, the Abwehr radio station in Hamburg-Wohldorf received almost daily detailed reports from their head agent in America: interesting information about new aircraft, convoys and troop movements and political chit-chat from New York drawing rooms that moved Major Ritter, alias Dr Renken, to raptures of delight. And this operation, planned with Prussian thoroughness, had only started seven months ago . . .

Now Ritter had his hands full: on the one hand he had to 'keep an eye on his people in the USA' and on the other he was beginning to construct his network in England. When he was getting Schmidt and Caroli ready for their mission to England (the dispatching team had meanwhile moved from Brussels and Amsterdam to Paris) he had just received his eightieth radio report from his super spy Harry Sebold in America. That was on 5 September 1940.

Goesta Caroli spent that day in Paris. But by the following day the British Ordnance Survey map of the area between Oxford and Buckingham, which Caroli could have drawn in his sleep, was to become a frightening reality. His departure had been planned for midnight. A few hours later, somewhere in the area shown on Caroli's map, English policemen might be asking him for his identity card . . .

Like a chess player, Ritter liked changing his tactics several times at the start of a game. Finally he decided to dispatch the two parachute agents to England by separate flights.

The first German soldier to land in England within the framework of Operation Sealion was to be Goesta Caroli. This was definite. What was equally certain within twenty-four hours was that 5 September 1940 was Caroli's last day as a free man. In the early hours of 6 September he was picked up hiding in a coppice north of Oxford by the English police. With this unexpected move the German Wehrmacht had lost their first and most important forward observer, who had set out to inform the German High Command of the defensive measures being taken in the British rear areas.

According to the plans, the Germans were to invade the British Isles at some time after 15 September and the heavy air raid on London, the blitz of 7 September. After Caroli's arrest there were still some eight days to go before that target date. A week before Caroli's drop near Oxford, the fighting units were given the details of Hitler's plans for the invasion in the secret operational plans of the Army High Command dated 30 August 1940. Operation Sealion could proceed.

Gartenfeld's report that he had accomplished his mission – 'Agent dropped in area ordered, without incident' – was enough to convince Major Ritter that his first operation against England has succeeded.

'Excellent,' was all he said.

With this one word he savoured his own place in history: to be in the front line of the coming attack and the guide of the first landing operations.

But at the very hour when Major Ritter went back to the Paris Hotel Lutetia to phone Hamburg after the return of the agent's aircraft, Goesta Caroli was already explaining to the British how to work the Wehrmacht radio set that was placed on a long table at which sat some ten interrogation officers. Before Caroli was taken into the interrogation room on the first floor of a former nursing home in Surrey, his captors offered him a thin soup ('It's all you deserve'), which Caroli declined. That soup was the first meal in England, a country which, with its barbed wire, searchlights, machine-gun emplacements, watchtowers and single cells, was quite different from what Caroli had expected.

The officer facing Caroli looked like 'a devil wearing a monocle'. In fluent German he alternately drove the prisoner into a corner, switched from soft words to harsh, or fired a barbed remark at him. But worst of all were the long silences, as ten pairs of eyes carefully and deliberately watched his reactions.

'Who taught you to use a radio set?'

'I can't remember,' Caroli tried to evade the answer.

'But surely Trautmann must have allocated you to one of his men! Wein perhaps or Baruth, or was it Koehn or Sierk ...?' Without waiting for a reply the interrogator carried on: 'Why actually did you go to Hamburg of all places, from Königsberg?'

And Caroli realized with dismay that the 'devil with the monocle' seemed to know his way about the Knochenhauerstrasse in Hamburg better than the guard officer there. Caroli only had to nod or shake his head, for the dark-haired chief interrogator not only knew all about the Hamburg under-cover offices, but also the real and the cover names of all the Abwehr officers, starting with Dr Praetorius, Dr Kahler, Leutnant Sessler, Sonderführer Haller – right down to the secretaries, Fräulein Kammer and Fräulein Rehder.

'Where is Herr Ritter?'

The other officers, who up till then had sat silently at the long table, laughed. Nevertheless, Caroli's reaction did not escape them. Earlier on he had told the British about his training, of his last days in Hamburg, of his trip to Paris ... In the first three hours of his interrogation he had been squeezed out like a tube of toothpaste, until hardly anything remained. And that little concerned Ritter and above all his friend Wulf Schmidt, whom he wanted to spare his own miserable fate.

The MI5 interrogators carried on questioning Caroli about his past with a kind of bored routine. On the other hand, in view of the impending German invasion, it was a matter of life and death to find out about the enemy's plans. Where were the Germans going to land? What did Caroli know about their operations? Although he had not decided on the exact reply, Caroli was prepared for the decisive question in his final phase of his interrogation.

'Who's next?'

'What do you mean, next?' asked the Swede, playing for time.

'I mean, which of your friends is Ritter going to drop here next?'

Caroli shrugged his shoulders. But that did not help. The interrogator noted Caroli's reluctance and had him taken back to his cell.

During his first interrogation at night, the same question was put again and again and with increasing urgency, until at last the prisoner told what he knew.

'But you must give me your word of honour that nothing will happen to him if you catch him,' the Swede stammered.

Caroli's attempt to make a deal for the life of his friend Wulf Schmidt was cut short by the senior interrogator – he had once been the governor of a prison in Africa.

'Out with it, Caroli!'

'The man is short and thin . . .'

'What is his name?'

'Schmidt . . . Wulf Schmidt.'

'When is he coming?'

'I don't know.'

'Where is he going to land?'

'I don't know.'

'Where' and 'when' – these two questions were to put half the country on the alert. Hundreds of observers and police patrols with their dogs waited in the remotest parts of the country for a twin-engined German plane that would approach with its engines cut out. Day and night they waited for the 'little German' who would probably try to pass himself off as a Danish refugee.

At the Abwehr radio station in Hamburg-Wohldorf – a mansion situated in a large park – things remained very quiet for a while after Caroli's jump. Twelve operators sat at their sets day and night, waiting in vain for the agreed call sign from agent 3726. The mysterious delay was only interrupted by the impatient telephone calls from Ritter in Paris, always asking the same question – 'Has he called yet?'

Wulf Schmidt was even more nervous than Ritter about the fate of his friend Goesta. Schmidt's life depended to a considerable degree on that of his predecessor, who 'was to reconnoitre the land over there just to be on the safe side'. Only when Caroli had sent the agreed signal, 'Everything OK', was Schmidt to jump over the same area, on the night of 6 to 7 September, and try to meet up with Goesta.

But after four days of fruitless waiting Ritter gave the order for the operation to proceed, probably inspired by the stirring speech which Hitler had delivered on September 4, and about which Goesta had enthused before parachuting into England: 'How wonderful to see our people at war, with all their discipline,' Hitler had enthused. 'Now . . . Mr Churchill is demonstrating his invention, the night attacks . . . if they say that they will make large-scale attacks on our cities, we will erase their towns.' (The applause becomes ever more enthusiastic.) 'We will stop these night-time pirates, so help me God. The day will come when one of us will break. And it will not be National Socialist Germany.' (Cries of 'Never, never' mingle with the roar of applause!)

Apart from the belief, widely held in German airforce circles, that Britain would be crushed by 1 October at the latest, two other more mundane factors may have influenced Ritter. For one thing the moon would be at its brightest for only a few days more; for another, three hundred thousand German soldiers, ready to invade the island, wanted to know what defences the British had put up to meet the German Wehrmacht.

The risks to Schmidt's life after parachuting were to some extent balanced by the legendary flying skill of Hauptmann Gartenfeld: only fourteen days earlier, Hitler had personally handed the forty-year-old airforce captain the Medal for Saving Life. The secret war diary of the Abwehr records the incident that led up to it as follows:

On May 28 in an accident during parachute training disaster was only averted as a result of the outstanding ability of pilot Gartenfeld. After jumping from the aircraft, the parachute lines of parachutist Leutnant Loeber fouled the aileron. As a landing on the airfield would have meant the certain death of Loeber, pilot Gartenfeld managed to land his aircraft, with great skill, on a narrow canal. Leutnant Loeber suffered a slight concussion, but is already on the road to recovery.

After this kind of heroics Wulf Schmidt felt relatively safe when, late that evening, he climbed into the Heinkel 111 and entrusted his life to the Luftwaffe, who were at that time launching their heaviest attacks on London. After the terrible Blitz on London on 7 September the survivors crawling out of their cellars had to look on as a German airman, flying high above their city, drew a swastika in smoke in the sky, a somewhat early victory celebration that made the British even more determined to resist the German jackboot trampling down their country.

At the time that Schmidt set off for England, a report from the German news agency DNB (which was however suppressed in Germany) stated that Reichsmarschal Goering had personally flown to England in a Junkers 88, escorted by two fighter planes. When he returned to base that Sunday morning he was deeply impressed by the destruction. 'I am proud to have made such a strong weapon of our airforce,' he told the DNB reporter. 'It brought us victory in Poland, Norway and in the West – now it will bring about the decision in the battle against Britain!'

The men who boarded the 'agent's taxi' at Orly airport wore grey overalls over their airforce uniform, all except Schmidt, who was in a close-fitting tweed suit. In his breast pocket he had four hundred pounds in notes, a faked identity card and a British ration book. In his trouser pocket he had a bottle of benzedrine tablets to keep him awake and alert in case he had to remain in hiding for a long time after his jump. Then Ritter gave him a revolver and finally something which might help him put an end to any unpleasant experiences if he were captured: a lethal cyanide pill.

The only thing he left behind was the address of his next-of-kin, his father in Berlin 'Unter den Eichen 16'. Gartenfeld had asked that in the event of his being killed his wife should be informed: Margarete Gartenfeld, née Benz, Oranienburg nr. Berlin, Officers' Quarters. Apart from his decorations Gartenfeld was only permitted to take with him on his secret mission his oval identity disk with his number '53658 A/8 – blood group O'.

The flight from Paris to England, which Harry Johnson refused to discuss, was described to me in 1971 by the observer of the aircraft, Karl-Heinz Süssmann, who after the war worked at Hamburg-Fuhlsbüttel airport:

I was at the airport an hour and a half before we left. I made the usual flight preparations: running the engines to warm up the oil and cooling fluid. The oil temperature was about 70 degrees, the coolant temperature about 100. Only when these temperatures had been reached was it possible to check the engine performance, and then to give full power. That was about 2100 rpm. After these checks, the fuel tanks were topped up again and the plane was ready for take-off. First though, the radio and electrical systems were checked. Finally I reported to Gartenfeld: 'Aircraft ready for take-off.'

We always needed a moon for our agent-dropping expeditions to England. We always flew alone. It was the same that time we took off from Orly with Schmidt. Paris was dark – it was wartime and only a few lights could be seen. Then we had to take our bearings from the rivers we knew which lay below us like strips of silver, only occasionally obscured by drifting mist. We flew at between 7200 and 7600 metres.

On take off, Schmidt and the dispatcher Achtelik from Upper Silesia had each been given an oxygen cylinder, made by the firm of Dräger. Both received a tube with a mouthpiece. The hold of the plane, in which the dispatcher and the agent sat, was connected to the cockpit by an intercom. Gartenfeld spoke to Achtelik over the intercom and the latter was to give Schmidt the signal to jump. The dispatcher had to watch the altimeter.

At 3000 metres, Schmidt prepared for flying at altitude by putting on the mask that was hanging over his seat. The noise in the plane where they were sitting, which was normally the bomb bay, was intolerable. With the mask on it was a little more bearable, but then no conversation was possible and smoking was strictly forbidden, of course.

Before take-off Schmidt had put on a fur-lined overall and under that he had his civilian clothes and an overcoat. It was icy in the plane. Schmidt's parachute was on his back, and secured across his chest by webbing belts. Before actually jumping, his radio set was strapped to his chest. In addition he also carried a small spade to bury his parachute.

After crossing the Channel we were almost always greeted by British ack-ack fire. After passing the Isle of Wight we flew along the coast in a north-easterly direction and then turned north towards London. After carefully feeling our way along the northern edge of the town we turned west again and then came Gartenfeld's orders: 'Get ready . . . another twenty-five minutes . . . twenty minutes . . . fifteen . . .'

Meanwhile in the hold everything was being got ready for the jump. We were down to approach height. Oberleutnant Nebel, sitting next to Gartenfeld, throttled back to cut out the engine noise. Then just before the actual jump we started to glide, with the propellers feathered.

Right up to the last seconds before the jump we flew in a kind of slalom run through the barrage balloon cables on to our target area, the road from High Wycombe to Oxford. We felt relatively safe between the balloon cables, because the British fighters could not follow us. At this point our altitude was about 800 metres.

About ten minutes before the jump Achtelik had taken Wulf Schmidt to the jump door. His parachute belts were once more checked by the light of a pocket torch. Achtelik had to shout because Schmidt could hardly understand him with his crash helmet on. Then Schmidt stood over the exit, his lifeline hooked up. Achtelik shouted: 'Good luck'.

Before Schmidt jumped, Gartenfeld gave Achtelik his final instructions to pass on to Schmidt: 'Look out, we are almost there!'.

Then Gartenfeld went on tensely reporting what he could see as he approached the target.

'Damn these balloons . . . just a sec . . . there it is . . . that was the coppice with the crossroads!'

Then we circled again and approached the target. Again Achtelik heard Gartenfeld's voice: 'Attention, here it is . . . look out . . . just a sec . . . careful . . . jump!'

At that moment Achtelik gave the agent a shove and Schmidt dived head-first into the night.

All that remained of the agent was the lifeline of his parachute and, at the end of it, the dark container in which his parachute had been packed.

After we had dropped Schmidt from a height of about 500 metres we carried on gliding for as long as we could and throttled up again when there was no longer any danger to the agent.

4 The great web: a study in Prussian thoroughness

According to Ritter, Harry Sawyer's engineering office in 42nd Street West was a howling success. Ritter was proud of his catch and satisfied that he could rely one hundred per cent on his fellow countryman Sebold, alias Sawyer, especially at a time when he himself was almost completely absorbed with the problems involved in Operation Sealion. 'Canaris,' he told me, 'wanted to appoint me head of the Abwehr in Britain!'

This appointment was actually discussed in all seriousness in September 1940 in spite of the fact that – though they themselves were not to know – Canaris and his model officer Nikolaus Ritter had already lost their secret war against the United States. The unsuspecting Abwehr were to go on financing their expensive American network until 28 June 1941. It was then that the bombshell exploded – six months before the United States declared war on Germany – and the boastful Ritter became more modest and the calm Canaris a trifle more ruffled. On that day thirty-three members of the espionage ring built up by Ritter in New York and other cities of the United States were arrested by FBI agents and charged with espionage on behalf of a foreign power. The court proceedings were to open on 3 September, and but for the fact that human lives were at stake the whole thing would have been a comedy with the Abwehr in the leading role.

But this was still in the future; in September 1940 the focus was on England and Canaris was happy in the knowledge that across the Atlantic everything was working according to plan. Had not Ritter said: 'None of the agents know my real name, Herr Admiral – I know how to behave'? Ritter was to give further proof of his determination and flair. Although the members of the espionage network were all in jail, the innocent Abwehr sent yet another radio message to Sawyer:

'Cease transmissions for two months stop have impression you are under surveillance by US counter-intelligence ends.'

The embarrassment was to be even worse when, on 3 September, agent Harry Sebold, alias Sawyer, appeared as chief witness for the prosecution and amid the laughter of the jury of eight men and three women described how he had been recruited as the chief Abwehr agent for America and produced hundreds of photographs, thousands of feet of film and tape-recordings as evidence for the treasonable activities of the accused Duquesne, Roeder, Lilly Stein and others. The costs of this play staged by the American counter-intelligence agency (including the salary of the FBI radio operator who had for months supplied the Abwehr radio station in Hamburg-Wohldorf with false information) were punctually met by the Abwehr in Berlin.

With these 'qualifications' Ritter now sat at the controls of the German secret operations against Britain – and gingerly walked into the next trap. It was in the summer of 1940 that the British also began their counter-intelligence ploy against the Germans, anxious not to make any mistakes and to obtain as much information as possible about the German plans for the invasion of their island.

It was with Caroli's radio – set up in the interrogation centre of Ham Common, a former convalescent home for British officers – that the Secret Intelligence Service roused Ritter into frantic activity. The report, prepared by the British – 'Have injured ankle on landing stop will try to go to ground as refugee between Oxford and Buckingham' – awakened the Samaritan instincts in Ritter who, promptly forgetting his principles of letting the mind dictate to the heart, neatly walked into the trap the British had prepared.

As they had expected, Ritter immediately alerted the best spy he had in Britain at the time, agent 3504, a forty-year-old Welshman and dealer in electrical goods, Arthur G. Owens, known to his Hamburg employers as 'Johnny'. This small, slightly crooked man, with a stiff neck and one shoulder higher than the other and who could only pronounce two German words properly (i.e. 'ein Bier!'), was now 'to proceed immediately and cautiously' and get the injured agent Goesta Caroli to safety.

'Johnny Owens, whom Ritter fondly believed to be in his flat in Hampstead, actually received his chief's message in a cell in Wandsworth Prison, for it was to that place that MI5 had taken the man who for years had been 'selling' the Germans to the British, and who, with even greater lack of scruple, had also been selling his countrymen to the

Germans. But whether they liked it or not the British still had to use Owens since the Germans still seemed to have complete confidence in him. And it was this confidence on the part of the Abwehr that henceforth made Owens (whose British cover name was Snow) one of the most important figures in the battle between the Secret Service and the Abwehr.

In my search for the Anglo–German double agent after the war, I discovered a trace of him in Ireland. For many years he had lived in Harristown under an assumed name, a fugitive from his own past, and it was there that I discovered the only thing that Johnny had left behind: a few hastily scribbled lines he had intended sending to a former fellow inmate in prison, before disappearing in the vast expanse of South America:

> Dear J., I have today recieved (sic) a letter from England, OHMS threatening me very strongly it seems they have cought up with me again and I am afraid I shall have to get moving. I am wondering if you are in touch with Hirsch in South America? Could you help me get there, or can you lend me some money so that I can disappear?

After the war the British authorities had deported the notorious traitor and so had saved his life, which was worthless now that the Germans had been defeated. But at the beginning of the war Owens was one of the most valuable prisoners in British hands, a hot potato that both sides wanted to use against the other, and one that might burn the handler as well as the intended victim.

This risky game entered its decisive phase in the night of 17/18 September 1940 as Owens sat in his cell, closely guarded, working the key to his transmitter. The 'chief Abwehr agent' had been told to send a lengthy message to Hamburg which had been prepared by the SIS German experts.

In the radio station in Hamburg-Wohldorf operators Koehn and Baruth received the message. They both knew the 'handwriting' of their Welsh agent ('we usually received him QSA (perfectly)') and so the Germans had no doubt at all that it was Owens himself who was working the set. For this reason Ritter completely swallowed the message which was telexed to the HQ in the Knochenhauerstrasse from the radio station, and which he now read with some emotion.

It appeared that Owens had arranged for a sub-agent to pick up the injured Caroli at High Wycombe station: '3726 (Caroli's Abwehr number) caught cold in the rain and is now completely safe and in bed with a high temperature in my friend's London flat.'

Ritter sighed.

'Thank God for that!'

On 27 September Ritter learned, again from Owens, that Caroli had recovered, whereupon the Abwehr instructed him to proceed to the area bounded by London, Colchester and Southend. In fact Goesta Caroli was in no position to go on any excursions. On the contrary, the husky sailor had to be guarded more closely than the other prisoners, as he was inclined to threaten the guards and shout at them. 'Just wait till the Wehrmacht gets here,' he would bluster, 'then you'll pay for this.' These outbursts were usually followed by crying fits, alternating with attempts to wreck his cell.

But by 23 October the British had managed to calm their prisoner down sufficiently to get him to agree to send a radio message to Hamburg. With this move they risked losing everything they had so patiently built up, but the risk was worth taking.

Caroli was unpredictable. The two men guarding him were aware of this and ready to rap him smartly over the fingers if he had given the Germans the slightest indication that he was in custody. But Caroli keyed the message in his usual form: 'Am getting down to work in the area south of Cambridge need more money.'

This latter request successfully got Major Ritter even more ensnared in the British game – 'Of course we must help Caroli at once!' So Owens received another order from his boss who, remembering the many evenings spent together in the 'Münchener Kindl' on the Reeperbahn, always referred to him as the 'Biermann': 'Please pay thirty-seven twenty-six two hundred pounds'.

Johnny Owens – or rather the British Secret Service – drew the money from the last transfer from Berlin. The cash was sent from Madrid to London by means of 'Operation Steinbutt' and there handed over to a friend of Owens, George Williams, a former police inspector from Swansea, who was also of great importance to the Germans, or so they believed in Hamburg and Berlin.

'Steinbutt' – a Spanish journalist by name of del Pozo – and Williams – the man from Swansea who supposedly hated the English – were only concerned with the Germans in so far as they had their intelligence activities paid for by the senior Abwehr finance officer in Berlin. In fact, however, they were a pair of very smart agents who had been active on behalf of British Intelligence on the London–Lisbon–Madrid run for years. The extent to which the Abwehr believed in 'its' agents Steinbutt and Williams emerges from an entry in the secret war diary of the Abwehr sabotage section dated 14 November 1940:

> According to a report from Section II, 1 West, the Spanish agent Steinbutt, sent to England by Abwehr II (the sabotage department) had a meeting in London with the Welsh nationalist leader Williams. Steinbutt has sent a report in secret ink on the position of the Welsh nationalist organization describing the energetic activities of the Welsh agents in pursuit of the tasks set by Abwehr II. Williams needs money in support of this sabotage activity.

The Welsh group run by Owens, and assisted to the tune of 20,000 Reichsmarks was to 'sabotage the three main railway lines so that the British army will be unable to move rolling stock to the north. This is important for the German operations owing to the narrower loading gauge of the British railways.'

This is a quotation from the secret war diary dated 6 September 1940. Goesta Caroli, who parachuted into England that day, had also been instructed to blow up British railway lines, and Ritter expected that Caroli, fit again and supplied with cash, would now get to work. But he waited in vain; there were no explosions nor were any more radio messages from him received at Wohldorf.

What really happened during the ensuing radio silence could only be told – if they were not bound by the Official Secrets Act – by the army doctors who managed to save Caroli's life after two suicide attempts. Then there was the British soldier, who was detailed to guard Caroli for a few days in a house in Hinxton, whom Caroli knocked down and tied up in order to make a getaway on the defenceless man's motorbike. Thousands of British policemen were involved in the chase, which ended with Caroli's capture near Ely. Again the doctors were called in, and this time they diagnosed retrograde amnesia, which in layman's language means that Goesta Caroli had lost his memory.

Wulf Schmidt's parachute landing in England had apparently gone according to plan, both from the Abwehr point of view and also from the point of view of the British Secret Service's expectations, for Major Ritter had personally informed them of the impending arrival of a 'new agent from South Africa' (Schmidt had been in the Cameroons before being taken up by the Abwehr) during a 'secret' meeting he had with Arthur Owens in Lisbon on 27 April 1940.

'We will send the agent in by parachute,' he disclosed to Owens.

'This man is intended to be your assistant. I am sure you will get on well together.'

Ritter could speak quite frankly to his British confidant, all the more so as Owens had brought along another of his friends from the 'Welsh resistance movement', who was responsible for sabotage. To him, Ritter described the sophisticated sabotage material he would supply and where and when it would be dropped. 'It will be of British manufacture . . . after all, we don't want them to recognize our handiwork,' he joked.

The meeting of the three took place in Lisbon, in the private apartment of Señora Rodriguez, whose mother came from North Germany. The charming German-Portuguese was a confidential emloyee of the German State Railway Office for Tourism. Her greatest achievement was the recruitment of a Portuguese naval officer who supplied the Abwehr throughout the war with the cargo manifests of ships entering and leaving the port of Lisbon. Señora Rodriguez ran what has been described as the 'Lisbon Roundabout' on which everyone could get to know anyone and could hear all the gossip he wanted to in this international social world. It was on this roundabout that Major Ritter usually arranged his meetings with his agents when in Lisbon, taking every precaution for his security – 'One cannot be too careful.'

Major Ritter took the same security precautions when he met his British friends in Portugal. At the last meeting in August 1940 he had given Owens' companion £3000 and another radio set: 'Now, of all times, we must make sure our communications remain intact.' The same hopes for continuing communications were also cherished by Major Ritter's opposite numbers in SIS in London, who calculated that up to that point the Abwehr had supplied them, free of charge, with four army radio sets, complete with operating instructions and secret codes.

A fifth agent's set floated down from the skies during the night of 3/4 October 1940, accompanied by the Hamburg Abwehr agent 'Mr Gander', whose real name was Reysen. Ritter later remembered his protégé: 'Reysen was small, modest, ill and unfit for army service. But he insisted on doing his bit. He had an operation in Hamburg and then we sent him off on his suicide trip from which he never returned. Later we set up his widow, who lived with her parents near Bremen, in a smart hairdressing establishment.

The sixth radio set, captured by the British authorities on 2 January 1941, was the one brought over by the parachute agent Joseph Jakobs, also from the Abwehr station in Hamburg. He too had relied on Major Ritter's foresight as he happily climbed into Hauptmann Gartenfeld's plane and entrusted his life to the parachute that Achtelik strapped to his back. Achtelik's 'Good luck' were the last friendly words that Jakobs heard on his trip from heaven to the hell of arrest and endless interrogations. These ended at dawn on 15 August 1941 when a soldier of the execution squad blindfolded him and tied him to the post in the Tower of London. A few moments later Jakobs was dead.

In capturing him the British Secret Service had again taken one of the enemy's men, but after much thought they pulled him out of the game and executed him. All that remained of the German agent were his personal documents in the name of James Rymer. These papers were a veritable masterpiece of the forged-document section of the Abwehr in Berlin, and they were sincerely admired by SIS. But even greater than their admiration for the technical perfection was their delight at the fact that all the personal details in James Rymer's documents coincided completely with those provided by British Intelligence to the Hamburg Abwehr station through their agent Owens.

'Naturally the papers must be accurate in every detail,' the espionage expert Ritter had said, 'otherwise the agent would be rumbled the very first time he was asked to produce his documents!' And in order to show the bunglers how it should be done, the wily Ritter had sent a flood of radio messages to London instructing his head agent to provide the name of a suitable Englishman, who was at least temporarily out of circulation but who was registered at a certain address.

As Johnny's freedom of movement was somewhat curtailed (he could take four steps in one direction in his cell and two in the other), Ritter's request was fulfilled by two obliging members of the Secret Service. All Owens had to do was to pass the carefully assembled details on to Hamburg. Like Ritter's other head agent in America, Harry Sawyer, he was a mere catalyst, a human radio set that simply passed on what the British told him to and received whatever the Germans sent.

But though up to that point the German intelligence operations against Britain had been somewhat paradoxically dictated by the British and at a pace decided by them, an event now occurred which they had not anticipated. Apparently a trifle baffled by some of the information received, Ritter decided that it was high time to have another meeting in Lisbon with his head agent Owens, to discuss the latest developments, to look into his eyes and to hear his voice, to detect any tremor and to hear whether he spoke with conviction. But most of all Ritter wanted to meet a second man, the RAF officer who, as Owens had explained on his last trip to Lisbon, was up to his ears in debt, needed money urgently and wanted to desert in order to sell important information to the Germans.

The British Government had quickly realized that they had the opportunity of establishing a direct link with the nerve centre of the German High Command through half a dozen German radio sets and as many 'turned' agents. This direct link with the brain of the German operational planning centre might be decisive for the outcome of the war if they could succeed in maintaining the links between the Abwehr and 'their' agents in Britain.

In order therefore to maintain their Hamburg counterparts' blind faith, the British set up the so-called 'Double-Cross Committee' under the chairmanship of Sir John Masterman. This was a collection of outstanding specialists, of men who had all the intellectual qualities to wage this battle of wits, among them the famous Oxford historian Hugh Trevor-Roper. The team of deception specialists held its first meeting in London in January 1941. From then on the intentions of the German war planners were to be systematically probed via the antennae of the Hamburg Abwehr post in Wohldorf.

But as early as its first meeting the committee was confronted with the ticklish problem that Major Ritter had wittingly or unwittingly presented, and whose correct solution was to decide whether the SIS was to win or lose the battle against the Abwehr. Ritter's invitation to Owens and his friend who wanted to commit treason was a conundrum that involved danger for both sides. It was a fishing expedition that promised the SIS a major success; it might even be possible to kidnap Major Ritter and take him to England, where he could be questioned at leisure about German intentions towards Britain in Operation Sealion, which still presented a very real threat.

On the German side too, preparations went ahead for the meeting in Lisbon. The conditions under which Owens' great new catch was prepared to pass to the Abwehr 'important secrets of the British aircraft industry' were known. His price was known. The place and the time, as well as the secret recognition signals which had to be observed by all concerned at the meeting at the Avenida Palace Hotel, had been agreed in lengthy radio exchanges between Hamburg and London. The only question which the Hamburg Abwehr officers could not answer even after the most careful examination of all the details was the key question in the entire operation: Are Owens and his companion genuine, or are they a bait cast by the British SIS in the hope that the Germans will eagerly snap it up, never to get off the hook again?

When Owens' guards opened the door of his cell in Wandsworth Prison and handed him a return air ticket to Lisbon, the only thing they knew for sure was that the Welsh double agent would at least use the part for the outward journey. Whether he would ever return to England after his meeting with Ritter, only to be locked in his cell again, was something doubted by everyone concerned in the preparations for the risky operation. It could even be predicted with ninety-nine per cent certainty that Owens would disclose his true role to the Germans and ask Ritter for asylum, all the more so as the gambler from Hampstead was at the end of his tether at the start of the trip.

The chances that Owens would voluntarily return to England on the other hand could be rated at about one per cent. No one knew that better than 'Johnny' himself. In 1942, he told a cell mate, Jörgen Börresen, a Dane whom the British had captured spying for the Germans on Jan Mayen Island: 'Here were the British, there the Germans – and between them the fire. Had I not done as I was told I should have been hanged, either in Germany or in England. MI6 would have sold me to the Germans without any compunction, as a token of "gratitude" for having helped my countrymen.'

In the autumn of 1940 – the exact date is not certain – Owens boarded a Panam plane in London bound for Lisbon, in order to consolidate his German friends' confidence. The 'traitor', the RAF expert who was to introduce himself to the Germans as Mr Dickitts, left London by ship at about the same time. He was to watch Owens like a hawk and to make a favourable impression on Major Ritter with the 'chickenfeed' provided by SIS – apparently valuable information on British coastal defences and on technical developments in the aircraft industry. It was all the more important for Dickitts to gain the Germans' confidence, as London were beginning to fear that they might one day drop their chief agent Owens. If that happened the cosy dialogue between the British SIS and the German Wehrmacht might have been interrupted for ever. But that must never happen, least of all now, when every scrap of information on the German invasion plans was of vital importance.

Dickitts, who had served in the RAF in World War One but had not been called up again in 1939, had spent weeks preparing himself for the task. He studied all the available reports on the previous meetings between Owens and his opposite numbers in the Abwehr. He read the interrogation reports on Caroli, Reysen, and especially those on Wulf Schmidt, who after his parachute jump from Gartenfeld's plane had dropped straight into MI5's lap.

The fact and circumstances of his capture were guarded by the small number of those in the know like some atomic secret. But whereas the existence of the atom bomb and its effect became public knowledge, the British security authorities still firmly refuse to reveal how and why Wulf Schmidt changed camps and allowed himself to be fashioned into an effective and durable weapon in the fight against the Third Reich. At our first meeting in London, Wulf Dietrich Schmidt, alias Johnson, still pretended to be the German hero whom the British had never caught. He was still living undiscovered, in hiding as it were . . .

In 1960 Stanley P. Lovell, an American intelligence officer who had been in touch with high-level British intelligence officers during the war, gave me some of the information I had been denied in England. He recalled something Intelligence General Sir Colin Gubbins had told him which apparently pointed at Wulf Schmidt's double game. According to him, the British Secret Service had sent all German agents to jail with the exception of one spy whom they had left at liberty with his radio set. This man, who was 'of peasant stock', was a convinced Nazi and could not be impressed either by threats or by bribery.

Lovell, elaborating what Gubbins had allegedly told him, said he mentioned that his grandmother had been a member of the aristocracy. It was this remark that had alerted SIS to one of his weaknesses:

Just as the Saxe-Coburgs had become the Windsors and the Battenbergs had become the Mountbattens so, the man was told, he would be given a British title if he agreed to work for the British. It was even said that the King himself had seen the man and had repeated the promise. It might be true, because there is no doubt that shortly afterwards the unknown wireless agent became one of the most important captures of the war . . .

The next, rather sparse piece of information concerning Schmidt's capture was given – ten years after Lovell's statement – by the chairman of the Double-Cross Committee, Sir John Masterman:

Tate (Wulf Dietrich Schmidt) finally gave up of his own accord during the interrogations. He became a double agent and in the middle of October 1940 he established wireless contact with the Germans . . . He became one of our most reliable wireless agents . . . He was carefully guarded and his secret kept so strictly that to everyone he appeared to be an ordinary British citizen . . . His work was of great value, first for our counter-intelligence agents and later for our deception operations . . .

So Schmidt had saved his life by willingly placing his phenomenal memory at the disposal of the British and by describing in detail the characteristics of the important Hamburg Abwehr officers.

It was these personal descriptions which were of such importance for Dickitts, so that he could prepare himself to meet the men who would be interrogating him in Portugal and later in Germany. Dickitts was well aware that his life depended on the outcome of this impending game of questions and answers. The fact that he nevertheless placed his neck in the German noose, fully aware of the dangers of his action, and dared to enter the lion's den as a British agent, must surely rank this as one of the bravest deeds ever enacted during World War Two.

Perhaps Dickitts might not have gone about his task quite so bravely if he had known what traps the Abwehr had set for him meanwhile. Apart from a horde of intelligence-hungry army, navy and airforce experts who lay in wait, there was 'Anna', a prostitute employed by the District Command, hoping he would share her bed. Two technicians from the Wohldorf radio station had filled the love-nest – in which she hoped not only to test his masculinity but also to obtain some useful information – with concealed microphones. In a safe in the Knochen-hauerstrasse there were some potent drugs which were to render Dickitts rapidly unconscious.

But what was to prove more dangerous than all the microphones in Anna's bed, the knockout drops or the interrogations, was the Gestapo. They had profound misgivings about the secret goings-on and had in-stalled themselves with microphones, chloroform, pistols and handcuffs in the room next to the one that the Abwehr had booked for Dickitts in the Vier Jahreszeiten Hotel in Hamburg.

It is also questionable whether Dickitts would have gone to Germany had he known the man who was appointed to watch him: Georg Sessler of the Hamburg St Pauli boxing club, who had also been charged with looking after Wulf Schmidt before his departure for England and from whom no escape was possible. Leutnant Sessler prepared himself for his job with the same care with which Owens and Dickitts tried to anticipate any problems that might arise in their encounter with the Germans.

I met Ritter's former 'guard dog' Georg Sessler on his estate near Marseilles on 5 June 1973. For a long time he had refused to see me to talk about his intelligence activities. 'I am glad I got away with it last time,' he had repeatedly told me over the telephone, 'and I don't want to have any more to do with the dirty business.'

As with Wulf Schmidt, alias Harry Johnson, I tried to make Sessler change his mind: 'But these events have become history! They happened a quarter of a century ago!'

'That may be,' countered Monsieur Sessler. He had married a Corsican girl after the war and gone to ground in France, and now he had some difficulty in stringing together into intelligible sentences the words of his own mother tongue. '*D'accord*. Those times are past. You may be right. But a lot of those people survived the war and are in it again. People who got caught up in that kind of business do not get out of it again so easily!'

Eventually I was able to follow up the call with a visit to his country house near Aix-en-Provence.

'Make yourself at home!' he said, placing an old Belgian army pistol on the table. He took out the clip to show me that it was loaded. 'You might need it!'

Then, all of a sudden he roared 'Alush' a few times into the lonely hills. And when nothing moved in the hut that was hidden in a distant fruit plantation, he blew the referee's whistle he was wearing round his neck.

There was a movement in the bushes behind me and a Tunisian bodyguard with broken yellow teeth and a fierce dog appeared. The skinny man with a twinkle in his eye and a broad grin on his face bowed several times, gabbled away at me in a language which I could not understand and finished every sentence with: 'German man – good.'

With this conviction and with the safety catch of his gun permanently off, Alush was guarding the life of the former Hamburg Abwehr officer.

'He's as lazy as the devil,' said Georg Sessler. 'During the day he is only fit to pour out the whisky. But when it is dark he is worth his weight in gold. The fellow has night-vision, and I should like to see anyone try and sneak up to the windows!' With that, Sessler pointed to the embrasure that Alush had sawn in the door of his hut.

The safety precautions somehow did not fit the image of the intrepid Hamburg boxer. But it seemed that somewhere in the cupboards of the farmhouse there were some mementoes of the past war, and there was an atmosphere of fear about the place.

'Have you ever heard of the Red Orchestra?' Sessler asked me, nervously lifting his whisky glass. I did not understand why he should start talking about the Red Orchestra when in fact I had asked him about Mr Dickitts, whom he had accompanied to Hamburg early in the war.

'Did you ever find Dickitts?' he went on.

'No.'

'Do the British know where he is?'

'I've no idea.'

'Then you ought to try and trace him if you really want to write history and not just flog a story without an ending!'

'But what has Dickitts to do with the Red Orchestra?' I asked.

'Have you found Schmidt?'

'Yes I have, after years of searching!' I answered with a hint of pride.

'I don't mean Wulf Schmidt,' Sessler corrected me, 'I mean Dr Schmidt; he was another of Ritter's discoveries who worked for us as chief agent in the Balkans. I had to take him a radio set in Budapest.'

The story was getting too complicated. It seemed that I was getting caught up in a net that I should never be able to untangle. Suddenly, quite out of context, Sessler asked: 'Have you ever spoken to Kim Philby?'

'But he is in Moscow!' I replied.

Just then Sessler interrupted our conversation because Alush could not start the lawn-mower. He got up and left me.

The secret British documents concerning the operations of the Secret Service will certainly remain closed until the year 2000. But even if the British Government agreed to make them available to historians tomorrow, they would not contain the account that Georg Sessler gave me when he had managed to get the lawn-mower working again. This story not only describes the breathtaking action of an Allied secret agent who bravely walked into the German lion's den; it also explains much that has remained an enigma to Sir John Masterman and his colleagues of the Double-Cross Committee in connection with their Operation Celery – Dickitts' journey to Germany.

When Dickitts set off, his brief from the Secret Service consisted of five points, and he was given a completely free hand in obtaining the information. He was to establish:

to what extent German Intelligence still trusted their head agent Owens;

who were the people cooperating with the Germans;

what were the interests of the various persons he would meet in Germany;

what were the operational intentions of the Germans in connection with their planned invasion of the British Isles – he could deduce this from the questions he would be asked;

what value the Germans attached to the various parachute agents they had dropped in England and especially to Wulf Schmidt, whom British Intelligence with all the means at their disposal were proposing to build up into the most important link between London and Hamburg.

As 'head agent Owens' had apparently lost some of his status in German eyes it was intended from now on systematically to supply the Abwehr 'with the most important information from enemy territory' through Wulf Schmidt, agent 3725. It was to be Dickitts' job to estimate the chances of such an operation meeting with success. His observations would have a major effect on the outcome of the battle. Georg Sessler began his account of Operation Celery as seen from the German side:

Admiral Canaris was doubtful about the whole business, and thought Dickitts was probably a top Secret Service agent. But Major Ritter was willing to bet anything that Dickitts was genuine and really did want to sell us important military secrets.

I was not bothered by the speculations of my superiors. All I was concerned with was my brief, which was to shadow Owens and Dickitts unobtrusively before, during and after their talks with Major Ritter. I imagined that in neutral Portugal this would be comparatively simple.

The second part of my task seemed to present more problems: I had orders to take Dickitts, who allegedly spoke not a word of German, to Hamburg and to help him pass all the Wehrmacht and Gestapo controls in Portugal, Spain and France. No one was to know about the Englishman travelling through Germany on a secret mission!

Exercising the same caution as our two British agents, Major Ritter and I also flew to Lisbon from Hamburg by different routes. By the evening I was sitting in the lobby of the Avenida Palace Hotel and caught my first glimpse of our great British spy Arthur Owens, who passed by me twenty minutes before the agreed time, without paying me any attention. Dickitts was not due to arrive by ship until next day.

I saw Owens take a seat at a table near by, and briefly glance at the exit, while pretending not to be waiting for anyone. It was only at the time of his meeting with Major Ritter that I noticed a hint of fear in his eyes – and suddenly the aura of the 'great spy' in whom one had such faith in Hamburg began to wear off, and I began to see him look more like some boffin, or a niggling accountant who espected to be ticked off by his boss. I saw a waiter go up to Owens and come back with a glass of port.

Then Major Ritter, alias Dr Rantzau, entered the lobby, walked straight up to his old acquaintance Owens and sat down at the same table. Early on in their conversation I saw Ritter look across to me a few times and finally he waved me over and asked me to join them. For a moment I was astonished at the free and easy way in which my superior officer introduced me to his head agent, making it quite impossible for me to shadow the man, as I had been instructed to do in Hamburg.

'How nice to see you,' Ritter greeted me and introduced me to Owens as George Sinclair.

This had not been in the programme at all, and I suddenly found myself in the embarrassing position of trying to make Owens believe that I was an American sailor who had just arrived from New York and was at present in Lisbon with my boss. Having given this cover story with what I hope was some conviction, I was again astonished by the openness with which Ritter discussed his requirements with Owens. They concerned airfields in Southern England, output figures of certain aircraft factories and weather reports which Owens was to transmit to Hamburg. At that time I was a lieutenant in German Intelligence, aged twenty-three, and I must confess that there was something theatrical about our secret operation, with Ritter and Owens in the leading parts. But in the idealism with which I approached my job it never occurred to me that a man whom my superiors trusted one hundred per cent might possibly be 'turned' by enemy Intelligence. The word 'double agent' I had never even heard at that date.

While Ritter was issuing instructions to Owens it was the head agent who tried to put the brake on with a question addressed to me: 'When are you going back to the States, George?'

It was only then that Ritter remembered he had introduced me as an American, in whose presence he obviously should not have discussed such highly dangerous espionage briefs. But Ritter was in one of his jovial moods and tried to pacify the Welshman.

'You can trust our American friend, Johnny. We have known each other for more than ten years and we've downed a few drinks in our day, haven't we George?' he said in an exaggerated American accent.

Ten years ago I was thirteen, I thought. But Ritter laughed out loud. And so the obvious nonsense he had talked about our having known each other for ten years seemed to pass unnoticed.

Arthur Owens had probably felt safer in his cell in Wandsworth Prison than at liberty in sunny Portugal, where he was forced to stay trembling for his life, on SIS orders. For when Dickitts had finally arrived in Lisbon, Major Ritter had completely upset his plans and his hopes.

'Your RAF friend is coming to Germany with us alone.' he told Owens.

'And what am I to do?'

'You stay here in Estoril,' said the German Abwehr boss, and when he noticed the fear in Owens' eyes he added: 'Don't worry. We'll keep an eye on you. You'll be all right.'

Now that Georg Sessler had to keep track of Dickitts, the task of unobtrusively watching Owens fell to the legendary 'thug-Schmidt', equipped with knuckle-duster and pistol, beside whom the misshapen little Welshman looked like a Prussian Junker. 'Thug-Schmidt' was married to a Portuguese and was employed by the Abwehr station in Portugal as a kind of general handyman, whenever there was need to settle a matter noiselessly and without leaving a trace.

'This man with his narrow-shaped head could only go out at night,' I was told by the former Abwehr paymaster in the Iberian peninsula, Max Franzbach, alias Pago. 'In the daytime he scared people; he looked like the hunchback of Notre Dame!'

But during the interminable wait in Lisbon the British kept an even closer watch on Owens than the Germans. Their prisoner obviously meant a lot to them.

Georg Sessler went on to describe the further adventures of the SIS agent Dickitts, whom the British had given the cover-name Celery before his risky trip to Germany.

Dickitts did not know me; he did not know what I looked like. All he knew was that at a certain time and place he would be approached by a man and given a certain password. I, Georg Sessler, was that man, calling myself George Sinclair. I had the advantage of having been given a detailed description of the man whom I was to watch over day and night during the next few weeks by Major Ritter in Hamburg.

At last I caught sight of him sitting in the bar of the Avenida Palace Hotel, as I edged my way past the people crowding round. I went quite close to him and bumped into him as if by accident, edging him up to the end of the bar where we could sit down. I apologized with the word agreed by radio and told him my name, 'Sinclair'.

Now we knew that henceforth we belonged together: he the Englishman and I the German. At this short introduction we did not speak very much. We looked at one another, each trying to decide how far he could trust the other, though the Englishman needed more confidence in me than I did in him: it was he who was walking into the lion's den, I was simply his watchdog.

We can discuss the details of the journey some other time. It was obvious that the die would be cast for Dickitts that night: we were still in neutral Portugal and he could still refuse to accompany me to Germany. But once we had crossed the frontier into France he would no longer be able to turn back – he would have to go on to Hamburg with me at his side. Then we should know whether he was 'a traitor in need of money' as Ritter believed, or one of the toughest agents of the British Secret Service, as Canaris feared.

Dickitts seemed to have summed up his prospects quite clearly. He knew that a traitor would be very valuable to the Germans, particularly at that critical phase of 1940–1. But he also knew what happened to secret agents found spying in wartime.

That last evening before our trip to Germany we went out to Estoril and had a good time. We had lobster and then went out and sampled Lisbon night-life. We met exciting Portuguese girls, had drinks and listened to music. But none of this seemed to interest Dickitts. Although he always smiled pleasantly, one could read in his eyes the question: is this man going to bring me back alive? For the Englishman whom I had only met a few hours earlier I was simply an executioner's assistant.

I remember walking out of a bar into the night air and him suddenly stopping and saying: 'You are very young. I can only rely on the impression you have made on me. But I think you are sincere. George, my life is in your hands!'

I shook his hand and said: 'I shall bring you back safely. You can rely on that!'

At the time Dickitts was about forty. He was wearing an English suit. His eyes and his voice betrayed fear when I took him back to his hotel and said good bye to him at about three that morning.

Now, after this farewell, my real work was about to begin: contrary to what I had told Dickitts I did not return to my hotel but instead kept observation on his hotel. I had watched all his movements, or had them watched. Would he get in touch with anyone?

I had noted that shortly after we had said goodbye the light in his room had been switched off. Only a short time before our proposed meeting next morning did I return to my hotel, pretending that I had spent the night there.

When Dickitts fetched me I knew that shortly before leaving his hotel he had rung a certain Lisbon telephone number. The hotel porter was easily persuaded to give me this information. I had simply told him that my friend Dickitts was in the hotel: he was an important American importer but not in the best of health. He might well require to see a doctor or someone and I should like to know in case I could be of any assistance.

In this way I learned that Dickitts had rung the British Embassy, though what the conversation was about I could not discover. At any rate I knew that Dickitts had thrown out a lifeline before leaving for Hamburg.

That afternoon we went into town, where I left Mr Dickitts in a cafe while I went to the German Abwehr station on the first floor of the German Embassy. There I picked up two German diplomatic passports. Mine was in my real name, Georg Sessler: my English's companion's was in the name of Werner

Denker. The name Denker came to me quite spontaneously when I was asked to provide a German name at the Embassy in Lisbon. Werner Denker, the former owner of the Timmendorferstrand Hotel, was an old friend of mine. When I picked up Dickitts at the cafe I did not hand him his passport, but kept it as a further safety measure.

Before leaving we went out to Estoril for the last time and for the last time we built up our strength by eating lobster in anticipation of the hardships to come. During the meal he asked me several times whether I was sure I would bring him back safely and every time I answered: 'Quite sure!'

Then at midnight, we left Lisbon station on our journey north. Dickitts had no luggage at all, not even a spare shirt. I can't remember now whether he even had any washing things with him.

The train was quite full up to the French frontier, with people standing in the corridors, but the German Legation had booked a first class compartment for us, so we at least had enough room. Then came the frontier check. With our diplomatic passports this presented no problems.

Now that we had got over the first obstacle we soon discovered a subject of mutual interest: sport. Then as now, my hobbies were football and boxing. I told him that I had once been an active boxer first in the Hamburg Hansa Elf Club and then when I was fourteen for the St Pauli Club, the same one which had not only produced Max Schmeling but also the then European champion, Herbert Nürnberg.

From boxing the subject changed to St Pauli and the Reeperbahn, which, as a Hamburg man myself, I know very well and which I described vividly to Dickitts. Although we were still one and a half thousand kilometres from the place, Dickitts could hardly wait to meet the Reeperbahn girls. In order to prepare him for the woman agent waiting for him expectantly in Hamburg I told him that I knew a cracking girl, with long legs, full bosom, slender and – rare these days – with a romantic disposition!

During the long journey from Portugal to Germany the compartment door was frequently opened. In France a military patrol entered; they stood in front of the Englishman, who looked up speechlessly at the men with their steel helmets. Here in occupied France I only had to show my service pass, which every military patrol knew but rarely saw. There were only a few dozen holders of such passes, people on a secret mission and answerable only to the Führer or the High Command.

When we arrived in Hamburg on the second morning I took Dickitts straight across the station square to the Phoenix Hotel. There I left him alone for a few hours, while observation on him was continued by Herr Harbeck, the hotel licensee, and two Abwehr agents concealed in the delivery van of a margarine manufacturer standing outside the hotel.

Next morning I collected Dickitts from the hotel. Four months earlier I had collected Wulf Schmidt from the same place on our way to Brussels. But whereas I had merely to protect Schmidt, I had to keep a very sharp eye on Dickitts. He quietly wished me good morning and got into the car.

First, to make him lose his sense of direction we crisscrossed Hamburg before stopping near the Spaldingstrasse and going on foot to No 4, where we had our cover firm: Reinhold & Co.

The first civilian who shook hands with Dickitts was Kapitänleutnant Tornow, a man of Russian origin, who was head of the naval intelligence section of the Hamburg Abwehr station. Neither he nor any of the other Germans mentioned their names: this was one of the things I had agreed with Dickitts. For the next few weeks he was also not to use any pencils to make notes. He was given writing material only when he had to explain something to his interrogators on paper, such as certain aircraft parts, site plans of air defences in Southern England and, most important of all, the harbour defences of Dover.

This was of particular interest to Kapitänleutnant Tornow and me, for in the planned invasion we were to be among the first to land there: Tornow as a Russian refugee and I as his sailor companion!

When we went into the next room, my chief, Major Ritter, greeted the visitor from England with exaggerated friendliness and asked him to be seated. There were two other men in civilian clothes, whom I did not know. During this first conversation I had to wait outside.

About an hour later Major Ritter returned my protégé to me.

'Just take Mr Brown for a short sight-seeing tour of the town and show him what the RAF has been up to! We don't want him to think that we are inhuman!'

'Mr Brown', as we now had to call him, was the name the Abwehr had decided to give him for security reasons. I was to show him some of the damage the RAF raids had already caused in 1940.

'Just show him the bomb sites,' Ritter stressed again as we drove off.

The route we took during our city tour and the exact times spent at each bomb site had been carefully prepared beforehand with reference to the damage caused and formed part of the Englishman's psychological preparation for the coming interrogation. We still did not know who Dickitts really was. For that reason I was told to make a careful note of anything he said, however trivial, and report to I/Luft, the air intelligence section, in the Knochenhauerstrasse. But the only time Dickitts made any comment of consequence at all was when I showed him a hospital that had been bombed. When he saw it I thought he looked just a little bit ashamed, but still he tried to excuse his RAF friends: 'Our pilots are always told that German munitions factories are disguised with a Red Cross. How are they to know the difference?'

A few hours after our tour of the city, in the Hotel Vier Jahreszeiten, Dickitts was inundated with questions from a circle of Abwehr officers and experts from the German armaments industry. They had come from all over Germany to get their fill from the cup that the alleged RAF deserter had brought with him from London. Few of them realised that Dickitts could also be a sticky customer when he chose.

During the long interrogation that followed he was not only questioned, but occasionally threatened and sometimes contradicted.

'How are we to know that your information is correct and that you are sincere?' they asked him again and again, whereupon the Englishman blandly and disarmingly replied: 'Do you really believe for one moment that I would have come to Germany voluntarily as a spy, to be caught out and possibly hanged? Surely all you have to do is to have my statements checked by your agents in England!'

It should perhaps be mentioned here that Dickitts apparently made these remarks in the hope that the Germans might let slip some remark about their agents in England, especially Wulf Schmidt. The Double-Cross Committee had given Schmidt the code name Tate, though the actual details of the game he was to play were not to be settled until Dickitts got back.

In fact for a time the events behind the scenes in the Hotel Vier Jahreszeiten made it seem unlikely that Dickitts would ever get home alive. Major Ritter had arranged an operation in a bar on the Reeperbahn, which involved Dickitts passing out for a short while. The last Dickitts was to remember before this incident was Ritter saying: 'Your health!' Then Dickitts drained his glass of whisky and collapsed.

Ritter now drew from Dickitts' finger a ring he was wearing and which had aroused the professional suspicions of Ritter's wife. On the inside of the ring was an inscription in minute letters which when photographed turned out to be a letter code which was deciphered, too late, in Berlin and discovered to be a cover address used by Soviet Intelligence in Lisbon. At that time the Ribbentrop/Molotov pact between Russia and Germany was still in force and for this reason alone investigations about a Russian Intelligence cover address in Lisbon would have been embarrassing. For that reason the Germans do not know to this day who supplied Dickitts with the secret Soviet address.

The Secret Intelligence Service will almost certainly remain silent about the details of its operations. Of course there is another possible source who could report on the true role of the secret agent Dickitts, and that is Kim Philby, one of the most capable British intelligence officers who is now known to have been working equally ably for the Soviets. Nowadays he is living in Moscow. Sometimes he can be seen crossing Dzerzinsky Square in Moscow, but it would not be wise to approach him, for in the KGB headquarters in Dzerzinsky Square they guard their secrets just as jealously as the British guard theirs or the Americans guard the information about their secret networks from World War Two, now being exploited by the Gehlen organization.

Efficient espionage is something that has grown organically, a spreading tree with countless branches, all grown from a few roots. One of the roots that nurtured the tree of Russian espionage was undoubtedly Kim Philby. During the long years of his activity he has squeezed the last bit of information from his phenomenal memory for the benefit of Soviet Russia. But as he wrote as recently as 1974 to a friend living on the Côte d'Azur, he is now a wreck: '. . . What do they want of me? . . . I have become a disagreeable old man. I would only annoy you!' Now, apparently, all that remains of him is a hopeless alcoholic.

When I started work on this book I thought I was on the track of a German master-spy in England. In fact I had already written a film script called *Bridge to London* that was to be a joint production by UFA and Rank. In this film Wulf Schmidt would have been shown as the intrepid German spy who kept MI5, the British Counter-Intelligence Service, guessing throughout the war, who had even married an English-woman and had then gone to ground in 1945 to live among the enemy he had fought so hard for so long.

UFA in Berlin had actually started negotiations with Rank about the co-production when a strange thing occurred: Wulf Schmidt, alias Harry Johnson, wrote me a letter of only eight lines, which gave me some of the information that had so carefully been kept from me by the British Official Secrets Act:

> I am proposing to spend my holidays in Germany this year and may also go to Hamburg. Perhaps we could meet there, or are you intending to visit England some time? You seem to be moving to and fro on the Bridge to London! How are things? Have you discovered anything useful yet? My sources of information are still very productive (and fast!). Best wishes, Harry.

Schmidt's reference to my moving about on the Bridge to London clearly referred to the title of my proposed film. I learned by way of a few telephone calls to Berlin and London that the British security authorities (to whom Rank had submitted the film script for security vetting) had asked Mr Johnson to read the book. From then on I knew which side Schmidt was on, and I did not doubt that the supposed German superspy 3725 had been a willing and valuable collaborator with the British from the moment of his capture.

In the light of this knowledge I again followed up the histories of all the spies who played a part in the game and learned with surprise how often there was some sidetrack leading to Moscow. It became more and more evident why Wulf Dietrich Schmidt had excused his silence with the remark: 'There is too much at stake, particularly as far as the Russians are concerned!' and why Georg Sessler, who was attacked by unknown assailants a few months after our interview at his house in Provence, had asked me about Philby.

In 1941, so it appeared, no one in London was more impatient for Dickitts' return than Kim Philby. It can be assumed with near certainty that any information the SIS agent brought back from Hamburg was also relayed to the Russians by Philby. But at the beginning of 1941 Dickitts was still in the hands of the Abwehr . . .

Suddenly during the interrogations in Hamburg it was no longer Dickitts alone who was in danger. The Abwehr officers concerned with the affair were themselves under surveillance, especially Leutnant Sessler, who as a result of jealous Gestapo surveillance was suddenly obliged to change his role from watchdog to hunted, and who in the middle of the war had to enter into a kind of conspiracy with his English charge so as not to finish up on the gallows himself.

Just as little fleas have lesser fleas upon their backs to bite them, so Operation Celery involved a chain of mutual distrust: Owens was to keep an eye on Dickitts; Dickitts on the other hand was under the watchful eye of Georg Sessler, who in turn was carefully watched by the competent Abwehr officers in Hamburg – until suddenly the feared Chief of the Reichssicherheitshauptamt (Reich Security Office), Reinhard Heydrich, stepped in. Heydrich disliked the set up of the Hotel Vier Jahreszeiten; as head of the RSHA he wanted to know what was going on and if necessary take control of the mattter himself.

And so one German Intelligence Service started spying on the other. In the neck-and-neck race between Heydrich's Security Service and Canaris' Military Intelligence Service, the Abwehr, the unscrupulous Heydrich was drawing ahead. One year earlier, on 9 November 1939, Heydrich had demonstrated to Hitler how it was possible to get hold of important enemy information without much expenditure but with resolute action. At that time Heydrich had taken over an operation painstakingly designed by Canaris in Holland and had simply pushed the initiators out of the picture.

It became evident at the time that Major Ritter was not a purely German phenomenon: two British officers, Captain Best and Major

Stevens, had not only rashly given some of their agents a radio set with which they were then fed with deception material, but had also allowed themselves to be lured into a trap. The brief description of the two officers in the files of the RSHA read: Captain S. Payne Best, 55. Peculiarities: always wears a monocle. Cover: partner in a firm in The Hague, in fact SIS officer. Major Richard Stevens, 45, professional soldier. Head of the Passport Control Office in The Hague. Controls British Intelligence activities in Holland.

When the two Englishmen arrived at the Cafe Backus on the Dutch frontier to meet their German partners, and Captain Best scanned the horizon for the expected resistance fighters from Berlin, it only needed two words from Heydrich, addressed to his old war horse from Kiel, Alfred Naujocks.

'Get them!'

In the Allied 'Wanted' lists, Naujocks's name figured prominently: 'Alfred Helmuth Naujocks, head of the technical section of the SD, Obersturmbannführer: born 2.9.1911 in Kiel; 185 cm tall; fair hair, blue eyes; special marks: skull wound, bullet wound on the right thigh, broken nose and burns on both hands.'

After Hitler's accession to power in 1933, Naujocks had played an important part in the formation of the Security Services (SD). His first operation took him to Czechoslovakia, where he blew up a radio propaganda station run by an émigré, Rudolf Formis.

During the Spanish Civil War the German Government managed to get hold of some important documents which were being sent to Spain from Moscow via the Spanish Consulate in Hamburg. Naujocks and his men simply set upon the Spanish Consul as he was leaving his residence and stole his briefcase. Later he was given a nominal sentence by a German court, and the briefcase was found and returned with the papers intact. The German authorities apologized to the Consul saying that the culprit had obviously only been after money.

Later, on 31 August 1939, Naujocks received orders from Hitler to carry out an operation that was to have disastrous results for the whole of mankind: on that day he and his men faked a Polish attack on the broadcasting transmitter in Gleiwitz near the Silesian border, and so provided the 'moral justification' for the attack on Poland next day.

In the *Guinness Book of Records* Naujocks is mentioned as the greatest forger in history, having been the initiator of an operation involving the forgery of £150,000,000 worth of £5 notes. The forged notes were put into the international market through a skilfully designed sales organization, and the effects continued to be felt by the British economy long after the war.

As has been mentioned, it was Naujocks who engineered the kidnapping of Stevens and Best on 9 November 1939. During the skirmish a man who was accompanying them was killed. He too was dragged across the frontier into Germany and identified as Lt Klop, of the Dutch General Staff. Klop's corpse was to provide another piece of 'evidence' in support of Hitler's plans. Here was a General Staff officer of a neutral country accompanying the secret service officers of a belligerent country to the frontier. So Klop became the 'moral justification' for the German invasion of Holland. The two intelligence officers, Stevens and Best, were also accused of having prepared the attempt on Hitler's life in the Burgerbraukeller in Munich.

With the capture of the two British intelligence officers Naujocks had placed 'two ripe lemons' into his chief's hand, with the result that the SD came to be regarded with special favour by Adolf Hitler, while Canaris stepped back into the shadows.

But now it appeared that, thanks to the machinations of his subordinate Ritter, Canaris had also found a 'ripe lemon' which was slowly being squeezed dry by the Abwehr officers in the Hotel Vier Jahreszeiten. Bearing in mind the Stevens and Best affair it is not difficult to guess at Heydrich's plan when, on a cold and wet winter morning of 1940/41 he called for his kidnapper Naujocks and the files on the two British officers who at that moment were sitting chained to their beds in the concentration camp at Sachsenhausen. Naujocks was to read the files carefully and then to confer, though not in depth, with Kriminalrat Dr Schambacher, Dr Schaefer, Grothe and Kriminal-kommissar Fehmer, in order to understand why the SD wanted to get hold of the RAF deserter Dickitts and take him to Berlin.

But Naujocks had paid even more attention to the reports from the Hamburg SD men than to the reports on Stevens and Best. They had managed to get some information on the interrogation of Dickitts in the Vier Jahreszeiten and there was a hint from Hamburg to the effect that Dickitts and his guard, a certain Leutnant Georg Sessler, were getting ready to depart for an unknown destination.

To ensure that Sessler did not take any unathorized steps, Heydrich now ordered SS-Sturmbannführer Naujocks to watch the watcher and to follow the trail of the Hamburg boxer. As a boxer Naujocks was not in the same class as Sessler, but against this he had far more experience in the sort of business that was now afoot. The man who had set the world alight with his attack on the Gleiwitz broadcasting station packed his suitcase in the apartment in Berlin, Derfflingerstrasse 8, II floor, ready to go to Hamburg to carry out his orders.

'I had been told to get hold of the Englishman, whom the Abwehr were handling like a raw egg, and take him to the Prinz Albrecht Palace in Berlin for a confrontation with Stevens and Best,' Naujocks told me in 1964 in a Hamburg nightclub where he was making himself useful as a chucker-out. 'I thought there should be no difficulty as it was, after all, in Germany and in Hamburg too, a place I know like the palm of my hand. I did not want to be recognized so before leaving Berlin I put on a pair of dark glasses . . .'

Although most Jewish shops had been smashed and looted in the 'Kristallnacht' of 1938, a Jew living in a small street behind the Hotel Vier Jahreszeiten not only managed to save his shop but also for a time his life by making himself useful to the Hamburg Abwehr station. When Dickitts and Georg Sessler entered his little shop, it was to be the Englishman's last test.

It was during our meeting at Aix-en-Provence that Sessler told me the story that has hitherto remained unknown to both the British and the German intelligence services:

To make one final test of Dickitts' genuineness I left him and the Jew alone for a few minutes, pretending that I had to go to the toilet in the café opposite. Before leaving the shop I said to Dickitts: 'Why don't you choose some little present for your girl friend?'

While the Englishman was selecting a suitable present it had been agreed with the owner of the shop, our agent, that he should approach the alleged RAF deserter for help, saying that as a Jew he was in constant danger and was trying to find some way of escaping from Germany. But Dickitts firmly but politely refused: 'I am awfully sorry, but I am afraid I cannot help.'

My idea of testing the Englishman by a 'threatened Jew' was to boomerang within the next few hours. A friend in the SD showed me a confidential telex message that had just arrived from HQ in Berlin to the effect that the Englishman in the care of the Abwehr in Hamburg was to be arrested on some suitable pretext and sent to the RSHA, Department VI in Berlin. It was only then that I realized that by involving the Jew the three of us, Dickitts, myself and the jeweller, had all walked into a trap of my design, which the SD might spring at any moment. Now I had to act quickly and on my own initiative. That night when I got Dickitts out of bed in his hotel I was confronted with another unexpected complication: Anna, our blonde, had fallen in love with Dickitts and refused to let him go off without her – a phenomenon apparently quite frequent in prostitutes when their maternal instincts are aroused by a man in danger. Anna's maternal protection was at that moment more important to Dickitts than her sexual complaisance, particularly when we managed to leave the hotel behind the backs of two SD men. The next stages of our flight were like hot frying pans on which we would certainly have got burned if we had stayed a minute longer than necessary. From Hamburg our first port of call was a hide-out on the Baltic, the Hotel Timmendorferstrand.

Two days later, as two SD men in brown leather jackets walked into the lobby of the hotel, we disappeared through the back door and drove back to Hamburg. There I hid Dickitts in a lodging house in the Königgrätzstrasse in the suburb of Hamburg-Hochkamp. And while he stayed in bed with Anna I took the night train to Berlin to get approval of my chief, Admiral Canaris.

The behaviour of the Admiral, whom I met by chance in the corridor of Abwehr headquarters in the Tirpitzufer, gave me the impression that he was well informed about the activities of the SD. For that reason our conversation was quite brief. All the chief said was: 'That man must be got back where he came from. Do you understand?'

No one could in fact have understood better than I did. I can no longer remember the number of the house where I had hidden Dickitts, but I shall never forget how to get there, for every yard of the way I reckoned on the Gestapo arresting us all just before our departure.

When I fetched Dickitts between two and three in the morning he was sitting, dressed and ready to leave, on Anna's bed. He kissed his German lover for the last time and said: 'Good bye Anna, God bless you.' And for the first time in the years I had known her, I saw Anna cry.

Now we had to rely on our luck and my green Abwehr service pass, which told the inquirer that I was travelling on the orders of the High Command of the Wehrmacht, Department Ausland/Abwehr, on a secret mission. Never had the pass been more important than that night as Dickitts and I left Hamburg across the Elbe bridge and down the autobahn in the direction of Stuttgart, where at any moment we might be stopped by army patrols.

The next hurdle was the check at Stuttgart airport, and this too we passed without mishap, but when the aircraft came in to land at Barcelona I discovered that the SD had already stretched out their tentacles to Spain. I realized that when I telephoned our Abwehr representative, who asked me with a frightened voice: 'Where are you?'

At that I put back the receiver and went to ground in Barcelona with Dickitts, until it was time to fly on to Madrid next morning.

There the same thing happened: an Abwehr officer of our Madrid station told me to come to the Palace Hotal immediately and to wait for him in the lobby – probably to be arrested. But such a meeting was far too risky, so I suggested waiting for him outside the town at a crossroads where I could observe the area more easily.

Before setting off to meet the Abwehr officer I had another talk with Dickitts, for I realized that the most important Allied secret agent we had ever had in our grasp could quite easily escape from me here in Spain.

'I have kept my word,' I told Dickitts, 'and have got you out of Germany safely. Now don't you let me down. If you disappear I shall certainly go to the wall when I get back.'

Before he had been in my power; now I was in his. I asked him to stay in the café until I got back from my meeting with the Abwehr officer. Now that I had left him, practically for the first time in three weeks, there were only two things that bound us to one another: in my pocket I had £5000 which I was to hand to him by way of fee, but not until we got to Lisbon, and then there was the Englishman's word of honour that he would wait for me. All the same I was surprised to see him sitting there when I returned four hours later. Was it really his sense of honour or was it the £5000? Next day I was to discover that it was neither: Dickitts wanted me!

At the end of the journey I seemed to be more important to him than the small attaché case that I collected from my Abwehr colleague in Madrid and which I was now to smuggle across the frontier to Portugal as diplomatic luggage. The case was sealed. I had been instructed always to keep it by me and never to let it out of my sight. All the same, I held the small brown case up to my ear on the long car journey to the border to make sure there was nothing ticking inside. It would have been just like the SD to send us into the next world with our own bomb.

We got out at the Spanish/Portuguese frontier and showed our diplomatic passports. For one last time Dickitts was the German Ministerialrat Werner Denker from Berlin, and then the formalities were over. Now we were in neutral Portugal, where we each had as much or as little authority as the other.

Our official connection ended where it had begun: in the bar of the Avenida Palace. First we had a drink and then Dickitts said he would like to treat me in return for all the hospitality we had shown towards him in Germany. In the meantime I had paid him his £5000 – his 'traitor's pay' as they thought in Berlin – and he could easily afford to pay for the last meal we would be having together.

'What will you have?' he asked.

'Lobster!' I answered, laughing.

And then, while we were waiting for our meal, Dickitts sat back in his chair and made me a strange offer that left no more doubt about the true nature of his mission: 'I will pay you anything you like if you will accompany me back to England. There you will be received with the same kindness as I met with in Hamburg.'

Without seriously going into this offer I asked him what guarantees he could offer for my survival. He replied that he himself could give no guarantee at all. First he would have to talk to London and that would take a few days. When I answered that he should save himself the trouble as I would much rather go back to Hamburg – I would manage somehow – he turned the conversation to SIS and Major Ritter.

'It was unfair to knock me out with those sleeping pills,' he complained, looking back to the incident on the Reeperbahn, then added: 'I suppose it is part of the game' – not to excuse Ritter's action but merely to justify what he had in store for me and which I can only vaguely remember. First we had our lobster. Our wine glasses were filled again and again and every time we klinked our glasses, German style, Dickitts said 'Prosit'. I noticed how he stressed the second syllable, but it was only in the Lisbon hospital that I remembered it, as I tried to reconstruct the events of the preceding day. I could only remember becoming violently ill and rushing off to the toilet to be sick before I passed out. I vaguely remember being taken somewhere by taxi and saying 'Cheerio' to Dickitts.

Dickitts had obviously tried to take me back to England as a kind of souvenir of his trip to Germany. This suspicion was confirmed a few days later in the military hospital in Hamburg-Wandsbeck where I lay for three weeks recovering from the effects of poisoning; my symptoms were identical with those of two German agents whom the Secret Service had tried to abduct via Gibraltar.

I again remembered that strange way of stressing the last syllable of 'Prosit', the word with which Dickitts had raised his glass before I passed out. As I know no Latin I asked one of the doctors what it could mean. He conjugated 'Prosim, prosis, prosit,' and added what it really means: 'I hope it does you good!'

After carrying out their instructions, the heroes of Operation Celery were not given decorations, as might have been presumed, but were actually treated with humiliating scepticism. The two double agents returned to England together and Dickitts was able to provide important information for British Intelligence. During his stay in Hamburg he had made the acquaintance of a number of important men who had already been allotted their tasks during the invasion: Kapitänleutnant Tornow, who was to be the first to land in Dover, and Major Ritter, who for years had been carrying out military intelligence work against Southern England and had detailed knowledge of the part the Luftwaffe was to play during the invasion. He had also met another man, the radio officer who controlled the sets that the German agents had established in England. Dickitts had become quite friendly with Leutnant Wein, the Hamburg radio officer, and had also met naval and airforce experts who had questioned him with great thoroughness on his knowledge of matters technical. Without doubt, Dickitts had been able to give the British authorities a lot of information on the vital question of where and how the Germans proposed to land.

Nevertheless, the differing accounts of their experiences on the Continent given by Owens and Dickitts started quite a lot of speculation in the British camp. Sir John Masterman, who, as chairman of the Double-Cross Committee had to try and resolve the discrepancies, still asks the question: 'If Snow really revealed all, why was Celery not executed by the Germans; unless of course he had gone over to the enemy. If on the other hand they both betrayed everything, why did the Germans give Snow another £10,000?'

On the German side, Georg Sessler sadly reflects that none of his Hamburg Abwehr colleagues bothered to visit him in hospital: 'Fräulein Rehder (the secretary to Kapitän Wichmann, the head of the Abwehr station) was the only one to look me up in Wandsbeck. I have never forgotten it!'

Sessler, who could hit so hard, could also be hard-hitting in his comments – and that was his mistake. For what he told his Abwehr colleagues about his experiences with Dickitts sounded very much as if he were trying to ruin Major Ritter's career: 'After I had realized how naively the officers responsible estimated the triumphs of their inter- rogations, I told him (Ritter) straight out what I thought of Dickitts and also reported on the unmistakable offer to take me back to England!'

But Ritter remained adamant: 'This man is never a double agent! I am absolutely certain that he gave us his information voluntarily; otherwise he would never have dared to come to Hamburg.'

What else could Ritter say, in fact, now that he had reached the summit of his career? All the more so as the newly-married pseudo- doctor now hoped to branch out into different fields and be sent to Brazil as Military Attaché?

In spite of some doubts about Dickitts' honesty, Ritter had given him some further briefs from which the British could deduce without much difficulty what the Germans had in mind. Dickitts was to report on electrically controlled landmines and gun emplacements in Southern England, on anti-tank guns and shipping in the Channel.

Ritter further stressed his friendship for Johnny by putting him in touch in Lisbon with a man with whom neither Owens nor British Intelligence had hitherto had much contact: Hauptmann Rudolf, the German sabotage boss in Portugal, who also heaped farewell presents on Ritter's 'head agent'. More important, he gave him a time fuse 'concealed' in a 'Pelikan' fountain pen of unmistakably German origin. As if that were not enough Major Ritter also pressed £10,000 into

Owens' hand. Said Ritter in 1953: 'He was a poor devil and somehow I felt sorry for him!'

Even if Owens had not continued to work for the Germans after his return, the detailed information he supplied on landing possibilities in Northern Ireland and which he brought with him on his last trip alone would have been worth the £10,000 he was given by Major Ritter.

The documents brought over by Owens were not only important for Operation Sealion in general but also for Major Ritter's own war against Britain, for Ritter did not rely only on direct action; he also believed in Schlieffen's dictum that one should never neglect the enemy's flank.

The eastern flank of the British Isles he handed over to a strikingly beautiful female spy, Viola, of whom we shall hear more in the next chapter, while he attacked the western flank through Northern Ireland with the aid of a number of male agents.

Among these intrepid agents I was later able to interview Walter Simon, the 'phantom sailor' Christian Nissen, and the parachute agent Günther Schütz; they arrived in submarines, aircraft and French fishing boats in order to join up with the IRA in their attacks against the British. All these German agents had landed in prison shortly after their arrival, with the exception of Hauptmann Dr Hermann Goertz from Lübeck, who managed to stay at liberty for nineteen months and who succeeded, with a lot of luck and courage, in completing his most important assignment for the Abwehr. Goertz was entrusted with an operation named 'Kathleen' a kind of curtain-raiser for the invasion of Britain, which entailed finding suitable landing areas for the parachute troops under General Student and transmitting details to Hamburg. German airborne troops were to land near Davis Head and Lisburn in order to cut off the military forces around Belfast from the rest of the country.

Major Ritter made preparations for Operation Kathleen with all his usual caution. The contact with Goertz had necessarily to be carried out through an IRA wireless operator of whose loyalties one could not be certain. For this reason Ritter operated his Irish networks in double harness. For their first meeting the IRA opreator was given complicated recognition signals to which Hauptmann Goertz, alias Dr Brandy, had to give certain answers when they met. When the two finally did meet their conversation went something like this:

'Which is the most important firm of exporters and importers in Hamburg?'

'Reinhold & Co.'

'Who is the owner?'

Then from Goertz the key phrase:

'Major Ritter!'

After that it seemed nothing could go wrong. For the name of Ritter was to prove a magic word in wartime Ireland, as Goertz discovered. Having personally reconnoitred the best landing areas he was then confronted with the usual problem of how to get actual materials – such as maps with the likely landing places, airfields and British garrisons marked in – safely and rapidly to Hamburg. But Ritter had provided for this too by giving Goertz the name and address of his British head agent Arthur Owens, who he said would always help when help was needed. It was this contact that Goertz used after having decided that all other means, such as dispatch via Lisbon and Madrid, had to be ruled out as unsafe.

Here too secret recognition signs had been agreed between Hamburg, Ireland and London in order to get the important material to Owens without delay. In practice it went like this: a Roman Catholic priest, a member of the nationalist organization who travelled to London several times a month, carried the documents sewn into his shirt. He had exact instructions how to get rid of them. As he set off from Ireland, the Abwehr sent a radio message to Owens (and of course to British Intelligence) who were thus alerted to the fact that the important documents were about to arrive at the Brompton Oratory.

As a result of this transaction Owens was again given a few hours of liberty. Under the watchful eye of two SIS men he went to the Brompton Oratory. He approached the Irish priest who was sitting at the end of a pew and asked him whether he would hear his confession. 'Of course, my son,' said the Irishman and led German agent 3504 to the confessional, where in effect British Intelligence took possession of the espionage material that Hauptmann Goertz had collected.

After the documents had been copied, Owens was sent off to Lisbon, where Ritter, with customary precautions, took possession of the material which was so important for the conduct of the war. These documents were worth the money spent on them, or so they thought in Hamburg. However, a few months later the Abwehr decided to drop their head agent Owens and ceased to answer his call sign.

But what happened to Dickitts, who was to maintain the contact between Hamburg and London after Owens had been dropped?

'We sent him back to Lisbon in March 1941 but he never came back,' is the British version. 'In March 1941 we were expecting him in Lisbon,' Georg Sessler told me, 'but he never showed up.'

'But he can't have vanished into thin air,' I objected.

Sessler laughed and advised me to make inquiries in Moscow – 'They are most likely to know what happened to Mr Dickitts!'

5 3725: Ace in both packs

As senior paymaster of the Abwehr, Dr Martin Toeppen was responsible for supplying its agents with foreign currency. Consequently he
was the only man who not only knew about all the secret operations
against the Western Allies but could also look at them dispassionately,
since he was not directly involved. In his estimate as an accountant, the
only investment that held any promise of a return was the hundred
pounds which Arthur Owens sent off to Wulf Schmidt by registered
letter after his return from Portugal. It was with this meagre starting
capital that Wulf Schmidt was to blossom forth as the top German
agent in Britain.

Ritter agreed with the paymaster, though not for the same reasons,
and exhorted his less experienced Abwehr colleagues to display even
greater psychological finesse in dealing with Wulf Schmidt.

'3725,' he said, 'is the surest pillar of our future work against
Britain.'

On the other side, the British government had naturally realized
Wulf Schmidt's potential value long ago: the flattering tone of the
German radio messages alone was proof enough of the blind confidence
they had in 'their man in England'. Little Schmidt had suddenly
become a kind of prodigy pampered and spoilt by the two warring
powers. The Germans were just as dependent on his cooperation as
were the British, who were now beginning to build up Schmidt, or
'Tate' as they called him, as their own principal agent against the
Abwehr. John Masterman and the other members of the Double-
Cross Committee waited with bated breath for the Germans' next
move. It was the turn of the Hamburg Abwehr strategists.

'Schmidt wants to do great things for Germany,' was the way
Hauptmann Huckriede-Schulz interpreted agent 3725's motives.

Major Ritter on the other hand thought that what Schmidt needed was self-esteem.

'Shouldn't we give him the Iron Cross, I wonder?'

In assessing how to influence their prisoner, whom they addressed as 'Harry', the British psychologists took far more trouble than the Germans. In the course of their week-long discussions with him they had drawn some inportant conclusions: in the first place 'Harry' needed confidence. He was sentimental and needed friends. He felt lonely and wanted contacts. He had always been on the move and needed a home. He had been strictly brought up by his father so he needed understanding. His mother had died early, so he longed for the warmth of family life.

This family background was provided by the head of the Double-Cross Department of British Intelligence, Major T. A. Robertson. He and his attractive wife Joan and their little daughter took him into their home and provided the visitor from Hamburg with warmth and security. This security, in their inconspicuous house in a London suburb, was safeguarded day and night by MI5 officers and unobtrusively watched over by the police. And while the British looked after the new German head agent 3725, Major Ritter's impression was this:

'Immediately after he had landed, 3725 was able to go into hiding with the help of a prostitute. Later he managed to get a job on a farm, where he became friendly with the farmer's daughter. It was through her that he got to know another girl who worked in a Ministry in London and had fantastic contacts . . .'

But his espionage experience had taught Ritter something else: 'The three most important conditions for successful work in the field of espionage are: firstly money, secondly money, and thirdly money!'

The British thought so too, and in order to make sure that agent 3725 was successfully established they hastened to dictate the next moves, which the Abwehr promptly carried out. In reply to Schmidt's radio message: 'Require more money' the blackened aircraft of Hauptmann Gartenfeld circled over a lonely stretch of country north of London in order to deliver £3000 to agent 3725. The former observer Karl-Heinz Süssman could recall this unusual financial transaction: 'On one occasion we had to go on an operational flight to drop money to an agent. The dropping point was indicated by three small fires. The pound notes were stowed away in hollow branches which had been tied into bundles. I cannot remember the exact location of the drop.

But it was north of London in an area stiff with barrage balloons . . .'

With these pound notes supplied by Berlin, the Abwehr base in London seemed set fair for further work. Relying on the principle that you can buy anything with money, groups of spies could now set out from every point of the compass to attack Britain, the final enemy, from all sides. For all these operations – whether launched direct or indirect (via Sweden, Spain or Portugal) – Wulf Dietrich Schmidt was now to act as a kind of supply base, and as a refuge for any agents who felt threatened by British Intelligence.

The strongest and most mysterious link with London, however, was forged without Major Ritter's help, in the shape of Operation Ostro in Lisbon. Although they tried for twenty years to find Ostro, the most highly paid German agent, no intelligence service had actually succeeded in discovering his identity by the end of the war: neither the Russians nor the Czechs, the French or the Americans – not even the British, who had mobilized one of their ablest agents, Kim Philby, against the Lisbon intelligence phantom. Before and during World War Two Ostro operated all over Europe, though some of his reports also came from the United States and Canada.

'A variety of schemes was put forward for the elimination of Ostro,' says Sir John Masterman in his report on German espionage against England. 'They did not succeed. Ostro continued to operate, and caused us anxiety till the end of the war!'

At the time that Sir John Masterman was writing his report after the war, a senior Abwehr officer, Generalleutnant Hans Piekenbrock, was asked by his Russian captors whom he considered the most successful Abwehr agent. Without hesitation he named Ostro and commented that he had been 'an outstanding example of successful work against Britain'.

During his interrogation in Moscow, Piekenbrock was careful not to mention that after 1933 Ostro, under a variety of aliases, had also been active in almost every Eastern European country. In Admiral Canaris' time he was considered 'the most reliable tracker dog' of the German Secret Service.

Before the German troops had occupied the Sudetenland Ostro had spied out the Czech defences and concentration areas. Before Hitler 'liberated' his native Austria it was Ostro who, thanks to his contacts in the Austrian Ministry of Defence, was able to obtain information about important Austrian defensive measures.

For Hitler's attack against Poland, Ostro had supplied his master Canaris with operational plans of the Polish General Staff. It was Ostro again who supplied the Germans with important data on the production plans and delivery contracts of the Ploesti oilfields before the Germans occupied the Balkans.

Before the start of the German offensive in the West Ostro had provided extensive information on the French and Belgian armaments industries. A short time later he had popped up in Copenhagen shortly before the occupation of Denmark. There he was arrested, together with his wife, after having carried out an espionage mission against the British and they were both sentenced to several years' imprisonment in a sensational trial. But almost before he could be taken to his cell the Germans were already moving heaven and earth to obtain his release. He was exchanged for four Scandinavian agents in German jails and sent to Berlin.

Now that Ostro had proved himself on practically all fronts in Europe he was to produce his masterpiece in the war against Britain and America. For this, the economics experts in Berlin had established a beautifully camouflaged trading company in Lisbon. With the Belgian businessman Brugger and an Austrian émigré, Camillo Frank, it was to do worldwide export and import trading, with Ostro as the third partner. In this business cover with international contacts he could play all the cards in his hand, which included intelligence, a charming manner, a phenomenal knowledge of languages and technical and commercial ability. In order to spy on the British and American armaments industries and their strategic planning, he also had unlimited means at his disposal. But more important even than all the treasures provided by the Abwehr was his wife, a beautiful, blonde Scandinavian with an angelic face, to whom admirers of all nations were eager to open their hearts and loosen their tongues.

Ostro's real identity was not even recorded in the Abwehr dossier in the Tirpitzufer. Only Canaris and a handful of trusted colleagues knew it. And my search for him, as in the case of Wulf Schmidt, took me to many places before it ended in the Barcelona cemetery where on 20 October 1958 Ostro had taken his many secrets to his grave.

Fortunately a Hamburg publishing firm was able to provide me with an address in a small and picturesque fishing village on the Costa Brava, and there I found the woman who had been Ostro's wife for thirty years. Her husband had left her a considerable amount of jewellery and she was living on the proceeds. She was quite unable to help regarding her husband's secrets: 'I never knew what my husband really did all those years, and frankly, I did not want to know!'

That was the discouraging start of my researches into the life story of one of the smartest of all German agents, who was also a link in the espionage web of which Wulf Schmidt in London was a member. The legendary spy himself could no longer answer my questions. But still, I was able to obtain a good account of his nebulous activities. In an old leather trunk that his widow had never bothered to open I discovered Ostro's memoirs, five hundred manuscript pages (the spy had written them after the war) in which the 'happy spy' revealed to his opponents in the British and American intelligence services how he had been able to get away again and again from pursuers who had been told to find Ostro and eliminate him!

Well-known historians investigated Ostro's story after the war. Some of them still doubt that he actually existed. From a distance he appeared even to me like some nebulous character, but he began to assume a form when I got to know the circle that he had left in 1958. The real name of the man who hid under the cover of Ostro was Paul Fidrmuc, born in Jägerndorf in Czechoslovakia on 28 June 1898, the son of a lawyer. He joined the Austro-Hungarian army and was taken prisoner by the Italians in 1918. After his return to Jägerndorf he was sentenced to a term of imprisonment for opposition to the Czech regime but managed to escape and went into business in Berlin, where in his spare time he was very active in athletics and rowing. In 1922 he moved to Lübeck, where he was employed in the sales department of a firm of steel exporters. In the following year he married his wife, who was seventeen. Their honeymoon took them to India, and after their return he worked as a journalist for a number of German and foreign commercial and technical journals. It was at this time that he offered his services and his connections with Austrian and Czech intelligence services to the old Reichswehr of the Weimar Republic, and after Hitler assumed power he was taken on as a reserve officer. He continued with his activities as a journalist and businessman in order to have a better cover for his varied intelligence activities.

The things that Paul Fidrmuc, alias Ostro, got up to in Lisbon in order to discover where the American troops went on board their troopship and where they were to land in Europe, or where General Eisenhower's headquarters were and how they were guarded, are reminiscent of some of the scenes in a James Bond film. Ostro not only stole one of the notebooks of the British Ambassador, Sir Ronald

Campbell, he also managed to break into the desk of the British Air Attaché, Air Commodore Fullard. As captured original material shows, Ostro gave the German High Command detailed information concerning important events in the war. He forecast both the American landings in North Africa and the date of the Allied invasion of Normandy. But whether Canaris actually believed the 'valuable reports' from his agent in Lisbon is another matter. At any rate, the reports from Lisbon were the cause (or the pretext) for money, paintings, gold and jewellery to be sent to Portugal in the German diplomatic bags during the war. The most valuable article that Canaris ever sent to Ostro in this way was a tobacco jar encrusted with diamonds, a collectors' piece which was said to have once belonged to Napoleon.

After the war the Spaniards arrested Ostro and deported him to Germany. The Americans doubled their security arrangements at the interrogation camp at Oberursel while he was there, though they were less concerned about his life than about the secrets he had collected in his twenty-five years as a spy. His secret contacts in Moscow, Prague and Warsaw resulted in his release and return to Spain in 1947. A Czech request for his deportation was refused. You do not hang a spy who knows so much!

The Spaniards realized this too when they arrested him after his return, only to release him again a few days later. The banquet that the Spanish intelligence service gave in Ostro's honour and in the presence of Admiral Canaris' widow was the start of a new liaison. This time it was General Franco who had made a profitable catch.

Although Ostro's new bosses were now in Madrid instead of in Berlin, he never gave up his cover occupation as a journalist: up to the date of his death in 1958, Hitler's most highly paid spy acted as Spanish correspondent for the Hamburg *Spiegel*. 'A spy,' Paul Fidrmuc wrote in his memoirs, 'should always be an expert in his cover job, so that people will believe it is genuine.'

'Viola', the next secret operation that Major Ritter – the jack of all trades on every scene of operations – was to undertake in support of Wulf Schmidt, was a tragicomedy. Contrary to what the producer had expected, the play ended with three dead. The woman, who had captivated everyone who met her, disappeared without trace as soon as she landed in England, a mystery which Major Ritter was unable to explain even years after the war. The story had begun so promisingly in 1939, though less so for German than for British Intelligence. Three women had been sent to Germany, all of them 'cuckoo's eggs' which Major Ritter carefully deposited in his own nest and hatched there.

Ritter met the first of these decoys at a tea party in a flat in the Isestrasse – apparently by sheer coincidence – and recruited her there and then as his agent. The name of the forty-five-year-old decoy from London was Mrs May Erikson. Major Ritter recalled that she had 'the soft brown eyes of a doe and chestnut-brown hair'. She was a German by birth, had married a Swede but was divorced, and was now the lady companion to the wife of a senior officer in the Royal Navy living near Grimsby.

An English country estate – open fires, parties at which many of the guests would be officers, whisky – and in the midst of it all the jolly Mrs Erikson, who wanted to serve her German fatherland in her hour of peril: it was difficult to imagine a more ideal situation for an agent of the Hamburg Abwehr station. And so Ritter's acquaintance from the tea party in the Isestrasse was immediately employed to act as a 'talent spotter' in Grimsby and London, with the task of introducing other reliable persons to the Abwehr. At that stage it never occurred to any-one that Mrs Erikson might also be in touch with sis: she was after all a German, so Major Ritter trusted her absolutely.

That same faith encouraged Major Ritter to undertake several journeys to The Hague, Oslo and Stockholm. In the latter place, where Mrs Erikson's children had just started their studies, he produced – with the speed of a conjurer pulling a rabbit out of a hat – a retired Swedish major, whom he recruited as a 'letterbox' for his espionage network. All he had to do was to receive the secret reports and put them into other envelopes addressed either to Mrs Erikson in Grimsby or Major Ritter in Hamburg.

After Ritter had established his 'Scandinavian channel of communica-tion' with much energy and not a little money, the British Secret Service brought the second lady spy into the picture, an Italian countess whom the Abwehr for cover reasons decided to call the 'Duchess of Château-Thierry'. The Duchess was a catch made by the 'talent spotter' Erikson, and her arrival had been announced to Ritter in a letter carefully designed to whet his appetite. Mrs Erikson had stressed the incredible possibilities opened up by the elderly Duchess whose house in Kensington was a meeting place of the highest-ranking British officers, of ministers, journalists and captains of industry.

'The Duchess could be very helpful,' Ritter read in the letter from his talent spotter, 'if . . .'

The 'if' was settled personally and promptly by Major Ritter. It appeared that the Duchess's late husband had left her some properties in Bavaria, and it was a small matter for Ritter to sell them and – what was more important – to have the money sent to the old lady in London by his own secret channels. As a result of this illegal transaction, Ritter reasoned, the Abwehr had got the Duchess firmly on their side, and he lost no time in letting her know what was expected of her. She should open a tea room in Mayfair, was the suggestion . . .

The trio was complete when the third of the intelligence agents, accompanied by her lover Hilmar Dierks, entered the Alsterpavillon in Hamburg, where Ritter was entertaining the 'Duchess'. Ritter had asked the Duchess to have a look at the young girl, Vera von Schalburg, to see whether she was suitable for intelligence work. If she was satisfactory, she might consider employing her in her tea room in London. Talking to his visitor from England Ritter made no secret of who Vera von Schalburg was: 'She has been working for us for some time. We call her Viola.'

It was more than a year after that meeting in the Alsterpavillon in Hamburg, where the Duchess had been acquainted with the Abwehr's intentions against England, that the proposal for a tea room in Mayfair was to take practical shape . . .

The following events occurred on the very day when Schmidt and his friend Goesta Caroli were in Paris waiting for favourable weather for their parachute drop over England. In spite of the dense fog over Hamburg it was lighter than usual when the Abwehr agent Erwin Druecke, a merchant by profession, settled himself behind the wheel of the grey DKW saloon belonging to his friend and boss, in order to drive back into town after a farewell meal at Jakob's, an expensive restaurant. At that meal three men had been trying to drown their sorrows in alcohol: Hilmar Dierks, who was due to go to Holland on a job, and the agents Druecke and Waelti, about to set off by flying boat for the Scottish coast, accompanied by the darling of the Hamburg Abwehr post, Vera von Schalburg, alias Viola.

At about the same time as her companions were finishing their drinking bout, Vera got back to the furnished rooms she rented in the Pappenhuderstrasse after a conference with Ritter's deputy, Hauptmann Julius Boeger. It must have been about midnight, for the Swiss-German

Waelti, who was sitting next to Druecke on the front seat of the car, remembered the bell of the Eppendorf church chiming twelve. Later he thought the bell might have been tolling for Dierks. He had been lying in the back seat, terribly drunk, with his head resting on the rear window frame when the car skidded on a bend and hit a tree.

Waelti rushed out to call an ambulance but when they arrived there was nothing they could do. And having looked at Dierks' papers the police also knew what to do – nothing. Dierks worked for a secret organization, so the details of the accident and especially the names of those involved were carefully suppressed.

While the ambulance men were lifting the unconscious naval espionage officer on to the stretcher, Waelti pulled his Mauser pistol out of his pocket and tried to shoot himself. It was the same pistol with which he was shortly afterwards to threaten an English policeman – two ill-considered actions which seemed to mark him out for the gallows.

In the absence of Major Ritter, who was in Budapest to make sure that the Balkan campaign would get off to a proper start, Hauptmann Boeger rushed first to the scene of the accident and then to the Hamburg Harbour Hospital. There they showed him the face of his former Abwehr colleague Dierks. It was as white as the sheet with which they covered it again immediately afterwards.

A worse experience than the confrontation with the deceased Dierks was Boeger's subsequent meeting with Vera von Schalburg. All her plans for the future were wiped out at three o'clock that morning when Boeger told her as gently as he could that Hilmar Dierks was dead.

Twenty years afterwards I asked Boeger, now a Hamburg business-man, how Vera had reacted to the news of the death of her lover. Vera's background seemed as unfathomable as the dark eyes that I had only seen in photographs. The officer who later in the war was also responsible for the Berlin end of the Karl Richter and Wulf Dietrich Schmidt operations recalled:

Vera's father was murdered by the Red Guards in St Petersburg, and that was the main reason why Vera von Schalburg hated the Russians and offered her services to the Abwehr. I repeatedly offered her large sums of money for the operation against England, but she did not want to take it. So I offered her a well-paid job in Germany instead in the event of her returning.

Vera was madly in love with Dierks. Now that Dierks was dead I reminded her that she was free to refuse to go on the operation to England. But she would not be dissuaded. Now more than ever she wanted to go on the dangerous mission. In memory of her lover, as it were . . .

When Boeger sat at Vera's bedside on that night of 1 September 1940, the attractive Russian's tears must also have dimmed his own vision. Otherwise he might at least have surmised that the seductive ballerina from Anna Pavlova's company had not come to Hamburg entirely by accident.

One of her closest friends, the Dane Jörgen Börresen, told me more about that dreamy, twenty-eight-year-old girl who had virtually loved her way from Russia via Paris, Brussels and London to the Hamburg Abwehr station. Börresen had once saved her life in Finland and he was probably the only person to whom the 'spy with the three faces' had revealed her past at the end of the war:

Vera spent her childhood in a small settlement on a river somewhere beyond the Urals. She had been born in Riga in 1910. When she was three her father, a government official, was posted to St Petersburg, but later banished to Siberia. Vera had an elder brother who later, under the cover name Alex, worked for me as an Abwehr agent. He was awarded the Iron Cross and fell at the Ilmensee as a Captain in the Danish guards. In Siberia Vera, her brother and her parents lived in very modest circumstances on a farm, but still it must have been something of an idyllic life for the children, for Vera often told me how she and her brother used to lie on the river bank watching the passing ships and how they had learned to read the names painted on the stern. In those days she had often spoken to animals and in her lively imagination she had pictured the animals with human heads, all of characters she knew. In 1916 an old teacher turned up at the farm and gave the children their first lessons.

In 1918 the Schalburg family fled to where they felt most at home – to St Petersburg. Here they hid in a cellar belonging to a shoemaker, until one day they were discovered and her father was shot on the spot. Vera told me how she and her mother and brother had fled to Paris and then on to Brussels, where the mother managed to keep them alive by working in a factory. Until 1926 they remained together in a small flat in one of the outer suburbs of Brussels, but then the family broke up. Vera had seen Anna Pavlova dancing when her tour took her to Brussels and she followed the company first to London and then to Paris. There she began to make the acquaintance of men, some of whom were involved in all kinds of shady business. Vera was a romantic and perhaps it was this that finally drew her to the world of espionage . . .

During the war I worked in the same line of business, as an Abwehr agent on Jan Mayen Island, where I pretended to be an explorer, but with instructions to report on British and American convoys. As a result of my arrest I lost contact with Vera for a time. One day I heard about her again: one of her companions who was later hanged, shared the condemned cell with me in Camp 001, Ham Common . . .

In the immediate post-war years Jörgen Börresen had met the mysterious woman spy a few times. For a while they even lived together in a small Paris hotel, Vera with a British passport in a false name.

Having found Wulf Dietrich Schmidt and the other members of the invisible spy network I also wanted to find Vera von Schalburg. Jörgen Börresen could have given me her name and address, but would not do so 'under any circumstances'. All he was prepared to say was: 'Vera is still alive!'

And he added something that threw a better light on her part in the British-German intelligence ploys: 'Before the war she worked in France for the Russian GPU and it was there that she was recruited by British Intelligence in order to penetrate the Abwehr.'

So it was as an agent of the British Secret Service that Vera von Schalburg had become the mistress of Hilmar Dierks, the naval intelligence expert of the Hamburg Abwehr station who, in that capacity, must have known valuable details about the German invasion plans in England. It was this knowledge that Vera had been after in their many nights of love-making!

And now that 'lover' was dead.

For the British Secret Service the events of that night merely had operational consequences: no more information could be expected from source Dierks! For the British SIS strategists the only question that remained was how to get hold of Vera's information as rapidly and as securely as possible.

It was Major Ritter who, unsuspectingly and always ready to help, provided the answer to their problem: with his idea of introducing Vera von Schalburg into the 'Duchess of Château-Thierry's' employment he arranged to have his seductive agent flown to Scotland in a German airforce seaplane. There the British would be able to interrogate their agent at leisure about the information she had been able to gather at the side of her Abwehr lover Hilmar Dierks in Hamburg and in occupied France, in Belgium and Holland, in Denmark and in Norway. To protect his agent Vera, alias Viola, Ritter had ordered the two agents Druecke and Waelti to accompany her on the journey from which there was to be no return.

At first light on 30 September 1940 Vera von Schalburg and her two companions were carefully put ashore on the Banffshire coast.

Even though Major Ritter, ignorant of the true facts, played straight into the hands of the British Secret Service with this operation – which had been given the code name *Hummer* (i.e. Lobster) – his intentions were perfectly sincere. Living up to his principle that no detail was too unimportant, he had paid much attention to the clothing and the equipment of his agents: Viola was wearing a dark-grey costume and wore a bonnet Scottish style. Druecke and Waelti were wearing tweed suits, naturally made of British cloth and in British style. Their papers were in order. Nothing could go wrong. They each had a Kodak camera. And we had even given them English bicycles that one of our agents had stolen from the British Consulate in Stavanger.'

The bicycles were one of the most important parts of their equipment, for on them the trio of German agents were to pedal their way – inconspicuously, as if on a cycling holiday and clad in tweeds and bonnets – through Scotland, right down to the Channel coast where they were to spy on the defences for Major Ritter.

'Druecke and the Swiss Waelti spoke very poor English,' Ritter told me after the war when he explained his Scottish secret strategy to me, 'so I sent Viola with them as interpreter.'

But the bicycle journey planned by Major Ritter ended before it had started, for shortly before they got ashore the three heavy machines fell out of the rubber dinghy in the heavy surf.

The comedy was continued at 7.30 on that morning of 30 September at a small Scottish railway station, where Vera and Erwin Druecke asked the porter, Geddes, the name of the station.

'Port Gordon, madam,' came the reply.

Their suspicions aroused by the unusual question, Geddes and the stationmaster, John Donald, watched the pair as they studied the timetable in the waiting room and then asked for two single tickets to Forres. Their suspicions about the couple were deepened when the man paid with money from a roll of brand-new pound notes, and when they noticed that although it was a dry day the feet of the man and the woman were soaked to well above their ankles. John Donald quietly slipped into his office and picked up the telephone. A few minutes later Grieve, the village policeman, appeared and asked the strangers for their identity cards. Their papers were made out in the names of Vera Erikson and François de Deeker, but the policeman noticed that where there should have been a letter 'I' there was a 'J' – a German habit.

Meanwhile police inspector John Simpson had arrived from Buckie and when he and Grieves checked the couple's luggage they found further evidence of their espionage mission: a Mauser pistol with a full ammunition clip, a box with nineteen rounds of German 6.5 ammunition, a list of contact addresses in England, a German army radio set with five spare batteries, a voltmeter, headphones and a tin of Frankfurter sausages . . .

On searching the beach where the Germans had landed, the Scottish police also found a pair of gumboots which however did not fit either of the two captives. The feet that they did fit had meanwhile carried their owner Waelti quite a considerable distance. He had soon separated from Vera and Erwin Druecke and had managed to get a train from Buckie to Aberdeen and on to Edinburgh. There he left his suitcase in the left-luggage office at Waverley station before going to a cinema in Princes Street, to pass the time before the next train was due to leave for London.

That act ended a few minutes after 11 pm that day at the Waverley left-luggage office. The men in the slouch hats and raincoats reacted silently and quickly when Waelti, returning from the cinema, made a lightning grab for the Mauser in his right-hand pocket; he found himself face to face with Chief Constable Merrilees and CID Inspector Sutherland.

In the final act of the tragedy of the *Hummer* operation, Druecke and Waelti made one more brief appearance on the stage – for their execution. Then the curtain descended. Not as a shroud for the dead but as a veil to conceal the fact that Vera von Schalburg was still alive.

Remembering the tragi-comedy after the war, Nikolaus Ritter still lamented in Hamburg: 'If only they had kept their bicycles and had followed our instructions, they would certainly have reached their operational areas without being intercepted, and the two men would still be alive today.'

What happened to Vera von Schalburg?

The British Secret Service allowed her to die formally, in order to let her go on living – under a new identity.

I tried very hard to trace Vera. In Copenhagen, where her mother lived, there was a parrot from their days in Siberia, who across the years and two world wars still repeated a word that a little girl had once taught him – 'Vera!'

Another hint regarding the whereabouts of the seductive agent from Siberia was given to me by Mrs Huntingford, whom I happened to meet on a skiing holiday in the Tyrol in 1959. She was the secretary to Lord Jowitt, who had been the judge in the cases brought against German spies during the war.

In his office in the House of Lords, Lord Jowitt received me courteously for the interview we had arranged, and willingly answered all my questions concerning the sentences against former German agents. When I asked him about Vera von Schalburg, however, he answered quietly: 'Naturally I cannot tell you any secrets, but it will suffice if I tell you that for certain reasons no charge was preferred against Mrs Erikson. All I know is that we kept her here in England, where she was still of some use to our authorities.'

In the first year of his career as a spy, Wulf Dietrich Schmidt had literally bombarded the Hamburg Abwehr station with 'reliable' reports about the tremendous British defences on the Channel coast. After Dunkirk he had managed virtually to defend Britain with his reports. In order to put a brake on the attacks of the German naval forces for instance, Schmidt transmitted to Germany details of alleged minefields, containing information which he claimed to have got from a contact in the Admiralty in London. As a result of this completely fabricated report, an area of some 3600 square miles was closed to German submarines.

Schmidt also managed to blow up the British air defences into an oversize barrage balloon with the help of the reports prepared for him by the Secret Service, which even impressed Reichsmarschall Hermann Goering. Things that the German reconnaissance planes could not observe on British airfields were reported on by agent 3725, thanks to his extraordinary contacts in underground RAF depots. The production figures for the British aircraft industry supplied by Schmidt were far in excess of those estimated by other informants.

Anyone in the German High Command who thought that the British Channel coast was largely undefended – 'harmless pasture and cornfields' – was taught otherwise by Wulf Dietrich Schmidt. According to him it would have been most inadvisable to attack the south coast of England. In the very places where the British Isles really were vulnerable in 1940–1, and where there were huge gaps in the defences, the British deception committee managed to construct frightening scarecrows: drifting mines, invisible tank traps and remote-controlled oil fire traps.

Naturally there were sceptics in the evaluation sections of Fremde Heere West, the department of the German General Staff where the enemy order of battle was studied, who had reservations about Schmidt's reports. But logical arguments counted for little amid the blast of war. The ones whose opinions prevailed were those who cast aside all doubts and loudly proclaimed: 'Schmidt is absolutely reliable!'

This was the opinion of one who was bound to know: Major Ritter. And with that the secret battle between London and Hamburg with its worldwide implications went on. As a reward for the 'exact details' with which Schmidt had so impressively described the British defences, he was to be given the Iron Cross, Second Class. And in addition Major Ritter felt that the patriotic endeavours of his star agent should be acknowledged with the sum of twenty thousand Reichsmarks.

'He was like an animal on the run,' Ritter reported in his memoirs. 'He slept rough or in barns and was on the point of starvation . . .'

In this situation the man obviously needed help and that was to be given him with German thoroughness:

Problem: In order to be able to expand his intelligence activities agent 3725 must be supplied with twenty thousand Reichsmarks, payable to him in London in English currency.

Proposal: In order to disguise the German connection, the money should be delivered by the Japanese, with whom the Abwehr in Berlin had long had close contacts.

Preparation: Dr Thoran of Abwehr Berlin will go to Hamburg to discuss the details of the handover with Major Ritter. Dr Thoran will then return to the Reich capital in order to make the necessary arrangements with the Japanese.

While the discussions were going on with the Japanese, the air between Berlin and Tokyo was thick with messages with details of the recognition signals to be used in contacting agent 3725 in London. And while these messages were being relayed from Tokyo to the Japanese Embassy in London, the radio station in Wohldorf was busy telling Schmidt about the arrangements that had been made for the safe transfer of the two thousand pounds.

In order to make doubly sure, a quarto page of white paper, without watermark, was torn in two, and one sent to Wulf Dietrich Schmidt by the Abwehr station in Lisbon, while the other matching piece would be produced by the Japanese emissary at the clandestine meeting as proof of his bona fides.

This is what happened: a Japanese Assistant Naval Attaché, Mitinori Yosii, carrying a copy of *The Times* in his right hand and a book in the other, boarded the first No. 11 bus to leave the Victoria bus station after 4 pm. Wulf Dietrich Schmidt, wearing a red tie, boarded the same bus and took the seat next to the Japanese. After a time Schmidt was to ask: 'Is there anything new in *The Times*?'

The Japanese answered: 'Nothing special, but you can have the paper if you like. I have read it.'

It was only after they had reached the fifth stop that the Japanese was allowed to hand over the folded newspaper with the two thousand pounds in it to Schmidt. Unnoticed by them, two photographers of British Intelligence had also managed to make a record of what Ritter had described as 'this unique solution of a very complex problem'. The pictures provided evidence of the next three points scored by British Intelligence in their game against the Abwehr.

As a result of the 'unique solution' of the currency deal via Berlin–Tokyo–London, British Intelligence had unexpectedly obtained confirmation of the close cooperation between the German and Japanese secret services. Secondly the lengths the Germans had gone to to arrange the delivery of the money impressed the British with the importance that the Abwehr attached to Wulf Dietrich Schmidt and the fact that Major Ritter clearly intended to entrust agent 3725 with other important work. The third point gave much pleasure to the paymaster of British Intelligence: in future he need not budget for the deception activities of the Double-Cross Committee; the Abwehr would go on paying for that, both in cash and in lives.

The ingenious delivery of cash to Schmidt was the last masterpiece to be executed by Major Ritter on the Western front. He had run out of grandiose ideas. All his agents had been blown up like so many colourful bubbles that would inevitably burst, one after the other, though Ritter either did not notice or refused to notice. Having carefully laid his cuckoo's eggs in America, in England and in the Balkans, and having come to grief with a well-advertised operation in Africa, he decided that it was time to conquer fresh fields: he would leave the grey, anonymous world of espionage and enter instead the glittering world of diplomacy, where, he felt, his talents would enable him to carry on his work for the Third Reich. But his new role was short-lived.

'I was to go to Turkey as Air Attaché and then on to Rio. I flew to Rome where I was asked to dinner by the service attachés and after that I went back to my hotel,' he recalled. 'Next morning I was to continue my flight at about five in the morning, when suddenly, the telephone rang: "Ritter, you are to come back to Berlin at once!"'

There the head of Abwehr I, Colonel Hans Piekenbrock, told him something he was never able to understand as long as he lived. Ritter's transfer to a diplomatic post had been firmly vetoed by Reich Foreign Minister Ribbentrop in person. The collapse of his espionage ring in the

United States and the resulting publicity had made Ritter's name a byword all over the world – and at that time the Germans were still unaware of what had happened to his agents in Britain!

It appears that Nikolaus Ritter never got over the sudden collapse of his careers both as a spy master and as a diplomat. Years later the ex-spy was anxious to continue the good work he had been prevented from pursuing under Hitler. 'After the war Minister Lehr worked on me again and again: "Ritter", he used to say, "you simply must write about your intelligence experience in the last war. Make it a primer. Our young officers could learn a lot from you!" '

Nor was the German Chancellor Konrad Adenauer safe from the advice offered by the secret veteran. On one occasion he suggested making use of his old Egyptian contacts in order to settle the Palestine problem and was baffled by the fact that his fellow-Rhinelander Adenauer did not even bother to answer his letter. The self-styled German top spy master of World War Two clearly had an outsize talent for putting his foot in it.

The details that Wulf Dietrich Schmidt and the other agents of the Hamburg Abwehr station had gathered while practising sabotage on the vulnerable spots in German power stations and shipyards were not merely intended for the British archives. The information supplied by the Anglo-German double agents was soon translated into action by the planners in British Intelligence.

In late March 1941 the former Hitler Youth leader Herbert Meyer, brimful with detailed information on the staff and technical layout of the Blohm & Voss shipyards in Hamburg, boarded a sailing boat in Aberdeen and was towed out to sea by a small ship of the Royal Navy before being cast off and setting course for Norway. The young sailor, who had been captured as one of the crew of a German weather ship, was setting out with a brief from the British Secret Service. His instructions were to report to the German authorities as soon as possible after landing on the Norwegian coast, claiming to be an escaped prisoner of war. In time he should try to obtain a job with Blohm & Voss with a view to sabotaging German submarine production. This done, he should obtain further instructions from a British radio agent based in Northern Germany whom he should contact by inserting an advertisement in the Hamburg *Fremdenblatt*. The agreed recognition phrase was a passage from the Bible: 'Come to me, all ye who are heavily laden.'

Three days after the escape, stage-managed by the British Secret Service, Corporal Erich Kokoschka of the Oslo Abwehr station was silently eyeing the young prisoner called Herbert Meyer who was sitting on his bed in his cell. He was at the end of his tether. During the last two hours of his interrogation his breathing had become quicker and quicker and Kokoschka figured that he would confess at any moment. For the story that the young man had told about his trip across the North Sea in a sailing boat he claimed to have stolen had not sounded very convincing to the Abwehr officers. On the contrary, some inconsistencies concerning the motives for his flight which he said he had undertaken during a storm and in fog had made them suspect that Meyer had been sent by British Intelligence.

But the interrogators could not be sure. What they had noticed was that the prisoner, who had been picked up by a coastal patrol south of Stavanger the previous morning and handed over to Hauptmann Grothe of the Oslo Abwehr station, had protested his devotion to Germany and to the Führer Adolf Hitler a little too much.

Kokoschka slowly and deliberately took off his dark-rimmed spectacles and leaning over quite close to the young man said: 'Look at me carefully and imagine me without a moustache.'

Then he covered his Hitler-moustache with two fingers and looking straight at the prisoner he fired his catch question: 'Don't you remember seeing me at the sabotage school in England, without glasses and without my moustache?'

The former Hitler Youth leader and present British agent collapsed and had to be revived. And then the young man, whose days were numbered, gave them the details of the important sabotage school near London:

The school is near St Albans and is run by British Intelligence officers. Apart from me, there were eight Norwegians, seven Frenchmen, six Belgians, two Austrians, a Czech and a Pole on the course. The students use cover names and wear civilian clothes. We were forbidden to use our real names. We were not allowed to leave the school precincts which were guarded by soldiers.

The lectures covered history, sabotage and intelligence work, explosives and their uses, map reading, tapping telephones, shooting with machine guns, sub-machine-guns, rifles and pistols, wireless, printing and propaganda.

We were also instructed in the handling of explosives, fuses, different time fuses for explosions on land and under water, limpet mines for attacking shipping, and small magnetic mines for destroying cars, petrol tanks etc. We were also taught how to destroy telephone cables.

From this description the German High Command deduced: 'The British Intelligence service is training members of the countries occupied by the Reich in the perpetration of acts of sabotage and in intelligence work in their native countries . . .'

The information about the British sabotage school also decided where the Abwehr were to strike their next blow: Operation *Hummer Nord III*, a repetition of Vera von Schalburg's ill-fated mission.

With the catch-phrase 'We must get through', it was now the turn of the Abwehr station in the large building near the Klingenberggatan in Oslo to show their colleagues in the Hamburg Knochenhauerstrasse how a perfect intelligence operation should be carried out.

The success of this operation was to be guaranteed by two young Norwegians, whom Hauptmann Müller had discovered in the course of a long and complex talent-spotting and recruiting campaign. The first man, whom he thought most suitable for the operation in England, had been found in the German censorship office run by Hauptmann Röhmer and had been given the cover name Tege. He was twenty-three years of age and already had some qualifications for the job: he was employed, in that first year of the German occupation, to read the mail going abroad and to look out for any suspicious expression and hidden meaning. Anything he discovered he could report to his superiors in faultless German, which he had picked up before the war when he had been in Wiesbaden as secretary to the Minister Samheyde, who together with Professor Birkeland had built up the famous Norsk-hydro concern.

The second man, whom the Germans simply called Jack, was twenty-one. Before installing him in the export offices of Herr Andersen, alias Angermaier (well known on account of his herring-bone overcoats), at the Johansgatan, Jack had been an assistant in his father's barber shop. His mother had been an Englishwoman, a dancer in the old Mayol Theatre. His grandfather had at one time been mayor of Manchester. This ideal background was further improved by the fact that Jack could not only play the piano divinely, he was also a pronounced lady's man.

Equipped with these talents Jack was to be the contact man in the agent duet. Tege, who had been trained in a school for Norwegian NCOs before the war, was to tackle the technical problems they would run across during their illegal work in England. At that time British Intelligence had an efficient network of informants at its disposal in Norway, and they were relatively well informed about German moves, so the Germans were obliged to make a special effort to explain away the sudden disappearance of Tege and Jack: first of all the rumour was put about in Norwegian resistance circles that the two had made some anti-German remarks and had therefore thought it prudent to disappear from Oslo for a while. On the night of 9 April, while German police were carrying out the second part of this smokescreen operation by making inquiries about the whereabouts of Tege and Jack among their friends and acquaintances, the two 'refugees' were boarding a German double-decker Arado seaplane, bound for Scotland, in support of Wulf Dietrich Schmidt.

It was intended that Jack and Tege should also get to their operational areas by bicycle and for this purpose two ancient English-made bicycles that Angermaier had somehow got hold of were loaded on the plane. The funds for their expedition were one hundred pounds in notes, for which they had to sign a receipt and which they subsequently discovered were of a type no longer in circulation.

Still, the agent runner Angermaier, who had to supervise their departure from Stavanger, thought the two potential suicide candidates looked 'very smart in their sky-blue boilersuits and gumboots'. Around midnight while they were making a last check of their equipment – bicycle, radio, pistols and rucksacks – Angermaier, whose knowledge about England had been picked up at school, was telling them how easy it would be for them to go to ground: 'You won't have any difficulty in getting around Scotland without being detected. The roads are packed with refugees from the bombed-out cities, so no one is going to ask you where you have come from. And if things should get too hot you have always got your guns!'

In Stavanger Tege and Jack left only two traces behind: one, for the benefit of the British, was in a small harbour south of Stavanger. There Corporal Erich Kokoschka had arranged to have an old and dilapidated fishing boat stolen, not to help the two escape but to act as proof of their escape. If the British caught them, at least that statement could be checked.

The other souvenir of the cheerful couple was a swingeing bill for their farewell party in the Victoria Hotel in Stavanger which caused some raised eyebrows among the Abwehr accounts officers in Oslo and Berlin, as they saw the long list of champagne, caviare and lobster that had been consumed and which prompted one of them to ask: 'I suppose this really was necessary?'

The two agents had hardly recovered from their meal at the hotel when the aircraft touched down on the water off the Scottish coast. While the plane rose and sank with the swell, Tege and Jack hurriedly and silently went on with the task they had practised so often back in Stavanger in very similar weather conditions, of transferring their gear into the inflated rubber dinghy. When they had got their bicycles, radio set and rucksacks full of sabotage materials aboard, the aircraft turned and got ready to take off again in an easterly direction.

The dinghy was tossing about like a cockleshell in the surf as the crew of the Arado took a last look at them during take-off. They were the last Germans to see them. For years after that, there were to be only the radio reports of the exploits of the two successful spies . . .

As the Germans saw it, their landing and the operations that followed had all the elements of tension that arise in a cinema when the picture fades out at the most interesting moment and only the sound is audible, for Jack and Tege soon started sending their messages, first from a hide-out in Glasgow, then from London and then again from Scotland. These radio reports made the then head of the sabotage department of the Abwehr, Colonel Erwin von Lahousen, almost lyrical.

Though the British interrogating officers in the camp at Bad Nenn-dorf had knocked his front teeth out after the war, the eyes of the Austrian aristocrat von Lahousen-Vivremont sparkled with pride as he told me the success story of Jack and Tege in his apartment in Solbad Hall in the Tyrol. In the room where we sat there were also some mementoes of Wulf Dietrich Schmidt: daggers and some photgraphs of his Japanese colleagues whom Lahousen had involved in Ritter's currency transaction for '3725' in London.

The ex-sabotage boss was suffering from a weak heart and his review of the 'outstanding success' of the two Norwegians Tege and Jack was greatly assisted by some notes for a book that Admiral Canaris had intended writing after the war as a vindication of his Abwehr. It appeared that Canaris was going to devote a special panegyric to Jack and Tege, whose first mention in the notes is dated 1 May 1941: 'The dispatch of two agents to Britain as part of Operation *Hummer Nord III* was successful. The agents (Jack and Tege) have reported from London by means of the radio set they had taken with them.'

After this brief sign of life Jack and Tege were to report to the Norwegian authorities in London in the hope of joining one of the Norwegian units in exile and there continue their espionage and sabo-tage activities. On 3 June Lahousen again heard from his energetic

Norwegians: 'The agents sent to Britain as part of Operation *Hummer Nord III*, who in the interests of their own safety had been forbidden to use their radio set until 1 June, have again reported now that date is past and have resumed radio contact with the Oslo Abwehr station.'

On 10 June Canaris' friend Lahousen noted in his diary that the two agents had radioed an interesting report to Oslo on the identity and ration cards in use and on the procedures for registering and handling Scandinavian refugees.

Well supplied with cash and basking in praise, Jack and Tege, together with Wulf Dietrich Schmidt, were the pride and joy of the Abwehr. After all the agents' success also reflected great credit on the officers running them and on their superiors. Understandably therefore Lahousen remembered this great moment of his career with pride.

'Tege had even succeeded in getting himself posted to a Norwegian battalion that was originally stationed in Scotland but was then transferred to Iceland. There obviously our man was right in the centre of things,' Lahousen enthused, rather in the style of Leutnant Wein, who had sung the praises of 3725 in similar terms when I started my investigations.

On the next page of Lahousen's secret diary, work was to begin in earnest for Jack and Tege. I could detect that from the sombre tone in which the German sabotage chief read out to me the order he had sent to England on 7 July 1941: 'The agents of Operation *Hummer Nord III* were ordered to begin sabotage operations.'

And so the two agents – or at least so Lahousen told me – set off once more for Scotland, where they retrieved the sabotage materials they had buried in order to transport them to the target areas by bicycle. After that a number of radio messages announced their alleged successes in setting fire to British ammunition dumps, food stores, timber yards and factories.

With great empathy Lahousen could remember all the difficulties and dangers that his agents faced in Britain – 'To be able to commit acts of sabotage when practically every hut and every crossroad was watched by the Home Guard my men needed not only nerves of iron but also money and lots and lots of fuses and explosives!'

And while the former sabotage boss was still worried about his agents' welfare after all those years, he slowly turned the pages to the next event, recorded on page 248 of his diary:

A report on Operation *Hummer Nord III* has been submitted to the Chief of the High Command. The two agents sent to Britain in the course of this operation were supplied by air with a radio set and money on 20 February in an operation carried out in exemplary cooperation with the fifth air fleet, while two neighbouring localities were bombed as a diversionary measure. This method of supplying agents under cover of an air attack has proved to be useful and successful.

Wilhelm Canaris, the credulous head of the Abwehr, needed some high-sounding reports in order to maintain his position vis-à-vis his competitor in the intelligence field, Reinhard Heydrich of the SD, all the more so as the American network established by Major Ritter had collapsed in the summer of 1941. To keep ahead of his fiendish opponent, Canaris needed trump cards, and his subordinates were only too eager to provide them for him. With hindsight it is possible to see that in this domestic battle for precedence in the intelligence field the Abwehr were the losers from the very start, for many of the supposed trump cards dealt to Canaris by members of his service were in reality jokers that the enemy intelligence services had managed to mix in with the pack. With this sort of hand, the Admiral was in time to lose the game against his SD rival completely and tragically.

But for the moment Canaris was still one of the senior yes-men, serving up reports of the Abwehr successes to Hitler: from the caviare-fortified outpost in Portugal the head of the station, Major Albert von Karsthof, sent him reports from his reliable agents Ivan and Ostro. In Stockholm a mysterious 'Dr K' sent piles of reports from Hector and Josephine, two of his agents in England. Madrid boasted of Alaric, a Spaniard who had managed to set up his own agent network in England. Hamburg supplied the chief with the strategically important reports from their star agent Wulf Dietrich Schmidt (assessed: very valuable) and Oslo provided the Tege and Jack reports, fresh from Scotland, all hinting at a landing in Norway, which made even Generalissimo Hitler a trifle unsure of himself.

'It is possible that they may attempt a landing up in Norway,' Hitler informed Admiral Voss (at that time naval representative in the Führer's headquarters). 'We will have to operate with packs of submarines off Northern Norway ... We will have to start sending submarines up there at once, before it is too late ...'

Who were the men concealed by these cover names, who with their deception reports were able at two critical stages of the war to tie down

German divisions in Norway and to keep tank formations in readiness at the wrong place, while Field Marshal Rommel badly needed them for the defence of Alamein? Who were the men who were able to spread rumours about an impending Allied landing in Norway and so force Hitler to make the miscalculation for the 'longest day' of the war – the invasion on 6 June 1944?

Where could I find them – Tege, the commercial corrsepondent, and Jack, the lady's hairdresser, who like Wulf Dietrich Schmidt had lured Germany into a trap with their radio sets and who, like puppets manipulated by London were to help destroy the Africa Corps and decide the outcome of the Normandy invasion in the Allies' favour?'

After the war, when Tege and Jack had finished playing their double agent role, the British – who called them Mutt and Jeff – made even more strenuous efforts to conceal their identities than the Germans had made during the war. The British produced a number of arguments for their attempts to throw people off their scent; they would very much like to help, I was told, but: 'It would be against the law!'

In spite of that, in 1970 it took me less time to track down Tege and Jack than it had taken me to find Wulf Dietrich Schmidt. I noticed that the cover name Tege sounded like the contraction of the two letters T and G, and I tried out my idea on the Oslo telephone directory. After a few false starts my call was answered by someone called Tor Glad, and when I spoke to him in German and told him I was calling from Munich he greeted me with a 'Grüss Gott!'

And that was how I met that reliable agent in a 'beer tent' at the Munich Oktoberfest and persuaded him to tell me things that no German was aware of up to that time, and which the British had made such efforts to conceal.

At first Tor Glad was not too anxious to revive memories of the most dramatic moments of his life; he was employed by Norwegian television as an expert on British affairs and would have preferred to leave the whole matter buried in the past. I managed to wear down his resistance by firing hundreds of questions at him: first the name of his companion, whom the American historian Ladislas Farago thought was a man by the name of Olaf Klausen.

'My friend's name is John Helge Neal Moe; that is his real name!' the ex-Abwehr agent informed me, but immediately threw up a defence against my curiosity on behalf of his friend: 'After the war Moe got a job teaching English to SAS air crews. He lived in Stockholm for a time.

But I am afraid that will not help you very much. I am sure Jack will tell you nothing about his work in England. He is not allowed to. They made him sign the Official Secrets Acts in London and that means: keep mum for ever!'

Wulf Schmidt had also sworn this oath of eternal silence. Now I realize what he really meant by his ambiguous statement during my first visit: 'I cannot talk about my past, because to do so would mean betraying old friends who gave me important information during the war.'

Those 'friends' were Sir John Masterman, Major T. A. Robertson and the other British intelligence officers who planned and directed the deception game against the German Wehrmacht and who had all been sworn to secrecy about the tricks they had played, just like their agents.

Whether it was the unrestrained Bavarian merrymaking at the Oktoberfest, or the Bavarian beer, or that the British had forgotten to tie Tor Glad's tongue, I do not know. But it is a fact that on that Theresienwiese in Munich, Tege, the Anglo-German spy, told me things that none of the other spies who had evaded the hangman had ever dared tell:

The Germans had ordered us to slit open the rubber dinghy with our knives after we had landed and fill it with stones to sink it. No one was to know where we had come from. Instead, we pulled the dinghy ashore and tried to find someone to give ourselves up to, but there was no one about.

In the end Jack went off and found a fisherman's hut. It was six o'clock. Jack knocked at the door and told the astonished fisherman that we had just landed in the bay from a German seaplane:

'We just want to know where the next military post is.'

Half an hour after we had landed the Chief Constable of Banffshire arrived in his car to fetch us in person. He gave us a friendly nod, as if we were old friends whom he had been expecting.

'. . . and where are you from?'

'Straight from Norway, from Stavanger,' I replied.

'And what have you brought for us?'

'Here is my pistol.'

'Have you got any ammunition?'

'Yes, twenty-five rounds.'

Jack and I gave the Chief Constable and the officer accompanying him our guns, our rucksacks and, most important of all, our radio set.

Then we drove off to Banff. Our bicycles were tied to the roofrack . . . In Banff there were a few hundred people waiting for us, who would have liked to lynch us!

The 'damned German spies' Jack and Tege were taken to Aberdeen jail late in the evening of 9 April 1941. There the interrogations started, to be continued next day in Scotland Yard and finally in Camp 001 at Ham Common, under the direction of Major Stevens. Their 'de-lousing' treatment was brief and thorough: within three days their blue boiler suits were parcelled up and stored away in the cellars of the interrogation centre.

Then the two Norwegians slipped into the tweed suits they had brought with them, ready for the parts that they were henceforth to act under the secret stage management of British Intelligence. Tor Glad told me how:

Four hours after our last interrogation they fetched Jack Moe and me out of our cells. Our radio set stayed behind in the interrogation room and we were surprised to be taken for a spot of London night-life. Our companions were six young MI5 officers who took us to a club – some sort of cellar in the West End. There they tried to fill us up with alcohol to loosen our tongues, but as it turned out, Jack and I were able to hold our liquor better than our English 'friends'.

After that wild party we finished up in the early morning in a mysterious house in Crespigny Road. Next door there was an even more mysterious villa. It had two floors and was empty. The house we were in was occupied by a man who called himself Mr Poulton, and his wife and son. He was the SIS radio expert and it was his job to supervise our transmissions to Oslo, although he said he could not speak a word of German.

We had told the British all about the radio instructions they had given us in Oslo. We showed them a book of crossword puzzles with which we were to encipher our own messages and decipher the ones we received from Oslo. We also told the British about the code word 'Henry' that we had to insert in our messages at certain intervals, to show that we were at liberty. If we were caught and obliged to transmit under duress we were to drop the word 'Henry'. In order to fool the Germans we naturally went on sending 'Henry', but in spite of this our double game with the Abwehr almost came to an end when it had hardly started: in order to make quite sure that our transmissions would reach the Germans, Mr Poulton had used his own aerial, and the strength of the signal had immediately been noticed by the Abwehr operators in Oslo. Promptly came the question: 'What aerial are you using.'

We answered without hesitation: 'Aerial as supplied.'

And the Germans seemed quite satisfied.

From the outside the suburban house and the villa in London's Crespigny Road were two completely different but ordinary buildings. The suburban house was occupied by a perfectly normal family – Joan and Thomas A. Robertson, with their little daughter and a grandmother who spent most of the time with the little girl. There was also a visitor, a pale little man whom the Robertson family treated with a solicitude that was quite touching, and whom they called Harry. Harry, alias Wulf Dietrich Schmidt, had apparently only recently come out of hospital, for he was fed and looked after like a convalescent.

It seemed a happy household. No wonder that the Robertsons had many friends, who were constantly coming and going.

The house in Crespigny Road and the life of the Poulton family gave the same impression of domestic bliss. Here however it was a little boy who provided the screen for what was actually going on in the house. In the first years of the war Mr and Mrs Poulton's little son was too young to remember the names of the visitors who arrived carrying briefcases and who spent hours talking to his father. Nor would he have been interested in the German army radio set that was hidden away somewhere in the villa. And he never inquired who the two strangers were who popped in now and again and called themselves Mutt and Jeff. The child was not interested in the man who accompanied them, a lieutenant in civilian clothes by the name of Chris Harmer, who lived nearby in Harley Street.

The secret British radio station in Crespigny Road and Wulf Dietrich Schmidt's hideout in the suburbs were so well camouflaged that none of the neighbours even guessed what went on inside. It was from these houses that the German secret battle front was continuously bombarded with misleading information. The two steel rod aerials on the roofs of the houses occupied by harmless British families were two of the heaviest guns for the defence of Winston Churchill's Britain.

With his two 'deception cannons' – one of them aimed at France and fired by Wulf Dietrich Schmidt, the other with its sights trained on Norway and serviced by Mutt and Jeff – the crafty British premier was actually able to persuade Hitler, in a grandiose deception scheme, to pull out several German divisions from the Eastern front and send them to France. The result was that there were forty-five German divisions on the Western front, strung out along a line from the Channel coast to Northern Norway, waiting for the first signs of the Allied invasion of Norway or France which Canaris' 'successful Abwehr agents' Wulf Dietrich Schmidt, Jack Moe and Tor Glad were constantly hinting about to Hamburg and Oslo.

In the meantime Wulf Dietrich Schmidt alias Tate had been awarded the Iron Cross by Hitler, in recognition of 'outstanding merit'. Jack Moe (Mutt) and Tor Glad (Jeff) had also proved to their masters in

Berlin that they had repeatedly been in mortal danger in contributing to the final German victory. They proudly reported a series of acts of sabotage which Colonel von Lahousen had ordered them to carry out and which the Abwehr officers responsible smugly added to their battle honours.

'Sabotage successes' like this presented some problems. They must have a real background if they were to appear credible to the Germans. For this reason, for instance, a food store in Wealdstone was actually set on fire by means of an explosion. When the depot was alight, the intelligence officers let everything happen that normally happens in such cases: the firemen poured water on the blaze, the photographers took photographs, the local press reported on the incident without anyone even guessing that the 'enemy act of sabotage' was a well-staged performance by John Masterman's Double-Cross Committee.

Now that the faith of the German Abwehr in their agents had been underpinned, the radio barrage could continue.

6 Some double-cross gambits

'Valuable information costs money.' That was Major Ritter's advice to his successor, Hauptmann Julius Boeger, before going off to North Africa in 1941 and leaving Boeger to run the agents he had sent to Britain. Boeger had hardly started in his new job when one of those agents, Wulf Dietrich Schmidt, presented him with a problem: Schmidt's valuable reports on troop movements in Southern England became increasingly interspersed with requests for money, which finally assumed the form of an ultimatum: 'Require money at once ... unless money received soon, you can go to hell ...'

Wulf Dietrich Schmidt, who was keeping a dozen radio operators busy in Wohldorf and whose reports made twice that number of officers in the Hamburg Knochenhauerstrasse and the Berlin Tirpitz-ufer indispensable, had to be treated like a spoilt child.

Thirty years later, on 11 September 1971, in his office in Hamburg, Herr Boeger sighed: 'Thank goodness, we were saved by an unexpected stroke of luck.'

Then he went on to give me some details which finally led me to a man I had been looking for for a long time. All Herr Boeger could remember was this:

One day we heard about an American actor who had twenty thousand pounds in England and wanted to transfer the money to the United States illegally. Naturally this was just the sort of thing we had been hoping for. There were a lot of telegrams whizzing to and fro between Berlin, Lisbon and Hamburg and Wulf Dietrich Schmidt in England, but in the end we managed to get the thing settled. Schmidt was to collect the money from a certain theatre agency in London. To make quite sure that only he could get hold of that large sum we naturally took all sorts of precautions. He had to go to the agency on three successive days and ask certain prearranged questions. We only telegraphed the questions to London just before he was due to set off to make the call . . . The entire operation worked beautifully. Schmidt got his money and then of course he was able to recruit even better sources. In addition he was able to pass on some of the money to other agents . . . If I remember rightly we gave the American actor the equivalent sum in dollars when he passed through Lisbon.

Anyone earning twenty thousand pounds in those days must have been a very famous actor, I thought. But Herr Boeger was unable to tell me his name.

Who in the Abwehr dealt with foreign currencies in 1941? Who was the courier who took a large sum of dollars to Lisbon? Who was the intermediary who handed over the money to the mysterious American actor? My journey – which was concerned only with this small aspect of Wulf Dietrich Schmidt's past – took me on 17 October 1974 to the secluded country residence of a Monsieur Dusko Popov, in Opio, a few kilometres north of Cannes.

As I drove through the gateway of what had once been the summer residence of the bishops of Grasse, where Dusko Popov, now sixty-four years of age, could relax with his family after a life of adventure, I already knew in general terms whom I was about to meet: one of the most successful agents of World War Two. It has been said that Ian Fleming modelled his James Bond on Dusko Popov.

A taciturn Tunisian servant, the quaint old ivy-covered house, and Jill, a flaxen-haired Swedish girl in sky-blue jeans, provided the right kind of James Bond setting, but the mental picture I had formed of Popov was rather different: the man who emerged from the house to greet me was, if anything, rather small and slightly bowed. His voice had a soft, smoky quality, conspiratorial in fact, like the voice of a patroling soldier trying to avoid being overheard by the enemy.

That evening we sat till far into the night in front of the open fire, whisky glass in hand, while he told me the story of his life. Since his birth in Dubrovnik he has lived in many places, usually where the sun shines. A wealthy man nowadays, he has been living in the South of France for a long time, in his medieval mansion furnished with priceless Louis XIV antiques. His parties were highlights of the social round of the Côte d'Azur. Money is something one has – one does not talk about it.

It was this recipe that helped Dusko Popov get through the war unharmed. While his Yugoslav countrymen were fighting the Germans in bloody guerrilla warfare, Popov was handling large bundles of dollar bills and 'navycerts', the wartime British trading permits, in the obscure intelligence jungle between London and Lisbon. Under the cover name Ivan he was the most successful agent of the Lisbon Abwehr station – apart from Paul Fidrmuc, alias Ostro.

At least that was the opinion of Major Albert von Karsthof, the head of that station. He and his secretary, with whom he lived in an informal relationship sanctioned by Canaris, owed four of the best years of their lives to the legendary espionage successes of Dusko Popov, alias Ivan. The most outstanding service he ever rendered was undoubtedly that 'clever and well-thought-out cash transfer' to Wulf Dietrich Schmidt that Herr Boeger had proudly told me about in Hamburg. The supply of the necessary working funds to the German agents was after all of the greatest importance for the future military operations, and what Haupt-mann Gartenfeld's squadron had failed to achieve with their direct drop of pound notes concealed in bundles of wood, the head of the Lisbon Abwehr station, with Dusko Popov's help, had managed with a mere flick of the wrist.

The radio message from Schmidt confirming his receipt of the money was greeted like the report of a great victory by all who had been involved in the complicated secret operation: Leutnant Wein, responsible for the radio side of the job, was jubilant. Hauptmann Boeger, Schmidt's new controlling officer could breathe more freely again. Martin Toeppen, responsible for the accountancy side of the cash transfer, could now sleep peacefully. And the chief of the espionage department, Piekenbrock, had another feather in his cap, while Canaris personally congratulated his skilful staff at the Abwehr station in Lisbon. Now that Wulf Dietrich Schmidt could use all that money to go hunting for more agents in the London ministries, the real heroes of the operation – Popov and the officers of the Lisbon station – had yet another excuse for celebrating.

And thirty years after those events, my meeting with Dusko Popov enabled me to fill in yet another chapter in the involved life story of Wulf Dietrich Schmidt. Eagerly I asked Ivan; 'How did Wulf Dietrich Schmidt react when you handed him all that money?'

Popov smiled mischievously as he gave me his surprising answer.

'You know that I was a colonel in British Intelligence, so there is a lot I cannot tell you, much though I would like to. But I do know that Schmidt – we called him Tate – never got his hand on a single penny of the money that the Abwehr bosses had sent him through me.'

Popov, whom the trusting Germans called Ivan and the even more trusting British called Tricycle, then told me about his life as a double agent, implying that only exceptional people were suitable for the job. While Jill remarked: 'Dusko is the most devoted of fathers to his sons,' James Bond's prototype gave a glimpse of the other side of his character: 'You have to have nerves like steel hawsers ... While you are encouraging your opponent to have complete confidence in you, you must be capable of ice-cold detachment and be able – if need be – to kill.'

Thanks to Popov's ability to dissimulate, he has remained a controversial character to this day. The former head of the FBI, Edgar Hoover, considered him 'a Balkan playboy'. The historian Ladislas Farago called him an arms trafficker and dope smuggler. Some thought him a superspy, others a small-time confidence trickster.

But his most extraordinary piece of deception concerned his own wife, thirty years younger than he, who only realized who her husband really was after they had been married for some ten years. In fact the revelation of his secret past seems to have caused a temporary crisis in their marriage, but the shock soon wore off. More than that, the beautiful Swedish girl seems to admire him more than ever for all the dangers he has overcome in such a masterly fashion: 'Dusko is a real man. He is quite unafraid. He has incredibly strong nerves. He knows everything. He is never at a loss for an excuse ...'

If there is one thing in her husband's make-up that worries the romantic Swede, it is his restlessness, which every now and again makes him get up and go out into the world. 'Dusko is quite capable of forgetting everything he has got her and settling somewhere else,' she remarked and her husband commented: 'I am at home practically anywhere ... The only thing that reminds people of my origin is my accent. I have kept that accent and whatever language I speak, you can always tell that I am from Dubrovnik!'

During the war this inspired quick-change artist enjoyed the confidence of both sides, the British even more than the German. In London he was even honoured by a personal invitation from Canaris' counterpart, Stewart Menzies, to spend a weekend on his brother Ian's Surrey estate. This kind of direct contact between the chief of the Secret Service and a double agent was contrary to the most elementary principles of secret intelligence work, but Popov's charm had evidently overcome his boss's professional scepticism. And not only his: brother Ian even asked the 'man from Dubrovnik' to be godfather to his first child.

'We have an agent in London who sends us up to twenty-nine reports a day.'
The former agent 3725, alias Tate, with the mayor of Mainz, 1959.

Leutnant Richard Wein, 3725's radio officer. 'The war might have turned out differently if those fatheads in Berlin had made better use of our reports . . .'

Captain Edmund Gartenfeld, the pilot who flew 3725 over the Channel in 1940.

The Phönix Hotel where 3725 and other German agents were stationed.

RIGHT Canaris, Chief of the Abwehr.

BELOW LEFT Dr Praetorius, the head of the economic intelligence section of the Hamburg Abwehr.

BELOW RIGHT Dr Scholz, alias Huckriede-Schulz – a talent spotter.

BELOW One of Ritter's watchdogs, Georg Sessler of the St Pauli boxing club.

RIGHT The first German soldier to
land in England as part of Operation
Sealion – Goesta Caroli, a Swede.

BELOW The Abwehr radio station
in Hamburg-Wohldorf.

Dear Jörger

I have today recieved a letter from England, O.H.M.S. threatening me very strongly it seems they have caught up with me again; & I am afraid I shall have to get moving. I am wondering if you are in touch with Hirsch in South America & can you somehow arrange for me to get there, or are you in a position to loan me sufficient money to get going?

Can you manage to come to Ireland from where you are

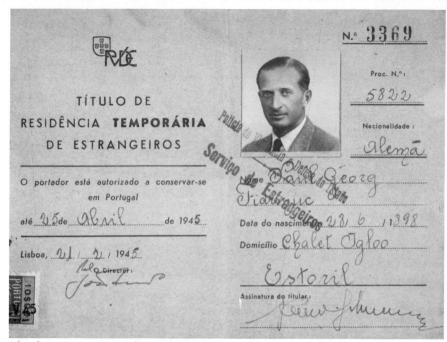

N.º **3369**

TÍTULO DE
RESIDÊNCIA **TEMPORÁRIA**
DE ESTRANGEIROS

Proc. N.º: **5822**

Nacionalidade: *Alemã*

O portador está autorizado a conservar-se
em Portugal

até 25 de *Abril* de 1945

Nome *Paul Georg Fidrmuc*

Data do nascimento *28/ 6/ 1898*

Domicílio *Chalet Igloo Estoril*

Lisboa, *21/ 2/ 1945*

P/o Director:

Assinatura do titular:

The phantom spy, Ostro, alias Paul Fidrmuc, one of the smartest of all German agents. 'A spy should always be an expert in his cover job so that people will believe it's genuine.'

BELOW RIGHT 'You won't have any difficulty in getting around Scotland without being detected. The roads are packed with refugees from the bombed-out cities, so no one is going to ask you where you have come from . . .' These were the instructions given to Tor Glad, alias Tege, alias Jeff, a Norwegian Abwehr agent.

BELOW LEFT Colonel Erwin von Lahousen, head of the sabotage department of the Abwehr. 'To be able to commit acts of sabotage when practically every hut and every crossroad was watched by the Home Guard, my men needed not only nerves of iron but also money and lots and lots of fuses and explosives!'

Dusko Popov, said to have been the inspiration for Ian Fleming's spy, James Bond.

Robbey Leibbrandt was supposed to undermine singlehanded a country three times as large as Germany: the aim was to infiltrate South Africa. Canaris had a film made of the agent's journey across the Atlantic.

It was in the course of these weekend chats in Surrey that the sis chief appears to have hit on the idea that the German secret service front could be bombarded by other means than just the radio aerials in outer London and Crespigny Road. Popov's charm could be utilized to good effect in the battle against the Third Reich.

With the aid of this Popov talent, the Allies managed to make deep inroads in the German defences during the war. Always anxious to please, Popov went back and forth between the German Abwehr and British Intelligence, like an experienced waiter. Quick off the mark, he took note of the wishes of the Abwehr in Lisbon and passed them on to the Double-Cross cooks in their London kitchen. There John Masterman and his chef T. A. Roberts prepared the menu as ordered – deception material on the Royal Navy, the Royal Air Force and the service ministries – which Popov then served up to his boss, Major Albert von Karsthof.

Also served up by this messenger between the front lines were the Leica films which had been given to him by von Karsthof. With the films he managed to photograph British troop convoys, factories, airfields and ports, always 'at great risk to himself'; in fact his pictures were of unimportant sites which the Secret Service had selected in order to build up his reputation as a tried and reliable agent. No wonder the Germans entrusted that enormous sum of money, about twenty thousand pounds, to their trusty agent Ivan, money that would now enable Wulf Dietrich Schmidt's British masters and fellow warriors in the secret war to operate in style at last. Popov's charm had succeeded in storming the Abwehr fortress in Lisbon, with the result, as the Germans were later to discover to their horror, that their most important Abwehr station abroad, in which the secret lines from Britain, the United States, Canada, Mexico, Shanghai and Africa converged, was 'almost completely in British hands'.

Popov's description of the German officers' gullibility was so fantastic that I could hardly believe it. I thought that his account of how he had wormed his way into the most important Abwehr station of all was highly exaggerated. I simply could not imagine that Major von Karsthof of all people, whom Canaris had sent to Lisbon, 'the porthole of the Abwehr battleship', because he considered him to be one of his most capable officers, had never in all those years seen through his star agent's double dealings. But every chain is as strong as its weakest link, or – to illustrate Popov's unsuspected infiltration of the Lisbon Abwehr station – there is a chink in every fortress wall.

One of the people sitting near that chink was the former head secretary, 'Mausi' who, according to other former members of the Abwehr, practically ran the show. Mausi was not only the secretary, she was also Karsthof's mistress and later his wife. She must know best how Popov was able to gain her confidence and that of her husband. In this assault on the most confidential areas of the Abwehr, of such importance for later Allied operations, two thoroughbred dachshunds, a present from Popov, played an important part . . .

I found Mausi, now a widow, living comfortably in a luxury apartment in her home town in the Ruhr valley, where at the outbreak of war she had met her husband and from where she had followed him into the exciting world of espionage. So as not to influence the former Abwehr secretary I purposely refrained from mentioning what I knew about the double role of her star agent Ivan. I did not tell her that Popov had really been a colonel in the British Secret Service and that he had come to Estoril on instructions from his chief in London, with the express intention of spying out highly explosive military secrets in her charming company. Recalling her first meeting with Dusko Popov, the former Abwehr secretary rhapsodized:

I have had quite a few flowers given me in my time, but I shall never forget the roses he gave me that time . . . Ivan was still very young then. He was not handsome, but very charming . . . he was so completely genuine . . . Ivan and my husband always spoke either Serbo-Croat or Italian. One of them was from Trieste and the other from Dubrovnik and they got on famously together . . . Our meetings reminded Ivan of home . . . I really do believe that he felt he was among friends when he stayed with us!

Then she told me about the exciting reports that Ivan brought back from England and which she had to take down in shorthand. She could well remember his description of a dinner at which Ivan claimed that he had sat at the same table as Winston Churchill.

'But surely,' I asked with surprise, 'a German agent able to get right into Churchill's entourage must have been cared for by you almost to the extent of being wrapped in cotton wool?'

'Oh yes, you bet he was,' my companion agreed, and went on to describe with what circumspection she and her husband guarded Ivan's secret. The mysterious Yugoslav had of course also been invited to her Christmas party. The only other guests were other members of the Abwehr station, so that the party would be small and secure. 'Of course they all knew who Ivan was.' But none of them apparently suspected that the friendly Ivan was a hard-boiled British agent.

The men pushing the old piano into the smoky room in the Phoenix Hotel that Herr Harbeck had placed at their disposal for a farewell party were drunk. Only the giant with the reddish-blond hair, who suddenly lifted the heavy instrument all by himself, pushed his tired companions aside and pulled the piano into the room, was in command of his senses to a certain extent. But this remnant of consciousness was limited to a sense of rage directed against his superior officer, Hauptmann Huckriede-Schulz – 'Hucki' to everyone for that evening only. Outwardly the party was to have appeared perfectly harmless.

The farewell party was for the agent Karl Richter, whose jokes and tricks had up till then been the centrepiece of the evening's entertainment. Up to the moment that is, when he had banged the piano up against the wall and standing in front of Hucki had roared a provocative: 'Orders executed, Herr Hauptmann!'

Huckriede looked at Richter for a moment and then said: 'Alright my friend . . . take it easy.' Then he raised the lid of the piano and started his party piece, in English: 'Happy days are here again, the sun is shining clear again . . .'

Richter felt that he was being pushed out of the limelight. But Hucki went on playing and singing the same ditty over and over again.

Then Richter, resentful at his boss stealing the show, slowly poured the contents of his beer mug into the piano. That only made Hucki play all the louder, so Richter smashed the empty glass into the works. Not even that could stop Hucki. For a few more moments he went on with 'Happy days are here again', the glass splinters tinkling an accompaniment as he hit the keys, until, finally, beside himself with rage, Richter smashed the piano to bits.

Next day in the Knochenhauerstrasse there was a discreet silence concerning the incident in the Phoenix Hotel. No one wanted to risk a secret mission for the sake of a smashed piano, an operation moreover that was of great importance to the Abwehr in those early days of May 1941 and which they had prepared over a long period. In any case, the officers responsible had a lot of sympathy with Richter's unruly behaviour. Hauptmann Huckriede's opinion was: 'With his operation repeatedly being postponed, Richter was like a nervous racehorse.'

But now, after waiting for the best part of a year, things had reached the stage where Artiste could set off at last. His chances of success were good, for unlike the other parachute agents before him, Richter did not have to jump into the unknown. Moreover he would not be dependent on the slightly crooked Arthur G. Owens, who would probably hand him over to the British police as soon as he got to England. After his jump, Richter was to join up with 3725, Wulf Dietrich Schmidt, who would look after the new arrival from Hamburg, if only for his own safety's sake. For carefully stowed away in his luggage Richter was bringing over something in the nature of a lifeline, without which – so Hamburg believed – Wulf Dietrich Schmidt would soon be irretrievably lost.

This lifeline consisted of a small dark-brown bakelite box, about three centimetres high, with two thin pins rather like those used in modern electric razors. Inside it there was a crystal which the firm of Telefunken had tuned to a certain frequency. Wulf Dietrich Schmidt was to instal this new crystal in his set without delay, for it had suddenly become very important not only for Schmidt himself but also for the German High Command. For some months now, Schmidt's messages had hinted that the British were trying to locate his set. Were it to be discovered it would mean not only the end of Schmidt's life but also the destruction of Germany's most important link with Britain. And that must not be allowed to happen in any circumstances, otherwise Hitler would no longer be able to boast, as he had done in 1940: 'We have an agent in London who sends us up to twenty-nine reports a day!' Now that Wulf Dietrich Schmidt's espionage network in Britain had been propped up again with the twenty thousand pounds supplied via Lisbon through Dusko Popov, only the tiny crystal was needed to make the threatened radio link with Hamburg-Wohldorf secure again.

Two days after the farewell party in the Phoenix Hotel, as Richter was sewing the Telefunken crystal, wrapped in cotton wool, into the inside pocket of his tweed jacket, he was not to know that the little bakelite box was in fact a hook pulling him towards England. Still less was he to know that the long line with the Double-Cross hook at one end of it was knotted at its other end into a noose in the Tower of London.

The clandestine meeting with Wulf Dietrich Schmidt had been carefully prepared in a series of radio messages. The two men were friends who had lived in the Phoenix Hotel together and had done their parachute training on Lüneburg Heath together – two agents quite unlike one another in appearance and in temperament, who were now to be welded together again in a fateful unit in order to complement one another by their very dissimilarity. Now they would jointly carry out the difficult task they had been given by Berlin: Schmidt as the careful, observant analyst, Richter as the fearless go-getter.

Originally the two men were to meet in London's Tate Gallery 'in front of some statue by Rodin', Oberleutnant Wein remembers. 'Then we altered the arrangements. Schmidt was to wait for Richter in the National Gallery on three successive days. I believe the first contact was arranged for 15 May.'

Hauptmann Julius Boeger, who had already dispatched Waelti, Druecke, Jakobs and Reysen on their journey to the beyond, shook hands with Karl Richter at Schiphol airport near Amsterdam shortly before midnight on 12 May 1941. Richter could speak only a little English and Boeger warned him: 'Don't be careless ... for heaven's sake man, be careful. And remember us all to Schmidt!'

As Richter was disappearing into the hold he looked back at his escort and laughed: 'Don't worry, Herr Hauptmann. I managed in Sweden all right, although I did not know the language. [A reference to the fact that a few months previously Richter had carried out a secret mission in Sweden, involving the sabotage of a British courier plane.] I shall manage in England just as well!'

Richter chuckled, as if to emphasize his lack of concern. Perhaps he was trying to suppress the fear that he really felt. In any case there was nothing left for him to laugh at a few brief moments later, nor was he a free man any longer. Shortly after take-off, Achtelik, the dispatching officer, passed him the oxygen mask and Richter got another last whiff of German air. Then the aircraft was over blacked-out England and the thin shafts of the searchlights were stabbing the night air.

When they were over St Albans, Richter was placed near the hatch while Achtelik fastened the safety line to the same hook which had also been the last physical link with Germany for Wulf Dietrich Schmidt, Jakobs and Reysen.

On 13 May (a day which Richter had always considered a lucky one) a pair of British handcuffs were fastened round his wrists ... Prison doors opened and shut again behind him. Prison vans took him from one interrogation centre to another. Within hours, Richter had become a mere object on a conveyor belt that finally landed him in the Tower of London. His end came quickly. I described it at the beginning of this book.

As Dusko Popov pointed out, the members of the so-called 'hanging committee' in London were not to be envied their job. It was their task to select – purely on the basis of cold reason – from among the German agents who had been caught, those who had to be executed at intervals. Their death was one of the standard tricks, one of the conventions of the espionage game.

Those agents on whom the death sentence of the hanging committee fell knew that the game was up, that they were being sacrificed as mere pawns so that there would be more freedom of movement for the more important figures: knights like Mutt and Jeff for instance, or even the queen called Tate, otherwise known as Wulf Dietrich Schmidt.

There is really no more to be said about the life of the Abwehr agent Karl Richter, alias Artiste. Only a short footnote may be called for, just to show that the case was properly wound up from an accountancy point of view. It concerns the fulfilment of the contract that Karl Richter had signed on what was to happen in the event of his death: the Iron Cross, First Class, posthumously awarded, and – most important – twenty thousand Marks.

After his execution in London on 10 December 1942 payment was due, but the Abwehr Pay Office in Berlin simply refused to part with the money, on the pretext that Richter had done absolutely nothing while he was in England! After a lot of haggling the head of the Hamburg Abwehr station, Kapitän zur See Herbert Wichmann, a man of honour, managed to squeeze a 'handshake' of sorts out of them.

It fell to Hauptmann Huckriede-Schulz, who had taken on the happy-go-lucky sailor on behalf of the firm of Stegemann, to tell Frau Martha Richter in Graslitz about her son's death:

First I gave her the Iron Cross, to prepare her for the news of her son's death. When she asked me how it happened I said: 'During an air raid on England. We do not know the details ourselves.' Then I gave her the envelope with the three thousand Marks in it. I even had to ask her for a receipt for this paltry payment for her son's life – to satisfy the accountants in Berlin.

Hitler had inflated his power until it was like a balloon whose envelope becomes thinner and thinner the larger it gets. At the end of the summer of 1942 the balloon had reached the limits of its expansion. At a time when Rommel was victorious in Africa, when German troops had advanced to the Volga and Hitler's tanks were at the gates of Moscow, the balloon was all set to burst.

In the face of these threats Molotov, the Soviet Foreign Minister, flew to Washington in response to an invitation from President Roosevelt. His brief statement to the President sounded like a drowning man's cry for help: 'Hitler will reinforce his Eastern front with men and material. The Red Army cannot resist the pressure. The situation could be changed overnight if the United States and Britain were to open up a new front. Then some forty divisions would have to be withdrawn from the East.'

As Churchill had not given him any positive assurances during his stopover in London, Molotov now expected 'a straight answer' in Washington. Roosevelt spoke about the immense power of the United States and then went on to speak of the American people's desire to smash Hitler's Germany once and for all.

Molotov immediately put down in writing the promises of support that Roosevelt had made him: 'In the course of discussion, complete unanimity was reached on the urgent need to establish a second front in Europe in 1942.'

No sooner had Molotov received this assurance than General George Marshall wanted to shorten the text, and the promise, by two short words: he doubted whether it would be possible to establish a second front in Europe *in 1942*. But it was these very words that counted for Moscow as a kind of shot in the arm, and once he had got it Molotov was not going to let it slip out of his hands at any price. On the contrary, he used the Washington communiqué as a draft for the text of a pact of mutual assistance to which Churchill also assented in the end.

Although at that time the British premier, as he said later, was politically at his lowest ebb and without a glimmer of military success, he nevertheless loudly confirmed his promise to Russia on 11 June 1942: '. . . in the course of our discussions, full agreement was reached on the urgent necessity of opening a second front in Europe in 1942 . . .'

The primary purpose of Churchill's communiqué, couched as it was in general terms, was to impress the Germans and to induce them to keep a strong force in the West, but though Hitler might be impressed by the implied threat Molotov wanted more than mere words. What he wanted to know was exactly when and where something was going to happen in the West, so that the crumbling Russian front could be relieved at once and not at some uncertain date in the future.

Driven into a corner, Churchill then told his Soviet allies in confidence: 'We are making plans for a landing on the Continent in August or September 1942 . . . Naturally it would not be in the interest of either the Russians or their allies if we were to persist in carrying out, at any price, a landing operation which might end in disaster . . .'

Today there can be little doubt that the landing on the Continent which Churchill promised could only have referred to one operation: namely the mini-invasion at Dieppe which – as Churchill had clearly feared from the start – 'might end in disaster'. Why then did he commit five thousand Canadian soldiers to that disaster on 19 August 1942?

A great question mark hangs over the dead of Dieppe. Was their heroic sacrifice merely staged in order to test German preparedness on the Channel coast? Our historians have no definite explanation to offer for this bloody advance payment except for the comforting words: these men did not die in vain! Dieppe, they say, provided the Allies with important information which proved invaluable two years later during the invasion of Normandy.

The statement made by Lord Louis Mountbatten, the King's cousin and the strategist responsible for both the planning and the execution of the Dieppe raid is equally unsatisfactory: 'Dieppe was one of the most important operations of the Second World War. The enterprise provided the Allies with the invaluable secret of victory ... If I had to make the same decision again, I should do the same as I did then.'

The Prime Minister, Winston Churchill, in words just as vague as those of his protégé Mountbatten, and in an apparent effort to make something senseless appear sensible, said of the drama of Dieppe: 'Dieppe has its own place in the history of the war and the terrible losses must not be considered a failure ... Honour the dead who fell there. Their sacrifice was not in vain ...'

As far as I was concerned Dieppe would have remained a cold milestone in the history of the war had it not been for the fact that the name of Wulf Dietrich Schmidt became tied up with it. A passing reference that Leutnant Wein had made way back in 1959 in the course of our talks in the garden of his house in Hamburg-Ohlstedt induced me to try and shed some light on the Dieppe affair: 'In 1942 thirty-seven-two-five told us about a proposed landing in the Dieppe area.'

In the course of my researches these reports, which had become so tragically true at dawn on 19 August 1942, were to grow into a horrible suspicion: if Wulf Dietrich Schmidt or some other agent who had been dropped in England had in fact only been able to send back messages by permission of the British – as the chroniclers of the Secret Service always claim – the story seemed to prove that the Germans had, paradoxically, been forewarned of the raid by the British themselves. In the case of Dieppe this would mean that Churchill had knowingly, though not lightly, delivered up five thousand men, mostly Canadians, to the German bayonets waiting for them.

The order to proceed with Operation Jubilee, as the Dieppe raid came to be known latterly, was undoubtedly one of the most fateful, but also one of the most profitable of the last war, which brought victory to the Allies two years later. Most of the assistance I received when trying to unravel the mystery of Dieppe came from the very men who had been involved in camouflaging the suicidal landing operation in 1942: the veterans of the former Double-Cross Committee. While erecting their own 'monuments' after the war they have frankly described their tactics, which did not consist merely of misleading Hitler through the radio links of the agents they had captured. In order to make the information from their turned agents seem more credible, they had fed similar reports, by way of confirmation, to the Abwehr through other channels as well: through resistance groups in France for instance, or through middle men in Portugal and Turkey known to be trusted by the Germans.

In my inquiries I started out from the fact that – according to British accounts – all German radio agents in Britain had been captured and that they were only allowed to send to Germany those reports which had first been dictated to them by the British.

Proceeding along these lines, I found the double agents, intermediaries, radio operators and officers at the German end of the secret 'London sources' who were still able to confirm the fatal advance warning of the attack on Dieppe. The same picture came from several different sources:

On 13 August 1942 a 'very reliable, proven agent' who was living in Southern England reported to the Abwehr on an impending landing at Dieppe. (Was this the report of the turned agent Dragonfly, who had been established with great foresight in Southern England – according to Sir John Masterman – in order to be able more easily to observe the preparations being made on the Isle of Wight for the Dieppe raid?)

'In mid-August 1942,' the former head of the Hamburg Abwehr station, Kapitän zur See Herbert Wichmann, told me, 'a radio agent in England told us about preparations for a landing in the Fécamp area. Fécamp is only about fifty kilometres west of Dieppe.'

Do these reports not confirm another of the principles of the Double-Cross strategist, namely that the 'cover schemes ought to be as near the "real thing" as was safely possible?' (Or, to put it more bluntly: the targets to which the opponent's attention should be deflected must be as near the 'real thing' as considerations of safety will permit.)

Oberleutnant Wein recalled that a further advance warning reached the Germans through another direct radio contact from England to Hamburg-Wohldorf: 'In 1942 thirty-seven-two-five also warned us about a landing operation that was to take place near Dieppe.'

These three direct reports were also confirmed by an identical piece of information passed to the Germans through the agent Ostro in Lisbon. The former agent-controller of the Lisbon station, Herr von Carnap, confirmed that during one of their meetings in Lisbon Ostro had reported to him about an impending landing near Dieppe.

The former chief of counter-espionage of the Abwehr, Oberstleutnant Hans Freund, told me that the Abwehr had received yet another warning about Dieppe from a Croat agent in Istanbul. This man, a merchant, was suspected of being used by British Intelligence in Turkey to disseminate deception material.

The final and the most unambiguous advance warning about a 'landing at Dieppe in the immediate future' came from Istanbul. Here the informant was Abwehr agent E800, whom the British were using as a double agent. But the Germans could be quite sure of his loyalty: they had his Jewish mother in custody and consequently had him at their mercy. E800 is also still alive. He is a business man well known in Germany and abroad, and for this reason it is unfortunately not possible to reveal his identity.

Who was sending out all these reports about Dieppe? Who channelled them into the Abwehr through those intermediaries in Istanbul and Lisbon?

The British secret reports on Dieppe are not accessbile. Winston Churchill, the man who knew everything about this chapter but revealed practically nothing, is dead. And others in the know must remain silent, for Dieppe – so it now seems – was the deception operation par excellence! With Dieppe, Churchill had opened the door of the trap which was to seal Hitler's doom within the next few months, and not just two years later in Normandy.

This conclusion is logically inescapable if one starts to count the successes that Churchill was able to notch up immediately after the catastrophic landings on 19 August 1942, if one tries to balance his later strategic successes against the losses at Dieppe. It is only then that one can properly appreciate the words he wrote after he had drawn up the balance sheet: '. . . their sacrifice was not in vain!'

According to Abwehr reports from Southern England dated 29.9., an operation similar to the one at Dieppe is to be expected in the course of the next month. The Abwehr comments that it was the same very reliable agent who also predicted the raid on Dieppe on 13 August . . . (War diary of the German Naval Command.)

The above document shows quite clearly why the Germans fell for the later, decisive, Allied deception operation: what their 'very reliable agent' in Southern England told them about another operation similar to the one at Dieppe was bound to be true. There could be no doubting his report, because the informant was the same man who had told the Germans on 13 August about the Dieppe raid . . .

Such misleading reports aimed at inducing Hitler to concentrate his troops in the northern sector of the Western front, although the attack might equally well come on the French Channel coast. Both these possibilities were suggested to German Intelligence, mainly in radio messages from four of their most successful agents. While the reports from Wulf Dietrich Schmidt and Dragonfly, the double agent established in Southern England, suggested an invasion in Northern France, Mutt and Jeff were operating with the 'Scandinavian spectre' of an invasion of Norway. In London the 'French' deception schemes were known by the code name Overthrow and the Scandinavian ones as Solo 1.

The success of these diversionary manoeuvres was to a large extent to decide the fate of Operation Torch, the Allied invasion of North Africa, and the substitute for the second front that Stalin was so anxiously waiting for. This was the fatal stab in Germany's back that was to start the slow bleeding to death of the Third Reich.

This turning point in the war was introduced by the warning shot of Dieppe and continued in the convincing deception concert of the London Double-Cross quartet Tate, Dragonfly, Mutt and Jeff. The fate of Europe was to depend on whether the 'reliable Abwehr agents' could succeed in drawing Hitler's attention northwards.

When the preliminaries of this historic action began, its results hung on a very slender thread indeed, as Tor Glad, alias Jeff, told me. In fact, the middle finger of the twenty-five-year-old business correspondent from Oslo was of the utmost importance for the coming Allied operation, dependent in fact on whether it ever forgot – intentionally or otherwise – to transmit the code word 'Henry' when communicating with the Germans.

'At certain intervals I always had to get "Henry" into the text somehow,' Tor Glad recalled. 'If I omitted "Henry" the Germans would know that we were prisoners and operating under duress.'

This was a risk the Allies obviously could not take at that stage of so important a military operation. So Tor Glad was put on ice and allegedly posted to a Norwegian sapper battalion that was being posted to Scotland. Against this background Tor Glad's reports on impending landing operations in Norway seemed all the more credible to his masters in Berlin. As sabotage chief Oberst von Lahousen recalled, the Abwehr were very well informed at the time because: 'In Scotland of course our man was right at the heart of things.'

Tor Glad, the man at the heart of things, later told me what really happened during his alleged period of service with the Norwegian unit:

Before I was shipped off from London I had to teach a radio specialist from the Secret Service exactly how I transmitted, telling him that he had to pay particular attention to the code-word 'Henry'. That man learned all about my life, about every detail, such as the names of friends and of Abwehr officers I had met, so that he would be able to answer any unexpected questions immediately. Then we told Oslo about my posting to Scotland. In fact British Intelligence sent me to Carlisle, where I stayed with Andrew Corcoran for a few months. He was a social worker and his wife had just had a baby.

After that and right up to the end of the war I was in prison with the double agent Arthur G. Owens. So the German Abwehr was not in touch with me, but only with my radio set that was operated by my British understudy . . .

In the opinion of his British controller, Wulf Dietrich Schmidt, who was operating the second German radio set for Operation Overthrow, was one hundred per cent reliable. The German agent-running officers were even more full of praise for the taciturn man from Apenrade, as they dressed up his false reports and passed them on to the operational staffs, especially those of the navy, with the warmest commendations.

The double agent Dragonfly operated the third radio set, which he had brought to England concealed in a gramophone. Before that he had been a fairly unsuccessful Cologne businessman, whose profits had been increased by the British Secret Service, who made him a wine merchant for reasons of cover. Dragonfly was to play a decisive part in covering up Operation Torch.

Apart from their task of keeping Hitler's troops on the alert on the French Channel coast and in Norway, the reports from the double agents were also to mislead the much-feared German submarines, to prevent them attacking Eisenhower's North African invasion armada before it had time to form up.

One thousand five hundred ships with a quarter of a million men and a million tons of war materials went into battle against the Germans. The armada was led by General Dwight Eisenhower, who up to that time had no practical battle experience.

While Eisenhower was able to manoeuvre the masses of his second front across the stormy Atlantic almost unnoticed in the radio blackout, German air reconnaissance was by no means uniformed about the concentration and preparations of the Allied naval units along the English Channel coast. For this reason the radio reports of the London deception quartet were attuned to the picture that the German reconnaissance aircraft would be getting from the air. So the Abwehr learned from their valuable source being tapped by Mutt and Jeff that large convoys were being assembled in the Clyde and the Mersey. At the beginning of November Jack Moe, alias Mutt, worried the High Command with a report from the Clyde about 'the greatest concentration of ships I have ever seen'. The fictitious embellishment to this report was provided by Tor Glad: 'Landing exercises are being carried out on the Argyllshire coast. The troops, which include Norwegian units, have arctic equipment.'

The Secret Intelligence Service left it to the Germans to draw their own conclusions from these reports.

In this critical situation Wulf Dietrich Schmidt was repeatedly consulted like an oracle. But Schmidt, whose radio link was just as much at risk as before (his meeting with Richter and the delivery of the crystal 'unfortunately having failed to materialize'), left both options open in his reports.

In that respect the information supplied by the merry wine merchant from Cologne, now established in the south of England and christened Dragonfly by John Masterman, was of far more use to the Germans. In the second half of October he reported to the Abwehr: 'Some of the troops believe that there will soon be another raid on the French coast like Dieppe, but on a much larger scale. No sign on the English south coast of any operations in the Atlantic or against Africa . . .'

The deception played by Wulf Dietrich Schmidt and his colleagues sounded so convincing that Admiral Canaris simply ignored other important reports from his observers along the Western Mediterranean. Although agents in Algeciras, Ceuta, Tetuan and Melilla had personally observed an extraordinary concentration of enemy ships about the middle of October, the wise man from the Tirpitzufer, addressing the uneasy members of a briefing session, unhesitatingly supported the 'facts' so carefully compiled in London. In 1942 the Abwehr chief was still a mouthpiece of the 'tried and reliable agents in England', paradoxically acting as the most important representative of the London Double-Cross Committee and placing their false reports exactly where the Allies wanted them. His authority underlined and strengthened the countless morse signals pouring out of England and received by the radio station at Hamburg-Wohldorf: Canaris' money was on France!

As the Abwehr had concluded that there would be no significant occurrences in North Africa, Field Marshal Erwin Rommel could set off with a clear conscience for a well-earned rest in Germany. But he had hardly handed over to his deputy when disaster struck the German formations in North Africa. Hitler's desert front was destroyed to the rhythm of the v-signal of the BBC.

With more than a thousand tanks, eight hundred aircraft and one hundred and fifty thousand men, General Montgomery delivered the first blow to the Africa Corps on 23 October 1942. The next came on 2 November, when the British armour broke through the German lines at El Alamein and Rommel told the High Command of the coming end: 'In this situation we must reckon with the slow destruction of the army, in spite of the heroic resistance and magnificent morale of the troops . . .'

Hitler's reply, intended to sustain Rommel in the bloody sands of the desert, ended with the advice: 'You can show your troops no other road than to victory or death.'

Victory or death . . . in those days in early November 1942 it was not only Rommel who faced those two alternatives. In Russia too the German troops arrived at the crossroads. But there the icy snow storms had already barred the road to victory.

On Sunday 8 November 1942 the weather was bad all over Europe. Shortly before 6 o'clock in the evening Hitler had entered the Bürgerbräukeller in the Rosenheimerstrasse in Munich to fire his old companions with the enthusiasm to march on. He stood in front of the column, draped with the swastika flag stained with the blood of the first of the fallen, the men who had died for National Socialism at the Feldherrnhalle on 9 November 1923.

Hitler had returned from the Eastern front via Berlin, to the place where it had all started, amid the smell of sweat, beer and urine. Now, on 8 November at the beginning of the fourth year of the war, he wanted to tell his faithful beer-sodden followers once more about the immense power of the Third Reich and show them the path to victory: 'I wanted to get to the Volga, at a certain place, at a certain town. By coincidence, it is called after Stalin . . .'

At the same time as Hitler, with his mention of Stalingrad, had taken the lid off Germany's coffin, the runway of Gibraltar airport was flooded after a heavy downpour. Fortunately the rain had not fallen until after dark, so the Allied landing operations which had started at 13.20 hours that day had hardly been affected. While Hitler was talking in Munich, four hundred and sixty-six British and American aircraft had taken off from Gibraltar in support of the Allied invasion forces in North Africa. And when Hitler went to bed in his apartment in the Prinzregenten-platz after his meeting with his old comrades, General Dwight Eisenhower was sitting in his underpants in the damp, underground command post in the rock of Gibraltar. His adjutant was trying to remove an ink stain from the General's trousers while Eisenhower scanned the headlines of the London morning newspapers that had just arrived by air: 'Allied invasion of North Africa!'

The establishment of the Allied front in Africa was a serious blow by which Germany suddenly and unexpectedly found herself in a west-east pincer. With the Russian winter setting in and the Anglo–American knife pressed against his back, Hitler asked himself, too late, how he had managed to get himself into this fateful situation.

The writer of the war diary of the German Naval Command commented, on 8 November 1942 on the 'blindness' of the Abwehr with regards to Operation Torch:

The fact that a landing along the Mediterranean coast must lie within the scope of enemy planning had been known to us for months through a variety of channels. But as similar plans were reported at the same time from other areas, namely Norway, the Channel and France, the enemy succeeded, probably deliberately, in ensuring that none of these intelligence complexes were as energetically assessed as would have been necessary for the preparation of long-term defences against the enemy operations. In this intelligence battle we lost the round.

The Chief of Staff of the Wehrmacht expressed himself more bluntly: 'Once more we have been let down by Canaris' stupidity and incon-sistency.' Jodl's accusation is harsh, but it does show up the soft core of Canaris' character. He still believed what Wulf Dietrich Schmidt and the other 'reliable agents' told him. He had become the principal piece in the secret game of chess which the Allies were going to win.

After this failure in connection with the Allied invasion of North Africa on 8 November 1942, Canaris had also arrived at the crossroads. It was the beginning of the end, both for him and for his Abwehr.

7 Success (and other) stories

The male commercial travellers of the Hamburg export firm Stege-mann & Co did not work for their chief, party member Dr Praetorius, for very long. With the exception of Wulf Dietrich Schmidt they quickly disappeared either into British jails or beneath British soil, like Karl Richter, Jakobs or Reysen.

Hauptmann Huckriede-Schulz had made a realistic appraisal of his agents' chances from the start:

> Naturally you must expect losses in this kind of business. But even if only one of them gets through and sends back valuable information, the investment has been worthwhile. Fortunately Wulf Dietrich Schmidt got through, otherwise we might just as well have shut up shop, both in the Knochenhauerstrasse and at our radio station in Hamburg-Wohldorf. Of our women spies who had been targeted on the British oil wells in the Middle East, only Waltraut Oertel got through to the target area. As a refugee from Nazi oppression she managed to get into the enemy refinery areas. She collected valuable information about fuel depots in Tripoli and made detailed plans of the Commonwealth oil refineries in Haifa, but somehow they never reached us. Her final destination was to have been Abadan on the Persian Gulf, but she never made it. We lost track of her somewhere in the desert.

At the very beginning of my search for Wulf Dietrich Schmidt's companions more than fifteen years ago, I had realized that although Waltraut Oertel's tracks had ended in the desert, she herself had reappeared in Australia after the war. As I have already related, it was there that the worldly-wise Prussian with the perfect knowledge of English had managed to make herself indispensable at the German Embassy in Sydney under the name of Sophie Clapham. In those days, in the Fifties, I could well understand why she wanted to forget her past and why she did not answer any of my letters asking for information about her espionage activities in the Middle East.

Then, as the field of my researches widened, the espionage brief that Waltraut Oertel was to have carried out in Abadan presented me with a strange conundrum. The code name was Gulf. These four letters referred to the sudden destruction of the oil refineries in Abadan which Hitler intended as a fatal blow at the very heart of the British war machine. Owing to the importance of the project only seven men were informed about it, and of those three have died of natural causes and the fourth, Admiral Canaris, was executed in the concentration camp at Flossenburg in April 1945. The fifth, the man who had actually initiated the operation was captured by the Americans after their landing in North Africa on 8 November 1942 and flown from El Biar to the United States under military escort. He was carrying the German identity documents issued to him by the chief Wehrmacht administrator in Paris, Medicus.

The prisoner's real name was Charles Bedaux, a Frenchman by birth, but a naturalized American citizen, and the founder and owner of a very important firm of business consultants still in operation with subsidiary companies in practically every industrialized country in the world, including Germany.

It is certain that the Americans knew quite a lot about the French charmer's international business dealings, and especially about his friendship with the Duke of Windsor. But why and how he wanted to help Hitler achieve victory was something he did not disclose to the American interrogators in the prison in Miami. Bedaux kept quiet about Operation Gulf and took his own life with an overdose of sleeping tablets. When they lifted his body onto the stretcher in his closely guarded room in the hospital and took him away for burial, none of those present had any idea that it had been Bedaux's greatest ambition to become the 'uncrowned king of England' with Hitler's assistance.

In 1975 – fifteen years after my first interview with the agent-running officer Huckriede-Schulz – I decided to try to obtain more information on this unknown page of history; so once again I dialled the old Hamburg telephone number of the former partner in the firm of Stegemann. I was after more details of the espionage brief that the Abwehr agent Waltruat Oertel was to carry out in Abadan. This was because I suspected a connection between Charles Bedaux's planned destruction of the British oil refineries in the Persian Gulf and the brief that Huckriede-Schulz had given his agent in 1941.

If I could confirm that the plan for the sabotage attack against the centre of the British oil supply system had been drawn up by some of the Duke of Windsor's closest friends, there might be grounds for thinking that Charles Bedaux's project was one of the most curious features of the last war. As the powerful Bedaux organization with its worldwide ramifications has survived its founder down to the present day and will in future continue to bear his name, I had to be in possession of absolutely incontrovertible proof for my theory.

At my first attempt to clear up Bedaux's connections with German Intelligence, Frau Huckriede-Schulz answered the telephone and I explained to her what it was that I wanted to ask her husband.

'I am afraid you have come too late,' she told me. 'My husband cannot answer your questions. He died last February. But if you want to know about Waltraut Oertel why don't you ask her yourself? She is back from Australia and at the moment she is the publicity officer for a large firm in Bonn.'

Owing to the supreme principle of the espionage trade, that you should never let the right hand know what the left is doing, Frau Oertel could only tell me part of the story relating to the secret of Abadan when I interviewed her in the luxurious Jägerwinkel sanatorium on the Tegernsee in Bavaria:

Before I left Budapest it was emphasized again and again that Abadan was the main target of my espionage mission in the Middle East. There I was supposed to become friendly with the engineers employed in sensitive sectors of the refineries. My information would have provided the basis for subsequent acts of sabotage. Of course no one told me who was to be involved in the actual destruction of the plant, but I did know that I was not the only agent sent to Abadan. When I was interned in Cairo in 1941, a fellow internee told me that the Abwehr had prepared a massive attack against the refineries on the Persian Gulf. The enormous plant was to be destroyed with one blow . . .

What Waltraut Oertel had heard in the internment camp in Cairo was a distorted account of what was intended. In fact it was never proposed to destroy the oil refineries at Abadan at a stroke. On the contrary, all that was to happen was that they should be put out of action for a limited period, to cut off the oil supplies for the Allied tanks, aircraft and ships. Afterwards the oil was to be made to flow again for the benefit of the Wehrmacht, since the fuel stocks of Hitler's armoured formations in North Africa had reached a dangerously low level and everything indicated that they were eating into their reserves.

It was this problem that Charles Bedaux wanted to solve for the

Germans. His Renaissance château in the Touraine, which the Duke of Windsor had chosen as a fitting setting for his 'wedding of the century' to Mrs Simpson, provided the captain of industry with the necessary peace and quiet to ponder on Hitler's major problems. Here in the Château de Candé, with its badminton court, golf course and swimming pool, Bedaux waited for the great inspiration that would hasten the victory of the Third Reich.

What had persuaded the close friend of the former King Edward VIII to make common cause with the Germans in their efforts to destroy the peoples of that close friend? What reason could there be for a rich man like Bedaux to place his knowledge and his abilities at the disposal of the Abwehr and to start on a career as an Abwehr agent, like Waltraut Oertel, Karl Richter or Wulf Dietrich Schmidt?

In August 1975 I put these questions to the former president of the German Bedaux Company, Herr Schlindwein, at his secluded country house on the Austrian Ossiachersee. As far back as 1926 he had taken on the industrial consultancy of the Continental Rubber Factory in Hanover, Bedaux's first client in Germany:

It was not technical knowledge that was Charles Bedaux's strongest point, but his radiant humanity. He was irresistibly charming . . . Bedaux wanted to become the uncrowned king of England, that was the real reason for all the attention he paid to the Duke of Windsor. He believed that one day the Duke would regain the throne and Bedaux did everything in his power to make that belief come true. He liked to earn money and to spend it. That was the real purpose in life of that 'charming Napoleon' who had started life as a dishwasher in the United States during World War One . . . He was introduced to the highest German officials by the sister of the then Foreign Minister, Ribbentrop, whom he had met in Turkey before the war. He was enthusiastic about Germany – order and discipline were after all basic to his own work. After visiting a textile factory in Augsburg he told me how refreshing it was to visit a German factory, where all the workers were clean and neat. In France they would all have had cigarettes dangling out of the corners of their mouths. Their workers were unshaven and dirty.

Anyone who is still interested to know why the Duke of Windsor, who abdicated for love, went to Germany to be received by Hitler may well find that Charles Bedaux is the answer. Bedaux used the ex-King as a kind of visiting card with which he was able to bring himself to the notice of the most important departments and the highest officials of the Third Reich. These contacts, enhanced by the Duke of Windsor's German visit, were of the greatest importance to Bedaux, who had a keen eye for success, especially at a time when Hitler's lightning victories had made him the virtual master of Europe. It was at about that time that Bedaux – whose passport was the only thing American about him – left Paris for Berlin and the Adlon Hotel, where he always stayed. He planned to tell the head of the Abwehr sabotage department, von Lahousen, about his rough ideas for a sabotage attack on the Abadan refineries.

The place where the details of the plan were to be worked out was a safe house at 53 Avenue Hoche in Paris, which the Abwehr had found for him. The two-storey mansion, with stabling in the yard, had once belonged to the notorious international arms-dealer, Sir Basil Zaharoff.

At the time when Bedaux, together with two Abwehr officers and two secretaries, occupied two rooms in the Zaharoff villa near the Champs Elysées, the house was the headquarters of a secret purchasing agency. The organization was run by one of the craftiest members of German Military Intelligence, Andreas Folmer, who kept the coffers of the Abwehr full with the proceeds of his enormous deals on the French black market. Folmer's cashbox also helped to provide the funds delivered to Wulf Dietrich Schmidt or, to be more precise, the British Secret Service. Andreas Folmer, alias Pat, became a multimillionaire thanks to the commissions he received and could afford to employ the late Zaharoff's butler. After the war he was sentenced to death, but had his sentence commuted to life imprisonment. He now lives in somewhat straitened circumstances in a remote and not entirely weatherproof garden chalet not far from Garmisch-Partenkirchen. It was there that he told me what he could still remember about Bedaux:

I had an enormous office, about thirty feet long, some three hundred yards from the Arc de Triomphe, and with a view down the Avenue Hoche. It was there that I first met Monsieur Bedaux, whose arrival had been announced by our armed office guard. When the doors were opened a cloud of perfume drifted into the room, closely followed by an elegantly dressed Frenchman. I had been informed about the purpose of the visit by the Abwehr: Bedaux was to work out some plans on behalf of the Berlin office and all I knew about them was that they were to be kept very secret. In fact I had been told that I would be held personally responsible for ensuring that no one could discover what it was that Bedaux was working on in my office.

I offered Bedaux Zaharoff's former bedroom and dressing room, which lay on the opposite side of the house, facing the courtyard, as office accommodation. Bedaux and the two Abwehr officers and two secretaries worked on their project in those rooms for about four months. Before the team started on their mysterious task I had to have double safety locks fitted to all the doors, and whenever Bedaux's staff entered the rooms they immediately locked the doors from the inside.

Of course this somewhat exaggerated secrecy made me all the more curious to know what was going on in those offices facing my own. On one occasion I had a row with Bedaux, who was always a bit patronizing. He was standing in the open doorway to his office complaining that his project was being jeopardized by the many strangers who came to the house, and he threatened that if even the slightest suggestion of what he was doing ever leaked out, he would report to the highest levels in Berlin that I was responsible. While we were arguing I had an opportunity to look into his office. I noticed that apart from a lot of drawings and papers there was a map of the Persian Gulf on the floor, propped up against the desk.

The next item of information on the Abadan project was given to me by a former Abwehr sabotage expert, Karl Strojil, whom I met in Vienna after the war:

I distinctly remember my chief, Lahousen, putting a very extensive study of a planned sabotage attack on the Abadan refineries on my desk one day. He wanted my opinion, as a former sapper, whether the method suggested would really put the plant out of action.

Lahousen told me that the plan had been put forward by a Frenchman, an industrial adviser, whose engineers had worked in the plant. Lahousen actually told me his name but I am afraid I have forgotten it. When I was a prisoner of war in Wolfsberg in Carinthia in 1945 this almost proved my undoing, as the British interrogating officer threatened to keep me and my wife in prison until I told him the name of the man who had worked out the Abadan sabotage plan for us. I would have been quite willing to tell him, but with the best will in the world I simply could not remember it.

All I can remember about the details of the plot is that the Frenchman apparently had a hold over one of the senior men in Abadan as a result of some financial deal, and was in a position to blackmail him. It was claimed in the report from Paris that some fifteen thousand members of the work force would blindly obey that director in Abadan and that if each one of them put only one kilo of sand in his pocket and then put it in the pumps, machines and greasing points, Abadan would grind to a halt.

I spent several days studying the project in Berlin. The object of the plan would have been very difficult to achieve, because the plant was not to be destroyed but merely put out of action temporarily. The idea was after all that the refineries should eventually go on working for the Germans. In view of this, the opinion I gave on the proposals put forward by the French industrial consultant was as follows:

'If the claims made in this paper are justified and if the attack can be carried out with lightning speed, within one day in fact, I consider the prospects for a temporary closure and preservation of the enemy refineries in the Persian Gulf to be very promising.'

Charles Bedaux, bon viveur and lord of the manor of Candé, always saw to it that he was paid highly for his advice. For Operation Gulf he was even prepared to risk his neck, and that would certainly not have been cheap. As General Lahousen remarked: 'The financial conditions he laid down always seemed extremely high.'

But there was something else that meant more to Charles Bedaux than mere money. A secret document of German Military Intelligence reveals his secret ambition:

The American citizen of French origin Charles Bedaux who is to lead the expedition has made a number of conditions for his proposed activities as the leader of the oil protection operation. For himself personally he demands to be allowed to join the Wehrmacht in the capacity of military governor with the rank of Generalleutnant . . .

In the event of Hitler being victorious that would have been the crowning glory of his life: Charles Bedaux, in the uniform of a German general with the broad red stripes on his trousers and a chestful of decorations! Then he would enter Buckingham Palace as the protector of his friend, the Duke of Windsor. He would return Edward VIII to the throne again, and Charles Bedaux the military governor would be the figure behind that throne, directing the country's destiny.

Major Karl Strojil told me why that dream remained a dream:

After I had read his [Bedaux's] plans, I said to myself: we could do this much more cheaply on our own. So I left my desk in Berlin and had myself transferred to Persia under diplomatic cover. But there were so many upsets on the long road to Abadan that I literally got stuck in the desert . . .

The secret battle of Abadan was not the only Abwehr project to be launched to loud fanfares and drumrolls, only to get stuck in the sand like Major Strojil's car. When war broke out in 1939 Admiral Canaris was like a man letting balloons escape into the sky, not knowing where or how they would come down to earth again. 3725 was one of them, and when I traced him after the war he was no more than a sad shell, a prisoner of all the conflicts that the war had left him with. In the course of the years I have spent tracing the secret history of the Third Reich I have found most of the other people whom the Abwehr sent out into the world like so many ciphers, and having spoken to those victims of the battles fought by the Abwehr for its own glorification I hope I shall never again be told that Admiral Canaris would never countenance any operation involving a risk of human life, and that the Admiral was against all forms of bloodshed.

As a matter of fact the very first victim of World War Two, a young Polish soldier, must be debited to the Abwehr account. He died at dawn on 26 August 1939 in a German attack on the frontier station of Mosty in the Jablunka Pass. This *coup de main*, part of an operation called 'Bergbauernhilfe' was a terrible mistake: the Abwehr agents with their swastika armbands and led by Leutnant Hans-Albrecht Herzner had begun the war six days early. This incident was only the first in a long line of amateurish secret operations – supposed victories that Admiral Canaris was anxious to claim.

The deployment of the Abwehr troops who were to occupy and secure the Dutch and Belgian power stations and sluices a few hours in advance of the German attack in the West had been particularly well prepared at the Tirpitzufer: in the course of a sumptuous meal at the luxurious Horcher restaurant in Berlin, the monocled head of the Abwehr central office, Colonel Hans Oster, had told his old friend the Dutch Military Attaché Sas when the German military operations against his country were due to commence.

Another balloon sent up by Canaris on 10 June 1940 at the request of Reichsmarschall Hermann Goering was to land in Switzerland. Eight intrepid young men from the reserves of the specialist Brandenburg Battalion were to 'destroy at one stroke all the Swiss airforce planes standing ready for action on Swiss airfields'. For all those taking part the operation – code name Adler – was to end in Swiss jails. Many years after the war I had an opportunity of studying history with the aid of living eyewitnesses.

Number 3033 had not been expecting my visit. As I stepped into his cell he looked up into my face and then got up and came towards me, his back bent and his arms hanging at his side. Years of sitting on his bunk had reduced him to a human wreck. The Auditor-General of the Swiss army had authorized my visit to Regensdorf Jail to see Friedrich Freiberger, a former agent of the Abwehr, who was serving a life sentence and had spent eleven years in solitary confinement. With tears in his eyes he described a comedy which reminded me vividly of the games staged by Major Nikolaus Ritter.

The Abwehr expedition to Switzerland had been prepared in such an amateur fashion that it was bound to go wrong, in spite of a number of safeguards. The eight agents were all dressed in plus-fours all made of the identical material and in the same style. A further item of camouflage for the group, who were posing as men on a walking tour, was a cape made of brand-new cloth as used for Luftwaffe uniforms. To ensure that the men should walk softly among the Swiss population they all slipped into the same type of brown walking shoes before leaving Berlin. And to protect the suicidal volunteers from the suspicious glances of the Swiss security officers they were all provided with Basque berets. Each carried a rucksack full of explosives – oddly enough, these were not labelled 'Wehrmacht property'. Finally the eight agents pocketed Czech pistols that had jammed during practice firing.

In order to conceal their identity, the identity disks which they normally wore on a cord round their necks were taken away from them. And in order to make quite sure that they would arrive in a Swiss jail promptly and without undue difficulty, the manager of this Abwehr circus, who had the strangely appropriate name of Major Klug (i.e. clever), handed each one of them a brand-new Swiss hundred-franc note.

It was in this attire that the men of secret commando Adler appeared at Kreuzlingen station at dawn on 14 June 1940. They jumped on to the train bound for Zürich and Winterthur at the very last moment, but in order not to draw attention to themselves they split up into twos and settled down in different carriages.

When the ticket collector came along he informed the first two that their tickets were no longer valid and that they would have to pay for new ones, which they did, handing him brand-new hundred-franc notes. When exactly the same thing happened further down the train he thought he was seeing things, but by the time he reached the third carriage to find yet another pair of Germans wearing the same clothes, with tickets that were not valid and paying for new ones with new hundred-franc notes, he was quite certain that he was doing nothing of the sort.

And that is how the Abwehr's attack on Switzerland ended at dawn on 14 June 1940.

A similar fiasco – cover name Weissdorn – was launched by Admiral Canaris with the aim of capturing South Africa Abwehr-fashion. There, a single man, the former Boer boxer Robbey Leibbrandt, was to undermine a country three times as large as Greater Germany, with explosives supplied by Berlin. A well-trained Abwehr agent like Robbey – so the armchair strategists in the Tirpitzufer reasoned – would have little difficulty, on account of his enormous strength, in emerging as the victor in a boxing ring of some 473,733 square miles of veldt and jungle alone, against a population of thirteen million. The strategic aim that had been hammered into the heavyweight champion's skull was the little matter of stage-managing an insurrection against the British, which would hasten the collapse of the 'decadent British Empire'. And that, so the planners of the ambitious Weissdorn project thought, anticipating their victory, would seriously weaken the southern flank of the British Empire.

In order to publicize the promising one-man crusade against South Africa, Admiral Canaris even had a film made of his agent's journey across the Atlantic which as late as 1942 he would proudly show to anyone who doubted the success of his daring enterprise. But while the film of the hazardous trip was flickering across the screen in Berlin, Robbey Leibbrandt was already in chains in prison in Pretoria. I heard these details from ex-agent Leibbrandt himself, when I met him after his release in South Africa after the war.

After Leibbrandt's abortive efforts to capture South Africa, Canaris prepared his next great blow against the United States. There, as in Switzerland, his intrepid agents were to blow up armaments factories, power stations, bridges and skyscrapers, and with as loud a bang as possible, so that the Americans might learn to appreciate on their own soil how hard and unmercifully the German Abwehr soldiers could fight.

The attack on the United States, code name Pastorius, began on 26 and 27 May 1942. On those days two German submarines, the U 202 and U170, each with four pale-faced secret agents on board, slipped out of the port of Lorient.

In the interval between their departure from occupied France and their arrival off the coast of Florida and Long Island respectively, the actors in Operation Pastorius lay seasick in their bunks for sixteen long days and held their breath as the submarines crept silently under the keels of enemy convoys. Before U 202 reached Long Island Georg Dasch, the leader of the expedition, drew a cartoon of Uncle Sam with a knife in his back in the ship's visitor's book. The caption read 'Straight to the heart'.

So much for Georg Dasch's courage with a pencil. But he soon grew sick with fear as he saw the strange coastline looming up out of the sticky darkness, and coming nearer and nearer, like some sleeping monster.

The inflated dinghy ran ashore, slightly scraping the bottom. Four figures jumped out and hurried up the shore with long strides, dragging four crates behind them. In a few moments it was over and the dinghy turned back to sea, a few muttered 'goodbyes' and 'good lucks' swallowed up in the mist. Then the diesel engines started up again and the long low shadow of the submarine headed east again.

It was two o'clock in the morning on 14 June 1942. On the Long Island beach, Georg Dasch and his three companions stripped off their wet uniforms, changed into civilian clothes and buried the crates in the sand. The first Germans had landed in America!

The first people to become aware of this fact, a few hours later, were the Long Island coastguards who noticed some strange sandhills on the beach which on investigation were found to cover four crates containing German army uniforms and other items of clothing. Moreover, although the Abwehr camouflage experts, in their efforts to conceal the nature of the operation, had packed the explosives and detonators in perfectly innocuous cartons, they had carefully labelled them 'friction detonators – Wehrmacht property'.

To make discovery of the sabotage materials easier, the beach of Long Island was strewn with German cigarettes and bottles of schnapps, the label 'German brandy' proudly proclaiming its origin.

To convince the Americans that their curious discovery was not just some practical joke, Georg Dasch (who had been chosen as the leader of the party because the Abwehr psychologists considered him to be the most reliable and the most able) telephoned FBI headquarters forty-eight hours after landing in America. Speaking from a New York hotel he told them: 'My name is Pastorius. Make a note of that . . . Franz Daniel Pastorius.'

On 29 June 1942 President Roosevelt ordered the trial by court martial of the Pastorius men. The accused were convicted on the strength of a confession running to two hundred and fifty pages volunteered by their leader Georg Dasch. In the first week of August, in the stuffy courtroom of the Washington District Court, eight verdicts of guilty were returned and eight sentences of death were passed.

When Georg Dasch and his deputy Ernst Peter Burger were taken down the long corridor of their prison to see the governor, they noticed that the doors to the cells of their six companions were open.

'That's right,' said the warder in reply to Burger's inquiring look. 'Your friends went to the electric chair this morning.'

Reprieved, and sentenced to thirty years and life respectively, they were sent back to Germany after the war 'on provisional release'. There in his native country, where the relatives of the six men he betrayed still live, Dasch goes in constant fear. 'Franz Daniel Pastorius', who once wanted to blow up the United States, went to live in Mannheim, where he served behind the counter in a wool shop.

I went there to try and coax the ex-spy out of his post-war anonymity, but when I mentioned the code name Pastorius Dasch winced.

'You will never get anything out of me. I am bound by an oath.'

'I am not interested in the details of your secret mission. All I want to know is whether you betrayed your comrades out of fear or whether there were any other motives.'

The word 'motives' breached the dam of his silence. Georg Dasch poured out the story of his ruined past in short, jerky sentences. In an orgy of self-justification he told me the story of the Pastorius fiasco from his angle. He wanted to ease his conscience. When he finally pulled himself together, he realized that he had said too much and his parting words were a threat:

'If you publish one single sentence about me . . . if you mention my name, I'll blow up your publisher's firm. Think about it. I have nothing more to lose in this life.'

Looking back on the events of the year 1942 one could say that the explosives of the Pastorius commandos did a lot to decide the outcome of the war in favour of the Allies, even though they never actually went off. Georg Dasch, the man in the woolshop in Mannheim, had managed to frighten one hundred and sixty million Americans – aided by some dramatic banner headlines in the press – into expecting more invading Nazi hordes.

It was in that climate that Washington decided in the summer of 1942 to send American troops to Europe: Winston Churchill's wish had been fulfilled at last. For this American military aid the British people's thanks are due, at least in some measure, to Admiral Canaris. By staging the Pastorius spectacular he had unwittingly sounded the alarm and persuaded the Americans to go and help put out the fire that was raging in Europe.

On the other side of the world Canaris was busy too, trying to get a foothold in the distant and inscrutable East by launching an operation – code name Tiger – which is unique in the annals of international espionage. The idea was for the Abwehr to infiltrate into India and

Afghanistan with a view to recruiting the natives as espionage and sabotage agents, and it had been imported from England at the outbreak of war. The notion of an insurrection of the frontier tribes had been put to Canaris by the leprosy expert Professor Manfred Oberdörfer, who was half Jewish but had returned to Germany from London, and it appealed to the Admiral so much that he had the professor posted to the Brandenburg Regiment as a lance-corporal, to help him escape racial persecution. There were incidentally quite a number of Jews who were saved by Canaris only because they were useful to the Abwehr.

The plan to set up a 'leprosy study commission' with the aim of interrupting the supply of troops from India chopped and changed so often in the Abwehr headquarters that in the end it was difficult to make out the original purpose of the exercise. Overloaded with far-fetched embellishments – mostly the contributions of the fertile minds of German orientalists – the operation was far too top-heavy before it even started. One of the key figures of the 'brilliantly camouflaged scientific expedition' was a Lithuanian lepidopterist, Fred Brandt, of whom Canaris' old friend Erwin von Lahousen told me: 'Of course the man was able to run about quite harmlessly catching his butterflies – and at the same time he could unobtrusively train the Afghan frontier tribes and supply them with arms . . .'

But in fact the course of events as far as the incitement of the Afghans and the Indians were concerned was rather different from what Canaris had imagined. Fred Brandt, whose Abwehr career ended by his being sentenced to twenty-five years in a Siberian labour camp, told me when he had been released after suffering four heart attacks how the ponderous Abwehr project had suddenly and rapidly run out of steam:

The whole thing was given away before we even arrived in Afghanistan. As soon as we got to Herat, the first town in the south-west of the country, we were given an Afghan guard for our protection, but the fellow was in the pay of British Intelligence. When we arrived in Kabul, the Italian Ambassador, whose wife was a Russian, introduced us to an Indian Colonel who claimed to have escaped to Afghanistan from the British. The colonel, who accompanied Oberdörfer whenever he had any discussions in Kabul, proved to be our undoing.

The man led us straight into an ambush in which we were mercilessly shot up by pro-British bandits. Manfred Oberdörfer was hit in the chest and stomach. We got him into the back of a truck but he died on the way back to Kabul, his head in my lap.

After all these worldwide successes, Admiral Canaris proudly hoisted

one victory pennant after another to the masthead. There were cele-
brations on board and on the bridge. Neither the white-haired master
of the ship, nor his espionage chief Piekenbrock, and still less the Austrian
sabotage boss Erwin von Lahousen had the slightest idea that the
timbers of their ship were riddled with wormholes and that the whole
outfit might sink at any moment. The radio messages sent off all over
the world were being intercepted and decoded by the British, with the
result that after 24 December 1942 they were informed in advance
every time the old Abwehr ship altered course.

Wulf Dietrich Schmidt was one of the most active of the wood-
worms, busily burrowing away on behalf of the Western intelligence
services, but the Canaris Abwehr establishment also had a large hole on
its Eastern side. It was through this gap that the Harnacks in Berlin,
representatives of the famous 'Red Orchestra', were able with the help
of an unsuspecting intermediary to get direct access to a source of secret
information and of important decisions in the Abwehr headquarters in
the Tirpitzufer.

The intermediary was Oberleutnant Gollnow. Under Admiral
Canaris he was responsible for the assistance given by the Luftwaffe in
transporting agents far behind the enemy lines, mainly by the Gartenfeld special squadron.

Mrs Harnack not only gave Oberleutnant Gollnow English lessons,
she also made room for him in her bed, and it was there that the
Abwehr officer, a faithful follower of the Führer, cheered her up by
telling her of the inevitability of Germany's final victory. He was in a
position to know, he told her, what great things were afoot that would
bring the enemy to their knees.

But the agent of the Red Orchestra was unconvinced and was not
satisfied until she had some concrete details about the operations
carried out by Gartenfeld which Gollnow said were a guarantee of
victory. As a result of these hushed conversations in a bed in Berlin,
Moscow knew about most of the agent operations while they were
still in a preparatory stage. When Hauptmann Gartenfeld set off in his
'spy taxi' on some operation, the Russians knew exactly where he was
heading for. Oberleutnant Gollnow was also concerned with the agents
parachuted into England, and in view of this position in the nerve
centre in Berlin he became one of Moscow's most important west-east
transmission points.

By his involvement with the airforce side of the agents' flights to
England, Gollnow had also become a link between Wulf Dietrich

Schmidt and his brother Kai. It was he who had arranged for Wulf Dietrich Schmidt to be flown to England in 1940 and who later directed his brother Kai, the pilot of a Ju 52, to a lonely valley in the Caucasus far behind the Russian lines one night. That flight was almost the end of Kai Schmidt. By great good fortune he was able to make a steep turn over the moonlit banks of fog that hung over the mountains and head back for home, and so avoided sharing the fate of the 'Caucasian Eagles' who were dropped by parachute that night near the villages of Tschischki and Datschu-Barsoi. It was 25 August 1942.

The operation for which Kai Schmidt and the other pilots of the Gartenfeld squadron were supplying the transport had the code name Schamil. The object was to 'incite the Caucasians to insurrection and to break them away from Soviet Russia like the segments of an orange', and it all seemed perfectly simple from Berlin. But the execution of the plan, whose ultimate aim was to secure the oilfields of Maikop and Grozny, was disastrous.

Of an entire company of eager Caucasians who together with three dozen German subordinate leaders, most of them from South Tirol, had parachuted into their target areas that night, only five got back to the German lines. They were in a state of complete exhaustion after many months of lonely wandering. Two of those men, the party's leader Oberleutnant Kurt Lange and his deputy Hans Putzer, told me in the course of several days' conversation how the ambitious Abwehr plan to break up the Soviet Union ended.

Oberleutnant Lange was in the leading aircraft with twenty Caucasians and twelve Germans. Before he jumped, Gartenfeld had throttled the engines, shaken him by the hand and wished him good luck. In the days since dropping Wulf Dietrich Schmidt, Gartenfeld had reduced the farewell procedure for the agents he was dropping to something like a conveyor belt system. It was only three months since Karl Richter had jumped to his eventual death over St Albans with Gartenfeld's 'Good luck' ringing in his ears. Now it was the turn of Lange and his Caucasian volunteers.

'I had arranged with the High Command of the Wehrmacht that they would send my parents a card every six weeks, telling them that they had heard from me. My brother had been killed a short time ago and I wanted to spare my mother any unnecessary worry . . .' This was the only precaution that Oberleutnant Lange had arranged with his superiors in Berlin in the event of something happening to him.

Hans Putzer, flying in the other aircraft, never gave a thought to such a possibility. Only life figured in his Tyrolean imagination. He would get back somehow:

It was a beautiful picture as we seemed to hang in the air, suspended on our parachutes, like a long chain of pearls. A strange moonlight shone on the village far below, seemingly fast asleep. We all had our submachine-guns slung across our chests and a suicide tablet of cyanide in our pockets – just in case. When we were about a few hundred metres above the ground and could already feel the warm air rising up from below, all hell was let loose as an incredible fireworks display suddenly burst upon us. Tracer bullets came at us from all over the place, bullets were whistling about, puncturing our parachutes. So we came down faster and faster, straight into the mouths of the machine-guns. Two companies of a crack Soviet unit had been waiting for us . . .

The background to this catastrophe emerged some time later in Berlin, after Oberleutnant Gollnow's bedroom indiscretions had sounded a deadly echo in the lonely and distant valleys of the Caucasus. Gollnow was sentenced to death by a court martial for 'military disobedience' and executed in 1943. As the judges considered that he had not intentionally committed treason they allowed him to be shot rather than hanged.

After their return, the men who had survived the hail of bullets were awarded decorations. These were presented on 21 January 1943, a day of conflict in the history of the Abwehr, or rather a day on which the conscience of one of its members must have been under considerable strain. While Oberleutnant Gollnow was waiting in prison for the sentence of death to be carried out, Hans Oster, who had done exactly the same thing in 1940 when he intentionally betrayed the date for the opening of the German campaign in the West to his friend the Dutch Military Attaché Sas, and who had since been promoted to general, hung the Knight's Cross of the Iron Cross round the neck of Kurt Lange, awarded by the Führer on 15 January 1943 according to the Abwehr sabotage department's war diary.

For the Germans the year 1943 began with Stalingrad. In the spring the remnants of the once invincible Africa Corps surrendered in Tunisia. Their last commander, General von Arnim, was taken prisoner by the British after receiving an encouraging message from the Führer, dated 13 May 1943: 'The last stand, the bearing of your troops will be an example to all the forces of the Greater German Reich.'

With the last German resistance in North Africa smashed, the base for the Allied invasion armada was cleared. The leap across the Mediterranean to form the first bridgehead on the Continent was to take place three hours after midnight on 10 July 1942. Admiral Sir Andrew Cunningham, responsible for the 3266 ships involved in the landing, had outlined the strategic aims of the Allied invasion, shortly before the battle for a Europe still dominated by Hitler began: 'Our most important task consists in transporting this enormous expedition in the shortest possible time and in ensuring the merciless advance of our land and air forces into enemy-held territory. To achieve this aim great risks must and will be taken.'

It was to reduce these risks that the imaginative deception specialists in London sat down to their chessboard to construct an effective diversion. Which of the pieces that had proved so successful against the Germans in the last three years could now be used in the impending invasion of Sicily? Which of the double agents could draw the Germans' attention away from the real invasion area, so that Hitler would expect the attack to take place in Greece and not in Sicily?

Wulf Dietrich Schmidt, who had made himself particularly popular earlier in the war with the German Naval Command owing to his 'valuable reports' on the movement of convoys and his sensational secret mine-laying plans, might have been the best channel for a diversionary manoeuvre in the Mediterranean. But Schmidt must on no account be moved across the board just now. The other double agents, Mutt, Jeff and Dragonfly, were also temporarily on ice, for the German High Command had clearly discovered, at least by the time Eisenhower invaded North Africa on 8 November 1942, that their Norwegian couple's 'Scandinavian spectre' had been deception. It must also be assumed that Dragonfly and Schmidt were likely to have overdrawn on their credit in Berlin with their constant hints about an invasion on the northern coast of France. It was for this reason that the British now produced their trick with the corpse that a Spanish fisherman found floating on its back, in the sea off Huelva on the morning of 30 April 1943.

This macabre operation – code name Mincemeat – became familiar to audiences all over the world in the film, *The Man Who Never Was*. In a London mortuary a suitable corpse was selected which, in age and appearance, might play the part of a dead British major. Then the pale figure was dressed in British officer uniform and placed in a watertight container.

Having carefully calculated the effect of the tides off Huelva, they took the body by submarine and consigned it to the sea off the Spanish coast at a point where it would be washed ashore. The man chosen for this strategically important mission had a few love letters and cinema tickets in his pockets and, most important of all, his personal documents showing him to be Major W. Martin of Combined Operations Headquarters.

Major Martin was the personal liaison officer of the Chief of Combined Operations, Lord Louis Mountbatten. The impression to be created was that the Major had crashed in a courier aircraft while carrying top secret papers intended for General Alexander and Admiral Cunningham. The Germans were to gather from these documents that the real Allied attack was definitely to take place in the Eastern Mediterranean, with the main thrust directed at Greece, but that in order to ensure the surprise effect of this gigantic operation it would be necessary to launch a feint attack against Sicily a short time beforehand.

To make sure that the Germans took these London-made reports seriously and that the papers would not get lost in the water, the courier pouch was firmly attached to the body of the Major, who was wearing an inflated life jacket.

Operation Mincemeat was a masterpiece of intelligence technology, from Major Martin's collar stud to the production of the misleading letters which were signed by Lord Mountbatten personally. That perfection was no mere accident, but the outcome of the most careful thought and planning.

The first exercise involving forged top secret documents to be played into German hands also took place under Lord Mountbatten, during the Dieppe raid. On that occasion a British officer 'accidentally' lost his briefcase overboard during a minor naval engagement and the briefcase contained secret papers about an intended invasion of Norway. In the documents, which were washed ashore on the French coast, there was also mention of a feint attack in the Bay of Biscay, similar to the one in Operation Mincemeat.

In the next invasion, that in North Africa on 8 November 1942, some secret documents also played a part in circumstances which have so far remained unexplained. In this case the corpse of a British courier was washed ashore as if by accident near Cadiz. In his breast pocket were secret documents relating to Eisenhower's Operation Torch. The report, which mentioned a completely false date for the proposed landing, purported to be intended for General Mason MacFarlane, the Governor of Gibraltar.

If on three successive occasions, and always just before an important landing operation, highly secret documents are washed ashore as if by accident, it is not surprising that Operation Mincemeat achieved its greatest success after the war. Ten years after the successful landing in Sicily, the details of Operation Mincemeat were described in cinemas all over the world. They provided an ideal film script.

However, as the former head of the department for Home Defence in the German High Command, General Walter Warlimont, assured me: 'Although we never really doubted the genuineness of the documents, I am quite certain that our military operations were not influenced by Operation Mincemeat.'

With the aid of crime writers, theatre critics and journalists it was an easy matter for the Intelligence Service to fabricate documents which the Germans believed to be genuine. In the Secret Service's preparatory exercises for the subsequent Allied invasion in Normandy it had been demonstrated, however, that it was not the manufacture but the placing of such top secret documents that presented the difficulty. This was the problem that the dead 'Major Martin' was able to solve most convincingly – at least in the film.

However, in my researches I came across another British secret courier who passed five top secret letters over to the Germans in a far less complicated manner than in the somewhat involved Operation Mincemeat. Of course no film was ever made of this operation. The exact details have not so far even been told. Only two men knew about the secret negotiations, for which almost a thousand French resistance fighters were eventually to pay. One of the conspirators – an Austrian named Fleischmann, alias Fonseca – had travelled from Lisbon to Paris with four letters of introduction and a fifth letter which was to serve as his credentials, authorizing him to negotiate officially with the patriotic resistance fighters on behalf of the British government. The envelopes of the four letters of introduction were addressed by name to the leaders of four of the most active resistance groups in France.

Fleischmann decided to confide in Andreas Folmer who told me after his release by the Allies about the conditions which the British secret courier made for the handing over of the lethal letters of introduction:

In return for the addresses, the man wanted the restoration of his personal fortune, which had been confiscated by the Nazis after he had fled from Vienna. He estimated its value at about one and a half million Austrian schillings, and I handed him the equivalent amount in American dollars after the successful conclusion of Operation Porto – that was the name we gave the operation involving the arrest of about a thousand French men and women.

Five letters in one man's pocket. That was the kind of carelessness that opened the gates of the German concentration camps on 9 October 1941 to admit nine hundred and sixty-two French citizens, all because of a few letters of introduction from British Intelligence.

The same irresponsibility with which they passed the names and secret addresses of French resistance centres to the Germans in Lisbon was also demonstrated when in an S.O.E. operation British Intelligence betrayed its entire agents network in Holland with its badly made identity documents. There two German intelligence professionals, Abwehr Major Giskes and Kriminaldirektor Josef Schreieder, were able to establish a deception operation against the British that was even admired by the American head of intelligence, Allen Dulles: 'One of the most successful secret intelligence operations of all time was without doubt the radio ploy Nordpol by German counter-espionage.'

In the belief that it was in touch with genuine Dutch agents, British Intelligence ran a total of eighteen illegal radio links over a period of a year and a half, serviced on the other side by German Intelligence. While the British operated in the counterpart operation with Wulf Dietrich Schmidt and half a dozen other turned agents, no fewer than fifty-four British and Dutch agents walked into the trap prepared for them by Giskes and Schreieder. Moreover the Germans persuaded the British to make ninety-five supply flights, in the course of which five hundred and seventy containers and one hundred and fifty parcels were dropped. With great generosity the British also financed Giskes' and Schreieder's efforts to the tune of five hundred thousand guilders and quantities of other currencies. The secret German radio links with England were so well disguised that even the Dutch Queen who was in exile in England sent messages to her patriotic followers at home through them.

However interesting and impressive all this may be, the fact remains that in the majority of cases so-called espionage successes are the fickle children of fortune. The American victory over the entire German agent network in 1940 required an opponent of extraordinary naïvety, whom the American Intelligence Service found in Major Nikolaus Ritter. The 'victory' of the London Double-Cross Committee was a heaven-sent present in the person of the unstable Wulf Dietrich Schmidt. For the next great American success Edgar Hoover, the boss of the FBI, had to thank Georg Dasch whose sudden appearance in the United States no one would at first believe. Dasch had to call in person at FBI headquarters in Washington, his little suitcase crammed full with two hundred thousand dollars, before anyone would believe that the Germans had actually landed in America.

The Germans for their part owed their success in the Cicero affair partly to the fact that the British Ambassador, Sir Hugh Knatchbull-Hugessen, was a very sound sleeper, and partly to the fact that the documents that the butler photographed contained some reasonably useful information. Recently, however, even this legendary German intelligence success has been the subject of some doubt. As the British historian Professor Hugh Trevor-Roper told me in Oxford on 16 January 1976: 'With the help of the Enigma deciphering machine, which we were able to reconstruct, we were able to decipher the Cicero reports from Ankara from the very start.' And Professor Trevor-Roper added with a smile: 'Towards the end we may even have used Cicero to deceive the Germans.'

Another of the 'greatest spies of World War Two', Dusko Popov, was able to penetrate the Abwehr chiefly on account of the fact that his smartest opponent in Lisbon was not nearly as smart as he seemed at a distance. Albert von Karsthof was anything but hard and aggressive. Instead of concentrating on combating enemy spies he appears to have been far more concerned with his mistress and his pet monkey Simon.

And what, in this context, is the significance of Operation Nordpol, either 'one of the most successful secret intelligence operations of all time' or the most lamentable failure of all time, unless the massive British Intelligence invasion of Holland had another purpose, namely that of deception? It is quite conceivable that the British (though they would never admit it) wanted to create a feeling of alarm, as in the case of Dieppe, in order to keep German troops tied down on the Channel coast. Everything points to this and very little against it.

Did the London centre really fail to realize, over a period of almost two years, that none of the fifty-four radio operators and saboteurs they sent over to Holland ever operated from their target areas, but had in fact been sent to prison by the Germans? Did the British really fail to notice that of the 15,200 kilograms of explosive they dropped, not a single kilo ever blew up? Had it really passed unnoticed that of the 8000 small arms they dropped not a single pistol ever got into the hands of the Dutch freedom fighters? Or that not a single shot was ever heard of the 500,000 rounds of ammunition?

These impressive figures, which sum up the greatest 'Abwehr success' of the last war, contain a deadly secret. I believe that the lives of the many Dutch agents risked by the Allies in the dubious secret service game (if one believes that coordination of military projects exists) were already part of the second half of that deception operation in which the Germans were made to believe in an Allied invasion of Holland, only for them to land at an entirely different place on 6 June 1944, namely in Normandy.

On New Year's Eve 1943 the Germans looked back on Stalingrad and fervently prayed that the coming year might spare them from even worse. In order to conceal the enormous military effort involved, the forces that would be advancing on the Third Reich from a certain point along the extended German Western front were at first spread out all over the British Isles. They were not to be concentrated until the last possible moment before the secret date for the invasion, when they would be taken south in readiness for the decisive attack on the German forces in France in one of the most gigantic military operations in the history of mankind.

Twelve million Allied soldiers were ready for the onslaught on Germany. The 'small advance party' of two hundred thousand men were to occupy a bridgehead on the French Channel coast and, according to the operational plans of the Allied Supreme Command, once established the bridgehead was to be further strengthened by another ninety thousand troops and nineteen thousand vehicles. The first two waves of troops were to be carried in some five thousand ships, over one thousand transport planes and eight hundred gliders. Air support was to be provided by ten thousand bomber and fighter aircraft. Twelve thousand warships would protect the flanks of this mighty armada.

The Germans, unaware of the size of the threat, could only guess and fear in awful uncertainty. In the midst of their hopelessness they paradoxically profited from their experience during the Dieppe landings, when 'the Allies were able to gain valuable experience for their landing in Normandy.' It now emerged that the expensive test landings at Dieppe had not only shown the Allies how the Germans would react in the event of a real invasion. In the reverse sense the attack on Dieppe had shown the Germans to an even greater extent what tactics the enemy invaders would employ when thay landed on the Continent.

8 The last round

Wulf Dietrich Schmidt was chosen to transmit the fateful message that acted as a starting signal for the last round of the war for Germany and the world. On 16 January 1944 he, agent 3725, was allowed to pass on to the German High Command through his direct link with Hamburg-Wohldorf something that had been a closely guarded secret in England before that day – that the Supreme Commander of the Allied forces, General Dwight D. Eisenhower, had arrived in London. His special, train had been shunted into a siding near Primrose Hill and he had left it at midnight and been taken to his quarters at Hayes Lodge in a staff car.

On 28 January another message added to the disquiet of the German High Command: Eisenhower and a group of generals had inspected invasion troops, in particular the camp for armoured units at Petersfield and other camps near Guildford and Horsham. He then went on to visit camps near Salisbury and Exeter.

Before the Double-Cross producers handed Wulf Dietrich Schmidt the text for the Hamburg Abwehr station they had taken careful stock of the chances for their next deception ploy. The pieces with which they proposed to checkmate the Abwehr in the final phase of the secret battle had been carefully considered and the strategic moves to deceive the enemy had been thought out well in advance. In essence, the aims of the subsequent Double-Cross actions were to make the Germans believe: that the main blow for the destruction of the Third Reich would be coordinated with the Soviet formations in the East; that the extensive preparations necessary for the invasion were far from complete and the attack would certainly come much later than 6 June 1944; that the strategists in the Allied High Command were unable to agree on the actual site of the landing. This was to direct German speculation to the

Bay of Biscay, Norway or the Dutch coast (which was the shortest route to Northern Germany).

The fourth and most important part of the deception plan designed to coax the German defenders into the wrong corner of the goal, was not to be played until shortly before the commencement of the actual invasion! Hitler was to be persuaded through hundreds of secret channels, that the first attack – the one in Normandy – was only a feint and that the main thrust would be in the Pas de Calais area.

Those were the four lethal pills the Allies proposed to hand over to Admiral Canaris, disguised as a life-saving tonic. They reckoned that the Admiral would present the pills to Adolf Hitler who would choke on them.

And so the Allied deception specialists went to work on their last scheme, which they had been preparing for three years. As the old Chinese saying, reworded by Mao Tse-tung has it: 'By applying all kinds of deception it is often possible to make the enemy draw the wrong conclusion and take the wrong measures; in this way he is deprived of both his advantage and his initiative.'

For the benefit of the German radio monitoring system and their very efficient interceptors a handful of Englishmen were engaged day and night transmitting thousands of orders and inquiries. This orchestrated radio traffic, going backwards and forwards, up and down, conveyed information on the movements and postings of non-existent Allied formations. Generals were sent from A to B, and a non-existent Norwegian unit indented for ski bindings, giving a hint of an attack on Norway.

To draw Hitler's attention even more towards Calais, dummy tanks and vehicles were placed on the English coast where they could be seen by German reconnaissance aircraft, and in the East Anglian estuaries old and useless troop transport craft were moored for the benefit of the German cameras.

Now the Anglo-American players began to move their pieces into their final positions. To make quite sure that the Double-Cross net which had been knotted so carefully and so skilfully over the years was not torn by some act of carelessness, only the most valuable and secure double agents were to be used for the final encirclement of the enemy.

The first place among the radio agents was taken by Wulf Dietrich Schmidt, in whom the Abwehr appeared to have the greatest confidence. He was followed by a spy who had been recruited by the Madrid Abwehr station and whom the British referred to as Garbo.

This man seemed to have taken to heart the views of Dr Kurt Georg Kiesinger, the liaison officer between the German Foreign Office and Dr Goebbels' Propaganda Ministry, and later a German Chancellor: 'The fact that Germany has virtually no contact with Great Britain is almost unbelievable and represents an almost impossible situation . . . In this respect it could be said that all departments have failed . . . Surely it must be possible to find suitable people . . .'

Inspired by Dr Kiesinger's exhortation, Garbo, a Spaniard, immediately set about producing a veritable horde of fictitious sub-agents, like a rabbit producing its young – to the great delight of his controlling officer Erich Kühlenthal, a civilian employed in the Madrid Abwehr station. Garbo had fully appreciated Kiesinger's reference to suitable people, though they existed only in name. And these names operated, to the great satisfaction of the Abwehr, in an agent network which according to the sparse information available to the Tirpitzufer in Berlin was spread all over the British Isles.

According to the painstaking inquiries carried out by the famous British journalist Sefton Delmer, the master of this greatest of German Abwehr networks died in 1956 'without ever having discovered the truth about Alaric and the FUSAG bluff'. I actually found him, twenty years after his 'burial', as a well-to-do business man living in Koblenz. Erich Kühlenthal, the Abwehr officer and friend of Canaris, now risen from the dead, had once directed the allegedly most sophisticated of Abwehr networks from Madrid, with its twenty-five spies of whom only one in fact existed: Garbo, the Spanish agent who had been turned.

During our conversations at the end of 1974 Herr Kühlenthal naturally did not disclose any details about the extensive and complicated currency transactions and opium deals by which he had financed his Alaric network during the war. After all, Kühlenthal did receive over five hundred 'important military reports on the Anglo–American preparations for the invasion' from the Allied intelligence services in London in return for his precious pounds out of Abwehr funds. In addition their Allied opponents flooded the German radio monitoring post in Madrid with more than two thousand misleading reports, which Admiral Canaris and later his successor handed over to the High Command as gospel truth.

This meant that the Germans were paying dearly for the costly Allied deception operation: the double agent Garbo's fictitious Alaric network, whose twenty-five non-existent spies allegedly occupied

important positions at the focal points of the Allied invasion preparations, was in a position merely as a result of cleverly directed, misleading reports to construct a terrifying ghost. This entirely fictitious
army which cropped up repeatedly in the Allied deception concert was
named FUSAG (First US Army Group).

The units of the mighty FUSAG which were said to be stationed at
various centres in the Midlands and in Southern England were to persuade Hitler to make a fatal miscalculation in his defence plans against
the Allied invasion. And, like a continuous drizzle from innumerable
intelligence outlets, the spectre of FUSAG was spread all over Europe.

The 'First United States Army Group' was supposed to be the actual
invasion force which would attack in great strength, but only as a
second wave and only after the first had established a bridgehead by way
of diversion in an entirely different place. In short, Hitler was to believe
that the invasion which actually took place in Normandy was merely a
feint attack, so that he would keep the bulk of his defending forces in
the Calais area ready to repel the dreaded second wave, i.e. the 'main
attack' by the non-existent FUSAG.

As the FUSAG drizzle set in – when merchants in South America,
diplomats in Switzerland, pilots in Lisbon, doctors in Stockholm,
prostitutes in Paris, military attachés everywhere, telephone operators
in Budapest and barmen in Ankara had been thoroughly infected by the
Allied deception epidemic – the organism of the German Reich, as if
eaten up by a cancer, was already beginning to shrink. In this state of
affairs, Hitler had to grasp at any remedy that seemed to offer some
promise of salvation. Hauptmann Albrecht H. Zetzsche, in whose office
in the Luftwaffe High Command thousands of enemy reports arrived
every day, like so many germs, has described the feeling of helplessness in
the evaluation departments of the various branches of the armed forces
in those critical months:

> I still get the shivers when I think of our headquarters 'Kürfurst'. The 'case-
> mate bears' – old men who wandered about the corridors or sat in their offices
> doing nothing – turned the whole place into a mixture of prison, geriatric ward
> and madhouse . . . It was not just Canaris who was responsible for the German
> defeat in the secret war between the intelligence services by his failure on the
> espionage front. The deplorable breakdown in our intelligence effort against
> the enemy was caused just as much by the addle-brained senile intelligence
> officers sitting about, even in the Führer's headquarters, as if they were in some
> smoke-filled beer cellar, and who uncritically swallowed anything that the
> Allied intelligence services chose to set before them.

I threw stacks of reports from our agents Hector, Josephine, Ivan and Ostro into the waste-paper basket, for instance, because I could probe from their replies to our purely invented catch questions that they were under enemy control – certainly before the Allied invasion on 6 June 1944.

The next two characters the Allies considered suitable and secure enough for the final round were Jack Moe, alias Mutt, and Tor Glad, alias Jeff. Proof that the Abwehr still had confidence in them was provided by the fact that towards the end of 1943 they twice supplied them by air with money and a radio set.

In the meantime of course the Germans had also begun to have doubts about the *bona fides* of their two Scandinavian agents, owing to the repeated false alarms about impending Allied invasions in Scandinavia. For this reason they had arranged the last two supply flights to Scotland as tests, to discover whether Jack Moe and Tor Glad were – as seemed likely – turned agents or whether they were still genuinely working for the Abwehr. By a trick the British were put in a terrible quandary: the aircraft of the Fifth Air Fleet carrying the money flew in formation with other aircraft that were to bomb two neighbouring towns while the money was being dropped by the supply aircraft. As it turned out, the British were prepared to accept the bombing raid and to sacrifice homes and lives in order to preserve their two double agents Mutt and Jeff for the final battle, to cover up the Allied invasion of Normandy.

British Intelligence had to face up to a similar test when the Abwehr began to doubt the genuineness of their star agent Wulf Dietrich Schmidt. The test was a deadly game of question and answer that was to place the British government in a serious moral dilemma. So that they could destroy a certain target in the London area by a concentrated V-bomb attack, Wulf Dietrich Schmidt was ordered to go to a certain part of the town in which a first marker missile was to land. His instructions were to radio details of the exact location where the bomb had landed to Hamburg without delay. The British were given little time to consider the answer, and Schmidt's reply was checked by photographs taken by German air reconnaissance planes. In this case the British also accepted immense losses in order to maintain Schmidt's credibility in the eyes of the Abwehr officers.

Operating with captured radio agents was a kind of blind man's buff in which the intentions of the enemy could at best be guessed but never known for certain. In any case, discovering German military intentions was not the primary task of the double agents in the later stages of the war. Hitler's once daring plans had changed to cautious defence. On the secret front in the years 1943–4 the enemy Double-Cross agents moved away from spying and had gone into the attack. But in planning and execution, the secret intelligence thrust at the heart of the Abwehr camp was hardly distinguishable from the over-hasty operations with which Hamburg had started the German espionage offensive against Britain at the outbreak of war.

In preparing for the last, decisive battle of the secret intelligence services against the Germans, the British deception planners seem to have employed the same sort of tricks that their competitors in the Knochen-hauerstrasse had used: just as the German secret war against the British had started in the offices of the Hamburg firm of Stegemann, importers and exporters, in the same way the silent, destructive attack against the Germans began on the sixth floor of the Albany House in London, behind a door bearing the harmless looking nameplate: Tarlair Ltd, Export-Import. Here too the 'owner' of the firm of Tarlair was an experienced British agent runner and antagonist of the German intelligence service: Major T. A. Robertson.

As Wulf Dietrich Schmidt's superior in the Intelligence Service, Major Robertson had come to value one thing above all: the absolute reliability of his faithful 'foundling' from Apenrade. As Wulf Dietrich Schmidt had proved to the Allies, the Schleswig-Holsteiners from the South Danish border country keep to their word, especially when their lives are at stake.

Nevertheless, when it came to camouflaging the gigantic preparations for invasion that were going on in Southern England, the Allies were neither able nor prepared to rely solely on the proofs of loyalty that Wulf Dietrich Schmidt had repeatedly given since his arrival. As a result of the deceptions practised by the Allies, the radio links between Allied counter-espionage and Germany had worn rather thin and were less secure than formerly. Moreover the secret lines between London and Hamburg threatened to break altogether at the very moment when they were likely to be most valuable as a victory-bringing weapon for misleading the enemy and smashing Hitler's Reich.

Now more than ever the Allies needed a secure bridge to Berlin for their secret intelligence counter attack and ideally one that could operate as a direct line to the High Command of the Wehrmacht. This wonder weapon, the 'uncollapsible bridge to Berlin' was supplied from Lisbon to London, just in the nick of time and with many promising words by the Anglo–German double agent Dusko Popov. With his charm and his businesslike powers of persuasion he demonstrated the explosive force of a 'bomb' he had been keeping in a villa in Estoril in anticipation of the final Allied victory: his German friend Johnny Jebsen, whom he had known since their student days in Freiburg and who had recruited him for the Abwehr, was ready – now that the Germans were near the end of the road – to change camps.

According to Dusko Popov's account his close friend Jebsen was a fanatical Nazi-hater and one of the small circle of conspirators gathered around Admiral Canaris and General Oster. Moreover he was said to be in direct pesonal touch with the most senior generals in the High Command of the Wehrmacht. The slight, Anglophile, allegedly rich heir to the world-famous Jebsen shipyards would casually mention his friendship with the Rothschilds and his business contacts with Krupp, the German armaments king. It was from this source that the British espionage boss Stewart Menzies hoped to get some sensational secrets on the design of the newly-developed rocket missiles.

For the reddish-blond Johnny Jebsen, looking pale and sensitive as he drove about Lisbon in his Rolls Royce, there were no problems. Obstacles which sometimes threatened to get in the way of the world-wide expansion of his business interests he simply overcame with bundles of notes in every conceivable currency and which were always at hand in his attaché case, ready for use like the ammo belt of a machine-gun. With those banknotes – so he confided to his best friend Popov – he had managed to obtain a hold over influential officers and men in charge of the most important secrets in the Abwehr. No wonder that he only had to put in an appearance in Berlin for the doors of the most important command posts of the German Reich to open as if of their own accord.

The influence of Popov's friend and heir to the world-famous German-Danish shipping firm struck London as so extraordinary that a special delegation of experienced SIS officers hastily set off for Lisbon to discuss with Johnny Jebsen the possibility of penetrating the Abwehr in the Tirpitzufer. Considering the seemingly miraculous plans which he promised to realize for the sake of the final Allied victory, if need be at the risk of his own life, the British gave their new secret weapon the code name Artist.

In his startlingly subdued camouflage – umbrella, bowler hat, monocle, Rolls Royce, US dollar bills and British pound notes – the rich shipping magnate's son seemed, to the agent recruiters from London, almost to guarantee victory. Their blind faith was further underpinned by a strange coincidence, which looked almost like a good omen for the strategically important Operation Artist, with its aim of disguising the Allied invasion plans. Johnny Jebsen, so it turned out, came from the same small town north of the German–Danish border where Wulf Dietrich Schmidt had spent his childhood. So the actions of two boys from Apenrade were destined to seal the fate of the Third Reich!

Wulf Dietrich Schmidt, the slightly-built son of the Apenrade lawyer William Schmidt, had started the secret war against Britain when he had jumped by parachute. He had hardly landed when he started, by his double game, to place the deadly noose round Germany's neck.

Was it a coincidence or a secret intrigue, prepared long ago, that the great espionage ring of World War Two should be closed at the very point where Wulf Dietrich Schmidt had opened it? Was it ordained by fate, or was it due to the great foresight of the British, that the delicate hands of the rich shipping merchant from Apenrade were to tighten the noose that Wulf Dietrich Schmidt had so carefully put in place?

(When I asked myself what the connection was between Wulf Dietrich Schmidt and Johnny Jebsen I was not to know that my further researches would lead me to look into the fate of four other Abwehr members who mysteriously disappeared without trace shortly before the end of the war. Their relatives do not know to this day whether they were killed or murdered, or whether they are still alive.)

The proposal by the strategists in Combined Operations to lure Admiral Canaris' clumsy Abwehr ship on to the wrong course in the decisive final phase of the war was certainly no unrealistic piece of wishful thinking. The chance of misdirecting the German military intelligence machine through Tricycle (Dusko Popov) and Artist (Johnny Jebsen) really existed at the time, for both British agents had managed to secure a firm foothold in the Lisbon Abwehr station. They had wormed their way into the confidence of some of the secretaries, who were only too happy to pass them the odd copy of secret reports which were really intended solely for the information of Berlin.

Tricycle and Artist, now stationed beside Major Albert von Karsthof at the 'porthole of the German Abwehr ship', were also on the best of terms with the men on the bridge in Berlin. Some of these proud captains of intelligence were well padded, under their smart uniforms, with the dollar and pound notes that Johnny Jebsen had thoughtfully provided in case they might have to jump ship. These blackmailed captains could now be persuaded to alter course in whichever direction the shipping magnate's son indicated.

In its last race, the Secret Intelligence Service had put its money on two promising favourites who convincingly gave the impression that the great deception operation for the concealment of the Allied invasion plans could be achieved thanks to their excellent contacts with the High Command of the Wehrmacht.

The omens were favourable. But in the practical execution of the Allied deception ploy which was to start up in Lisbon there suddenly appeared a fundamental error of calculation which suddenly put at risk both the long build-up of the Double-Cross actors and the preliminary intelligence skirmish which was to precede the landing of millions of Allied soldiers in Normandy. The two principal actors, Dusko Popov, alias Tricycle, and Johnny Jebsen, alias Artist, who were to persuade Admiral Canaris to alter course against the Nazi regime which was 'fighting to the last drop of blood' suddenly discovered that they were on a sinking ship. In the ensuing panic Admiral Canaris was ceaselessly trying to whitewash the blemishes and to patch up the holes in order somehow to keep himself and his men above water right up to the bitter end.

The enemy that Canaris now had to fear was neither British nor American: the antagonists were in his own camp, in the competing intelligence service of the SD. The black sharks with the runic SS sign were steadily circling the sinking ship of the Abwehr, eagerly snapping up every crumb that dropped overboard. Canaris had to be on his guard against these predators with the sly eyes of a Heinrich Himmler, the cropped hair of Müller, chief of the Gestapo, the sabre-scarred faces of a coolly calculating Dr Ernst Kaltenbrunner, an ambitious Walter Schellenberg and a reckless Skorzeny. It was primarily from them that he had to conceal those slip-ups that were still being wrongly quoted as assets on his list of successes.

After the dismal failures in Switzerland and the United States, in the Caucasus, Africa, Afghanistan and Canada, to mention only a few, and after the complete failure of the Abwehr as regards Operation Torch in North Africa, the Sixth US Army Corps unexpectedly landed at Anzio beach south of Rome, behind the backs of the German defenders, on 22 January 1944. Once again Canaris, the omniscient man on the Tirpitzufer, stood there ignorant and helpless, quite unable to understand how three hundred ships had suddenly appeared from nowhere and off the very same thirty-five-kilometre strip of coast which he had only recently told Generalfeldmarschall Kesselring was not in any way threatened.

As more and more water seeped into the battered Abwehr ship, some of his Abwehr faithful began jumping overboard like rats, as those posted in stations abroad weighed up their chances of survival. In Ankara, Erich Vermehren, who had been employed under cover of press attaché, and his wife, née Countess Plettenberg, went over to the British. So as not to come empty-handed they brought with them a present in the shape of the newest secret codes and a some interesting details on Abwehr organizations.

At the same time, and also in Turkey, the Abwehr Leutnant Hamburger and two agents, a married couple named Kletzkowski, changed their employers, arriving with secret files hidden under their coats.

In Berne the Abwehr Oberstleutnant Prinz Auersperg, who had been enjoying a chocolate soldier war in Switzerland as Assistant Air Attaché, parted company with the Tirpitzufer overnight. The same thing happened in Sweden, where the Assistant Air Attaché, Hauptmann Riedel of the Abwehr, saved his skin by deserting.

By February 1944 only the mast of the Abwehr ship, sunk in the series of catastrophes, was still above water. The Admiral still held on, completely exhausted but convinced that he had steered his ship across the oceans of the world from success to success, and determined that posterity should know it.

Canaris' defiant voyage would almost certainly not have lasted as long as it did had the background of a dubious enterprise, in which three men tried to kidnap a member of the secret radio station in Madrid in broad daylight and in the heart of the city become known in 1943 when it occurred.

To be sure that there is no repetition of the mysterious car accident of 3 November 1969 near the precipices of the Sill Gorge near Innsbruck, I shall simply report on the event itself. As a precaution I shall not mention the names of the men involved, who are experts in the handling of chloroform pads, handcuffs and pistols, and who tried at the time to settle a compromising Abwehr matter.

The subject of the proposed kidnapping operation was a factotum of the Madrid Abwehr station, a stolid Bavarian whose duties included delivering to the station's various outposts, and in particular to the one at Algeciras, near the Straits of Gibraltar, some new, radar-like night-vision apparatus in which the British were very interested.

On his secret supply trips between Madrid, Bordeaux and Paris the Abwehr driver spoke freely to the British agents who, for a large fee, always accompanied him on part of his journey, and in particular about the most secret German secret: the wonderful cipher machine Enigma, three of which, sited under the green copper dome of the embassy building at 4 Castellana in Madrid, automatically enciphered hundreds of radio messages every day. The friendly, well-to-do passengers were not very interested in the cipher machine itself. What they were far more interested in was the cipher key, which was changed at short intervals and which they hoped the little Bavarian would get them.

It has been revealed only recently that the working method of the little magic box, which looked like some kind of a typewriter with flashing lights, had been known to the British since the beginning of the war. The British called the captured secret Ultra, and hid it in their code-breaking headquarters in Bletchley Park, where it was used throughout the war to decipher thousands of radio messages every day. It was there that the orders from the Führer were transcribed into plain language. It was the Ultra deciphering machine that monitored, for instance, the radio traffic between Rommel and Generalfeldmarschall Kesselring, the Supreme Commander South who was stationed in Italy.

The secret of Ultra, an invaluable weapon in the hands of the Allies, was threatened however by the jealous wife of the Abwehr soldier. He had become steadily wealthier, but she was annoyed that her formerly rather staid husband was spending the money he got from the British on a newly-acquired Spanish mistress and she betrayed her husband's long-standing contact with the British to his Abwehr masters.

Three sabotage pros saw to the rest. I found two of them and the first warned me: 'You keep out of this!' The man who was so reluctant to let me disturb his peaceful postwar life was born in a small town in Czechoslovakia, the son of a policeman. I just mention this so that he can recognize himself in this book and realize that I am not going to reveal his identity.

'My father, who was in the criminal police, taught me how to hold my tongue,' Herr W. told me, 'and the Americans could not loosen it either when they tried to frighten me in the interrogation centre near Würzburg, by tying a noose round my neck and pretending that they were going to hoist me up on the door frame. They asked me the same question as you did. I just told the interrogator: "You have knocked me silly – now I can't remember a thing." '

Then the former kidnapper gave me a similar answer: 'You won't believe this, but I really cannot remember a thing about the whole affair. It has gone clean out of my head.'

Herr W, whom I had found in a small town in Upper Austria, assured me as we said goodbye that I would not get anything out of the others either, and in fact the second Abwehr kidnapper, whom I discovered in Northern Italy twenty-five years after the incident, was as taciturn as his old accomplice W to start with. Fortunately he did not quite have the other's effective technique of fencing himself in behind a strong Czech accent and a determination to match. After I had promised him not to mention his name or to tell where he lived, he started, haltingly, to tell me his story:

One day W, K and I were called to the office of the sabotage chief of the Madrid Abwehr station. There we were told what it was all about. He said that one of the drivers, who spent a suspicious amount of time in our secret radio station, had been working for an enemy intelligence service for a considerable length of time. When he was about to be questioned he had disappeared from his quarters without trace. In the meantime however it had been possible to establish his probable whereabouts. It was thought that the man was hiding in the apartment of his Spanish mistress in the centre of Madrid. We were told the exact address, so that we could prepare ourselves for the operation.

Our instructions were to overpower the traitor – a Bavarian – and to take him to the Abwehr office alive and without causing a fuss. We were all in civilian clothes. Each carried a pistol and I also had a few tins containing cotton-wool chloroform pads. Then we went off to our destination.

While W waited in the car, ready to drive the captured deserter through the town quickly and quietly, I and the other man went into the house, which had a laundry on the ground floor. Then I rushed up a few flights of stairs on my own to the fourth floor where our victim was thought to be in hiding. I stepped into a small kitchen where two Spanish women started up in fright . . .

Just as I was inquiring about the German the door into the next room opened and there stood the man I was after. He only stood for a fraction of a second before dashing back into the bedroom. A few shots rang out as I ran after him and tried to overpower him, but he crumpled up, killed by his own gun, and fell backwards through the splintered door of the wardrobe.

Dead spies cannot talk. This fact was primarily an advantage for the Allies. Now the former Abwehr driver was no longer a threat to the Ultra secret so carefully guarded by the British in Bletchley Park. And for Canaris too the death of his subordinate was a stroke of luck. The Admiral's career would probably have ended earlier if, after the painful interrogation of a traitor who was in fact lucky to be dead, Hitler had discovered that the Allies had been able since 1940 to decipher his most secret orders with the help of the reconstructed German Enigma machine. Hitler would have shown no mercy towards his Abwehr chief, who was already out of favour, if it had been proved that it was from the ranks of the suspect Abwehr of all places that his enemies had been supplied not only with the first German radar sets but with other secrets of radio technology as well, especially with the constantly changing cipher key.

What the Allies were unable to uncover with the German deciphering machine – the residual secrets that were to expose the entire German Intelligence Service completely – fell into their laps without any effort on their part towards the end of 1943 in the Herrengasse No 23 in Berne. A forty-year-old man named Fritz Kolbe, assistant to Ambassador Karl Ritter, who was responsible in the German Foreign Office for matters relating to the armed forces and especially the Abwehr, presented Allen Dulles, the European head of oss, with a parcel tied up with string and containing one hundred and eighty-six specially selected documents from his office. Kolbe was well able to assess the strategic value of the material because it was his job, as Ritter's right-hand man, to sort out the incoming diplomatic mail and the radio messages from some twenty German missions abroad, and to group them according to their importance. Trained in the German Foreign Office to exercise a sense of priorities, Fritz Kolbe and his contribution, the so-called 'Berne Report', caused quite a sensation in the Pentagon.

Kolbe not only told the Americans in the Herrengasse about the existence of the wonder agent Cicero but also unmasked the Stockholm-based civilian Abwehr officer Dr Karl-Hans Kahle, who was operating in Sweden as one of the 'master spies of the war' and who, at the beginning of his career in espionage, had been concerned among other things with the Wulf Dietrich Schmidt operation.

Kahler, one-time member of the staff of Karl Kaufmann, the Nazi Gauleiter of Hamburg, started his secret service career as assistant to Major Nikolaus Ritter. Since then he had far outstripped his erstwhile master and with considerable ability, backed by substantial funds from Berlin, he had rocketed to become one of the most important Abwehr agents.

Kahler's espionage ploys in Sweden were simple but expensive: the agents who supplied him with top-level information from England and who all had mysterious-sounding cover names were said to have penetrated even into the Allied operations staffs. One of them, Hector, even claimed to have attended a meeting of the war cabinet.

The Germans at the receiving end of the reports in Berlin never discovered in detail how he obtained his valuable information. They only knew about the high prices paid to his outstanding secret links, which seemed to reach right into Downing Street. However valuable, false, or controlled by the enemy Kahler's activities might have been, Canaris at any rate considered them to be a masterpiece of rationally conducted secret intelligence work. And looking back, the American writer Ladislas Farago describes Kahler's obscure intelligence network as the 'most inventive and effective secret operation of World War Two'.

By mid-1943, however, a very different conclusion had been reached by an alert young officer in the airforce control staff *Kurfürst* in Potsdam, where he worked in the evaluation department for the Western airforces, sifting hundreds of agents' reports and reports on the interrogation of prisoners of war in search of useful information and assessing its credibility. In the course of this work Hauptmann Albrecht H. Zetzsche had noticed a curious similarity between the Stockholm group of agents Hector-Josephine and the Ostro network run by Paul Fidrmuc in Lisbon, who has already been mentioned.

Quite independent of Zetzsche, Department III F (counter-espionage) of the Abwehr had also begun to look into the obscure operations of the 'most successful Abwehr agents' in Lisbon and Stockholm. In Sweden Oberst Ehinger was to become a porter in the German Legation in order to inquire into Dr Kahler's possible enemy contacts, while at the same time the Abwehr station in Lisbon was also to be gone over with a fine-tooth comb 'as the Abwehr station in Lisbon was apparently saturated with agents of the Secret Intelligence Service'.

In this atmosphere of general collapse in Germany, one wave of distrust after another broke over the unhappy Canaris, already up to his neck in the water, feebly clinging to the lifebelts of former Abwehr successes of which even the most outstanding triumph, the one which his successful 3725 had brought him during all those years, was also to prove fraudulent.

While Tate, the double agent Wulf Dietrich Schmidt, was once more being groomed as one of the favourites in the Allied camp in London and allowed to transmit valuable, almost factual information to Hamburg in order to confirm Berlin's faith in him, agent 3725 had actually been written off at last in the Tirpitzufer. According to the former Abwehr officer Julius Boeger:

By the end of 1943 it had been shown quite conclusively that the British had found Schmidt and that he was transmitting his information to Germany under duress. Oberstleutnant Brede (the former head of the Abwehr air intelligence department) instructed me to stop the expensive radio traffic with Schmidt, which had been tying down a lot of our people, at once.

But after a long argument with the General Staff officer Brede I succeeded in having the radio traffic with Schmidt continued. Although we no longer believed in his reports we did go on pretending to play the secret service game. All I wanted to do was to save the life of 3725, who had been working for us bravely and successfully for a number of years. From a humanitarian point of view it would have been impossible to drop Schmidt the very moment it became apparent that the enemy had captured him. If the British were to notice that we no longer believed Schmidt he would have been useless to them and would probably have ended on the gallows.

To get away from the collapsing house of cards in the Tirpitzufer in Berlin, the unfortunate Canaris suddenly felt a longing in February 1944 to revisit Spain, the country in which he hoped to find some peace after the war. He longed for the sunny south, where he hoped to preserve some ground for his faithful followers beyond the bitter end, with the help of five 'Reichsbahn sacks filled with seven thousand gold coins weighing fifty kilos'. He also felt drawn towards the successful Abwehr men who were still on his side: to Erich Kühlenthal in Madrid, the civilian officer who in the Third Reich's hour of peril still had a functioning agent network covering the whole of the British Isles.

The Admiral was greatly affected by the twilight stage of his career when all his successes were being questioned. He felt that he had become the victim of intrigue, especially considering that two of his ablest agents who had provided Hitler with material of outstanding value from Britain and America for years, Dusko Popov, alias Ivan, and Paul Fidrmuc, alias Ostro, were even at that moment fighting the enemy with unabated vigour – or so he thought.

The depressed Abwehr chief also longed for the company of his most intimate friend Major von Karsthof and his secret fiancée, with whom he had whiled away so many peaceful wartime hours at Estoril. But above all the Admiral hoped that his friend Generalissimo Franco would afford him some protection against his enemies.

Wilhelm Canaris never dreamed that the journey to his second home would end in Biarritz after a conference on 10 February 1944. There he learned that General Franco was very annoyed with him. The dispute, and the subsequent clouding over of Spanish–German relations, had been caused by a British acid detonator, eight centimetres long, which in the final analysis was also to spell the end for Canaris by causing an explosion in a Spanish port, an event subsequently exploited by the SD to add another nail to the Abwehr coffin.

The Admiral heard about the disastrous effects of this comparatively minor incident through a teleprint message that reached him via the local Abwehr office just as he was about to go for a ride in his car in the countryside around Biarritz. It happened in Cartagena, of all places, the port where, according to the British writer Anthony Cave Brown, in the summer of 1916 the German naval spy Leutnant Canaris was to have been kidnapped or killed by a young British SIS officer named Stewart Menzies. Now, twenty-eight years after he had managed to elude his British kidnapper, Canaris was brought down in Cartagena by his British rival, advanced in the intervening years to the position of chief of the British Secret Service. The battle between Menzies and Canaris had ended where it had begun.

In January 1944 two Abwehr saboteurs had instructions to blow up the Italian tanker *Lavoro*, sailing for the Allies, with an underwater mine of British origin. But in setting the timing of the device, which usually worked with great precision, a fiendish trick had been played: the British Secret Service had palmed off on the Germans detonators on which the markings of the hours actually applied to mere minutes.

The Abwehr diver Carl Kampen tried to jump out of his rowing boat but was torn to pieces, though he was not the only one to suffer. The explosion of the underwater mine resulted in strong protests by General Franco about German secret activities on Spanish soil. For Adolf Hitler the blunder at Cartagena was a welcome opportunity to give the Secret Service chief his marching orders once and for all.

At the beginning of the secret war, agents were required to be brave men – spies who were prepared to fight their way through enemy country underground or swallow the cyanide capsule. Those daredevils were used up like so many logs thrown on a fire. Most of them came to grief in the centres of action in Europe and what remained of these eager young agents were mere shells, tragic figures who were too small and insignificant to play a part in the last, decisive round.

Those last, chancy and complicated Abwehr operations were mainly carried out by smart businessmen who gave the impression that they could still win the war with the cash that Canaris had left behind. That was the state of the game on the German side before the last battles of

1944. While German and Allied soldiers were engaged in bloody conflict in the east and the west, while Jewish emigrants were desperately trying to escape from a Europe in flames and while in the East fleeing women broke down and abandoned their babies in overcrowded cattle trucks rolling westwards, where they would hopefully live on as orphans, a golden roundabout went on turning and turning, its axle pivoted on the Tirpitzufer in Berlin. Mounted upon it, well above the catastrophic events, were the bullet-proof cabins in which a few businesslike agents were able to survey the scene calmly and with unclouded vision.

These spies were men of the world and could appreciate the value of diamonds and the influence of the exchange rate. Their attachment to Germany was secured by the golden chains that held them more firmly to the roundabout than any amount of loyalty would have done. The links of those chains had been forged with good Reichsmarks by the paymaster-general of the Abwehr, Oberstintendant Martin Toeppen. The motto of this last agent elite was: 'Money is on our side.'

With this motto a small group of the remaining Canaris intimates, Nazis and Jews, aristocrats, returnees and deserters, went about their profitable business under the wide umbrella of the Abwehr. Naturally these men never revealed the tricks of their trade, for as we shall see their dubious operations could be dangerous. On this front also, in the golden witches' cauldron of Lisbon, where the battle was carried on with bundles of banknotes, some 'fell' of whom it is not known to this day whether they were actually killed or whether they just wanted to cover their tracks.

The question about the precise attraction of his strenuous activity as an agent-runner (which Hauptmann Albrecht Zetzsche had asked during the war) was answered by Ostro, the Abwehr oracle of Lisbon, in the manuscript memoirs now in my possession:

The jewellery business has always been a profitable one ... In Portugal in 1940 a wave of émigrés besieged the visa offices of foreign countries. Terrible prices had to be paid for passages and visas. Often the émigrés had to wait for eight, ten or even more months. Many of them ran out of money. But with the émigrés a large quantity of jewellery had been brought to Portugal. Brooches from Germany, beautiful old earrings and gold boxes from Vienna. Unset diamonds had been brought from Holland and Belgium, necklaces from France, bracelets from the Balkans. Jewels were offered in large quantities. Why not make use of them?

The secret battlefields of Lisbon, on which the enemy spies claimed to be fighting a bitter war, were the casino at Estoril, the bar of the Palace Hotel and the bedrooms of the Ritz. Particularly close contact with one's enemies was possible in the tastefully decorated rooms of an old palace down near the port of Lisbon, which was occupied by the largest private bank in Portugal. Its owner, appropriately named Ricardo Spiritu Santo, blessed friend and foe alike and made peace with his warlike account holders. The secrets they had omitted to give away at the innumerable cocktail parties were revealed by many a spy, diplomat, officer and industrialist, impressed by the old porcelain, blinded by the precious silver and enraptured by the charming daughters of the house, at the dinners to which they were invited by a generous host.

One can well imagine how hard the underground battle must have been in this atmosphere of social jockeying for position, compared with the front line where people were only shooting at one another, and where all you could lose was your life.

Kim Philby, the British SIS officer responsible for the Iberian Peninsula and simultaneously Moscow's master spy, Dusko Popov and the shipping magnate's son Johnny Jebsen, who had recently been recruited by the British as 'Artist', were apparently prevented by the diversions available at Estoril from concentrating on the brief by which Allied headquarters set such store: the order that the Abwehr agent with the cover name Ostro who was conducting widespread espionage operations from Portugal should be found, abducted and if need be killed. And while these able British agents claimed to have failed in their efforts to find him, the phantom agent Ostro, known to all and sundry as 'jolly Paul Fidrmuc', was living right there in their midst.

From this caviare-fed, golden base of Estoril the Allies, with Dusko Popov and Johnny Jebsen, intended to carry out their main attack into the heart of the German High Command. Much would depend on the charm of Popov, in whom the Germans had complete confindence, if the plan for misleading the most senior commanders of the Wehrmacht was to succeed. Popov had been preparing for this strategically vital task for years, and the Allies rated his chances of success very high, for fighting at his side, with a keen intellect, high political contacts, fat wads of dollar bills and some blackmailing knowledge of corrupt dealings in high places, was Johnny Jebsen.

Jebsen's method of preparing for the last battle in his villa in Estoril was very different from the way in which Wulf Dietrich Schmidt, his shy, taciturn and unostentatious countryman, had prepared for his secret operation against Britain in the Phoenix Hotel way back in 1940, with his ration books and next to no expenses.

The source of my knowledge about Jebsen's time in Lisbon is his comrade-in-arms of those days, Dusko Popov. Johnny had unlimited funds at his disposal. He was a bachelor who lived out in Estoril, and when he became bored he would go to some bar or other, his umbrella over his arm. There he would stand against the bar, tap the floor with the tip of his umbrella until silence reigned, then point at girls with the umbrella: 'You, you, and you at the back there.'

Then Johnny would go back to his villa with the women he had never seen before and carry on until he fell asleep in a corner. In the morning it was always the same: the girls standing round his bed, trying to wake him up, shaking him and pouring water over his head. But nothing would wake Johnny, and he was deaf to their pleas for money. In the end the girls simply helped themselves to the expensive antique silver ashtrays, vases, plates and lighters that were strewn about the place and when Johnny did finally wake up the house would be stripped. Whereupon he would climb into his Rolls Royce and go to Lisbon, buying up old silver ready for the next night.

And this was one of the most important British agents who was to carry out vital deception operations on the German forces in advance of the Allied invasion. The life-style of his best friend and head of the so-called Tricycle network, Dusko Popov, was apparently very similar. He too had occasionally to flee from the morass that threatened to engulf him, nights spent 'in a stupefying whirl of alcohol and sex'.

The superspy Popov describes in his memoirs how he gained, so it seems to me, some additional battle experience for the secret death blow against Berlin from a newsreel he saw in a Lisbon cinema. There he saw German tanks advancing, flattening everything that lay in their path, and felt a kind of 'psychological delirium tremens, the professional disease of the spy'. He remembered those dramatic moments: 'I felt quite alone, fighting without comrades, I felt as if I was being overrun by those German tanks in the film. My shirt and forehead were drenched with sweat. I simply rushed out of the cinema.'

The bedroom stories and personal experiences of Jebsen and Popov are quite amusing, but talking to Dusko Popov in Opio I wanted more information for my book than just an account of the successes of the Tricycle team. How did he and in particular Johnny Jebsen succeed in misleading the German High Command in the decisive phase before the invasion?

I received no very concise answer to my question and in the absence of facts Popov described the many handicaps he had faced in 1944 when he tried to carry out his historic brief. The description of the secret operation, designed to get the 'reluctant resistance group within the Abwehr under control' with the assistance of his friend Johnny, and to get it moving, developed into a thrilling crime story, complete with a murdered man and his murderer.

Popov clenched his fist as he told me how Gestapo gangsters had in cold blood thwarted him in the move against Berlin that was so important for the coming Allied invasion: right in the heart of peaceful Portugal, ss assassins had attacked his friend Jebsen, locked him unconscious in the boot of a car and taken him to Berlin. The ex-spy's voice trembled as he told me of the tortures inflicted on Johnny in the cellars of the Gestapo building in the Prinz Albrechtstrasse in Berlin, and he faltered as he told me of Johnny's death in the Oranienburg concentration camp, where he was shot 'while attempting to escape'.

I was moved as I listened to Dusko Popov's story of Jebsen's tragic end, but when he started to tell me about his murderer I sat up – he was an under-cover SD man by the name of Walter Salzer, who had approached Jebsen claiming to represent Johnny's shipping interests vis-à-vis the ministries in Berlin and the Abwehr and SD.

Popov went on to describe how, as a British colonel he had combed every occupation zone in Germany after 1945 in his search for Salzer, whom he held responsible for the death of his best friend, and how he had finally cornered him living under an assumed name. As he told the story, Popov clearly relived the moment when he punched the 'SD swine' in the stomach and kicked him in the head, only to let him off. So Popov's story ended with a dead man (Jebsen) whom no one had seen die and a murderer who escaped with his life. It struck me as very odd.

Some time before my mysterious accident in 1969 I had wanted to clear up the hitherto unsolved problem of who the daredevil was who became world-famous as 'secret agent Lieven' in the successful German post-war novel *Es muss nicht immer Kaviar sein*. During my researches I had come across a man in Augsburg who called himself Dr Aloys Schreiber, and who was said to have been involved with the abduction of Mario Simmel's hero Lieven. Before Dr Schreiber would talk to me at all over the telephone I had to spell out my name and tell him my address. Only then did he say: 'You will get no information out of me about my Abwehr activities in Lisbon.'

That was the beginning and also the end of our conversation, but before replacing the receiver he added: 'If my name appears in the press you will be sorry for it!'

I respected the wish of the former Lisbon Abwehr officer until last year, when I thought of Dr Schreiber in connection with my search for the kidnapped son of the shipping magnate. I learned that he had died in the meantime. Then I spent another four months looking for Johnny Jebsen's kidnapper and murderer. Where could I find the former SD agent Walter Salzer, whom Dusko Popov had allowed to live in 1945?

I wrote to the famous SS Obersturmbannführer Otto Skorzeny in Madrid. The answer was 'I do not know any Walter Salzer.' A similar reply came from the former Gruppenleiter in the Central Reich Security Office, Walter Huppenkothen, who had carried out the preliminary investigations that led to General Oster and Admiral Canaris being brought to trial: 'I have never heard the name Salzer. I had nothing to do with the Jebsen case. I know nothing about it.'

All that the former head secretary of the Abwehr station in Lisbon, Frau von Karsthof ('Mausi'), knew was this: 'I do not know how Jebsen was abducted and who carried out the kidnapping. My husband and I had been ordered back to Germany before it happened.'

I asked Frau Lilli Craas, a former Lisbon Abwehr secretary. All she would say was: 'I was a close friend of Jebsen's. I do not know any details about Johnny's arrest and abduction. I had been sent back to Berlin just a short time before it happened.'

In Cologne I inquired from Otto Wolf von Amerongen, president of the German chamber of commerce and industry, about his friend Johnny Jebsen: 'I met Jebsen before the war through a mutual tennis partner and we met again in Lisbon in 1942 ... When Jebsen was abducted from Lisbon I was in Cologne and Berlin and later in Salzburg, where my daughter was born.'

Perhaps the sabotage expert of the Lisbon station, Dr Blaum, alias Baumann, who had posed as a Regierungsrat, might know about the Jebsen case. I found the former Abwehr officer in Bremen. 'Why don't you ask Ciro, the head of the Lisbon counter-espionage section, whose real name is Cramer? He is still alive.'

In fact Dr Blaum had unwittingly put me on a false scent, because Cramer had been dead for years. A long detour took me to Kempten, where the former Abwehr staff paymaster Max Franzbach was able to give me some details about Jebsen:

Johnny Jebsen looked on me as his friend. I had been instructed by Berlin to see to his every wish whenever he stayed in Madrid. Jebsen often took wads of dollar bills out of his pocket and offered them to me. Naturally I did not take them . . . Later I heard that Jebsen had been lured into the German Consulate in Lisbon by the SD. There he is said to have been given an injection and put in a crate.

The very able counter-espionage expert Oberstleutnant Hans Freund first realized that Johnny Jebsen was in touch with the enemy towards the end of 1943:

At first Jebsen enjoyed the complete confidence of the office. As compensation for his activities he was given preferential treatment in hiring neutral ships for journeys involving the use of sea lanes which the Germans controlled. Jebsen must have earned a lot of money. During 1943 he suddenly started taking a great interest in information about our station in Lisbon. He got most of the information through affairs with the secretaries there, so that a number of his friends and acquaintances had to be sent home to Berlin and replaced. Early in 1944 Jebsen was more or less forcibly removed to Berlin. I do not know the details of what happened.

Having received no more than a shrug of the shoulders from the two dozen or more of Johnny's old friends whom I asked about his kidnapping and murder, I at last stood face to face with Herr K, the director of a well-known German firm, who told me in his office about the secret he had kept for thirty years:

Yes. I planned and arranged the forcible removal of Jebsen from Portugal. It had become a matter of certainty that the British had penetrated our Lisbon office and that someone was working for the British Secret Service. We got the first tip-off from Ballhorn, a young half-Jew from Berlin who was working for the Abwehr in Portugal. Ballhorn was a big, fat man who had something wrong with his glands and had a very broad face. He kept us informed from Lisbon about Jebsen's movements. His reports showed that Jebsen was undoubtedly in touch with the British and was about to escape to England.

This information was all the more unpleasant for us since only a short time previously an Abwehr agent in Turkey called Vermehren, and his wife, had gone over to the enemy and Himmler had made this incident the excuse for going to Hitler to tell him that 'the Abwehr stank!' Now the SD were eagerly awaiting another Abwehr blunder . . .

It was the forcible abduction of Johnny Jebsen from Portugal that started the self-immolation of the Abwehr. Herr K, a former General Staff major and head of the Abwehr army intelligence branch, continued the story of this act of desperation:

In addition to the report from Ballhorn we were also informed by Dr Schreiber that Jebsen was no longer calling at his office. So we made a very careful study of the Jebsen file and noticed from a character portrait it contained that Jebsen had a strong streak of egotism.

It was the Anglophile Jebsen's egotism that suggested the following abduction plan to Major K:

We sent a teleprint message to Lisbon saying that in view of his outstanding services the Führer and supreme commander of the Wehrmacht had awarded Corporal Johann Jebsen the cross for meritorious war service, first class. The decoration was to be handed to Jebsen at the Abwehr office.

Jebsen fell for the bait. One morning he appeared at the Abwehr station, where Schreiber gave him the treatment, first a right and a left hook to the jaw, shouting 'there is your decoration', and then a few more blows for good measure – 'and here is your reward for working for the British.' Then they overpowered him, gave him an injection and packed him into a crate which was then taken across Portugal and Spain into occupied France as diplomatic luggage ... Dr Schreiber made a very good job of it.

After his arrival in Berlin, Jebsen was first lodged in the Wehrmacht prison. There Major K visited his catch: 'Jebsen was in prison garb. He was small, slightly built, a young man with reddish hair and freckles. He asked me who I was. But I did not tell him my name.'

A few days later Major K was informed by his chief, Colonel Hansen, who had succeeded Admiral Canaris, that the prisoner Johann Jebsen had been handed over to the Gestapo on the orders of Generalfeldmarschall Keitel. Then Major K did one last thing to conceal the Lisbon blunder from the SD and to preserve what remained of the Abwehr's good name for posterity: 'When I was told that Jebsen had been handed over to the Gestapo I immediately tore up all the files and reports on the incidents in Lisbon and threw them down the lavatory.'

When Major K pulled the chain to consign the Jebsen case to the Berlin sewers, all he was doing was destroying the documents on the case. What he could not get rid of was the impression left on him by his last visit to the Lisbon Abwehr station in the company of Admiral Canaris. This deeply shocked the honest Abwehr officer who had fought against Hitler and who was imprisoned as one of the conspirators in the abortive coup of 20 July 1944: 'When I returned to Berlin after my visit to Lisbon it was with a sense of outrage. The people down there – obviously concerned only with their own affairs – were living in the lap of luxury. When I think what our unfortunate soldiers had to put up with at the front, I am still disgusted!'

While Johnny Jebsen was in prison the Allied Operation Overlord commenced. The mightiest invasion armada in history landed with relatively little incident. This success was achieved despite – or perhaps because of – the fact that Tricycle's intelligence commando act, on which so many hopes had been pinned, (owing to the abduction of Johnny Jebsen, alias Artist) developed in a way which had not been anticipated by the deception strategists in London. After the landings in Northern France, the game against the Germans had been won.

On 6 June 1944 the British and Americans began their eastward thrust, while simultaneously the Soviets began to move in the opposite direction. Their two front lines were to meet among the ruins of Germany, on the banks of the Elbe. In the face of this threat the intelligence services both in the western and in the eastern camp began to prepare for a new and bitter battle long before that dreaded confrontation took place on the day of their final victory, on 8 May 1945.

On the British side this battle was opened by Kim Philby, who early in 1944 had taken his place in an office on the sixth floor of the Secret Intelligence Service Headquarters building opposite St James's Park underground station. There he was to run the new Russian station and build up a network of agents in Eastern Europe to work against the Soviet Union.

In tackling this complicated task Philby would perhaps have been glad of the assistance of the tried and tested collaborator from the Balkans and fellow Ostro-tracker Dusko Popov. But while Philby started weaving his invisible network in the East, Colonel Popov, 'the most successful spy of World War Two', claims to have given up his warlike activities and to have concentrated chiefly on trying to liberate his friend Johnny Jebsen from the clutches of the Gestapo.

When these efforts had failed, and after he had run Jebsen's supposed murderer to ground, he retired to the country of his former enemies. To earn a living he started up an export-import firm in Krefeld, the first to engage in east-west trading after the war. He did not strain his imagination to think of a name for the company: it traded under the name of 'Tarlair' which, so Popov said, was purely by coincidence the same as that used by the Secret Service as cover for its wartime operations against Germany.

In the business revival during the turbulent years after Germany's collapse it was often shown how valuable genuine friendships can be. In this respect, Popov told me, the old Lisbon hands did a lot to help one another back into the saddle. There was only one of them for whom there could be no help: Johnny Jebsen had disappeared without trace. The only eye-witness, who claimed also to have been the last man to have seen Johnny Jebsen in Oranienburg concentration camp, accompanied by an ss guard, was Jebsen's old friend Abwehr Hauptmann Kurrer, who wrote to me from Brazil: 'All I could take away with me was the shattering impression of having seen, probably for the last time, a man about to die.'

As Kurrer was also unable to confirm Jebsen's death I managed to get hold of the address of the man who had been responsible for the Abwehr finances, Oberstintendant Dr Martin Toeppen. I was looking forward to seeing what he could tell me about the shady currency transactions to and from Lisbon in those days. What I learned from my telephone conversation were fragments which, if it were possible to complete them and fit them together, would probably throw some light on one of the darkest chapters in the history of the Abwehr. The telephone was answered by Frau Ilse Toeppen, one of the first to suffer in the events of thirty years ago, which she cannot fathom to this day:

My husband completely disappeared in 1945. I have since had him declared presumed dead, so now I get a pension, but it is not very much. Before my husband disappeared at the end of the war he was locked up in the Lehrterstrasse. I had been evacuated to Misdroy with the children at the time and discovered practically nothing about the reasons for his arrest. Only once, when I was out for a walk in the woods with the children, some men came and searched the little flat we were living in. They were looking for a valuable Rubens painting. The officers had already found a number of old masters in our flat in Berlin, including an original painting by Caspar David Friedrich. But the pictures all belonged to Dr Ivo Popov, who often came to Berlin and looked us up . . .

I asked after the other acquaintances who might have visited the Toeppens:

There was a Herr Jebsen. He must have been what they called an agent. All I know about Herr Jebsen is that he also disappeared mysteriously . . . When meeting a lady he always kissed her hand. He was a handsome man, but as slippery as an eel. Jebsen was also in touch with Canaris and he was also connected with a man called Ruscheweih, an arms-dealer. But owing to the children I never bothered about these things, and when my husband came home with Jebsen or Popov I always had to leave the room, so I never did find out what they talked about . . . Herr Popov at any rate was a nice man. He was the godfather of our youngest son Michael, who was born in 1943. Popov promised that he would leave part of his estate in Yugoslavia to his godson Michael.

The solution of the riddle of the old masters, the Rubens and the Caspar David Friedrich and others, would fill a book on its own. And a search for the currency boss of the Abwehr, Martin Toeppen, or for Heinz Moldenhauer, son of the Reich minister of finance in the Weimar Republic, who had also mysteriously disappeared, might result in yet another wheel on my car working loose – who knows?

During my search for Johnny Jebsen, I recently had a curious experience in the bar of the Sporthotel in Igls, the same bar where I had a drink on 5 November 1969, ten minutes before my car accident in the Sill Gorge. I knew that the wife of the Tyrolean hotel proprietor, Didi Beck, was a member of the Howaldt family, founders of the famous shipyards in Hamburg and Kiel. Surely she must have known Johnny Jebsen when she was living in Kiel. I described him briefly: 'Reddish fair hair, well dressed in an English fashion, comes from Apenrade and is also said to have been an import-exporter in Hamburg.'

When I had finished my description of Johnny Jebsen, her eyes twinkled with amusement. 'That can only be Joko,' she laughed. 'Joko Jebsen, a respectable man. He was in Hamburg during the war and perhaps in Berlin as well. If I am not mistaken he is still alive.'

After my conversation with Didi Beck I simply had to ring the owner of the Jebsen shipping firm and ask him whether he was the man who had been abducted from Lisbon during the war, and what his connection was with Wulf Dietrich Schmidt.

Herr Jebsen, it appeared, had been expecting my call for some time. He had been told – though I do not know by whom – about my researches into the whereabouts of his namesake. So he surprised me when he got straight to the point.

'You obviously want to know about the man called Johnny Jebsen ...'

I only answered 'Yes' and there was no need for any further questioning on my part.

'Let me say at once that the man you are looking for is no relation of ours. Nor did he ever have anything to do with our firm – except insofar as he always mentioned our name when he got into hot water or was involved in some shady deal.'

The owner of the shipping firm suggested that I should make inquiries in Flensburg about Jebsen:

'There you will discover that Johnny was not the son of a shipowner, but of a well-known faith healer who lived at Nerongsallee No 5 ... You will find a lot of people in Flensburg who knew Johnny Jebsen very well and who will confirm that he was a very clever lad. Anyway a lot of very well-known people knew him.'

'But surely,' I interrupted him, 'these acquaintances must have known who they were dealing with – especially if they were Johnny's friends?'

Hans Jakob Jebsen laughed out loud. He still seemed to be amused by the ingenious confidence trickster: 'In that case all his friends must have fallen for his stories.'

At the end of our conversation I told him how I had started my researches in the very place he was speaking from, Apenrade: '. . . Then there was a man from Apenrade who worked for the German Secret Service. He was very young at the time and one night in 1940 he parachuted into England as one of the advance guard for the German invasion forces who were to follow a few weeks later. The famous Operation Sealion was called off, however, and I have been told that the man went into hiding somewhere in London. In this manner he remained of necessity the only Abwehr spy who went on transmitting important reports to Germany right through to the end of the war.'

Herr Jebsen listened to me attentively. Then he asked whether I had ever found the man.

'Is he still alive?'

'Yes,' I replied, 'I found him in London.'

At this Herr Jebsen laughed again and told me, to my great surprise, that the father of the spy I had sought so long, and whose name I had intentionally refrained from mentioning, had once been on the board of his firm.

'The name of the spy is Wulf Dietrich Schmidt,' he said with the self-assurance of an official certifying a document. 'Looking out of the window I can see the old house where the Schmidt family lived. My brother Michael, who is our representative in Hong Kong, went to school with Wulf Dietrich Schmidt.'

I should perhaps mention that towards the end of the Sixties a British journalist, Patrick Brangwyn, also sensed that there must be a remarkable story behind Mr Harry Johnson, a sensational story in fact, possibly one of historic significance. To avoid getting into trouble with the laws of his own country he first started, carefully and perfectly legitimately, to search the archives of the local newspaper for some leads that might throw some light on Mr Johnson's background, if only in general terms. Patrick Brangwyn did not think there should be any difficulty in getting hold of some facts. He had already discovered that Johnson was a journalist like himself, that on 26 April 1946 he had become engaged to a Hertfordshire girl, and that the marriage between the Englishwoman and the German spy had produced a little girl.

The Fleet Street researcher had also found out that Johnson was known to be one of the functionaries of his local football club, so he should have no difficulty in finding a photograph of the man he was looking for in the sports pages of the local paper. In this unobtrusive way Brangwyn hoped to be able to approach Mr Johnson, and he began his search through the dusty copies of the 1946–9 editions of the paper. But his search led to a curious discovery that had unfortunate results and persuaded Brangwyn to stop taking an interest in Mr Johnson then and there. He told me:

First I observed that two photographs had been cut out of the editions of the paper for 28 November 1947 and 24 September 1948. There were just two holes about six by eight inches. Those were the only references to Harry Johnson. I imagine that they had been removed on purpose. While I was collecting material for my Johnson story somebody broke into my flat in Notting Hill Gate. Curiously enough, nothing was stolen. My unwanted visitors had only gone through all my drawers and had mixed up all my journalist background materials. After that I stopped taking an interest in Harry Johnson's past.

Len Adams was the next English journalist who wanted to get to grips with the Harry Johnson story. On 24 September 1971 the Fleet Street reporter, who had got to hear of my researches, followed the ex-spy to a remote valley in the Scottish Highlands. There he learned that Johnson had gone out for the day with some friends and would not be back until the evening. The journalist waited near the blue Mini parked in front of the cottage belonging to the key secret agent of World War Two.

When Mr Johnson reappeared, accompanied by some friends, Len Adams introduced himself and handed him a visiting card on which he had made a note of the subject he wanted to discuss. A short time later, when the ex-spy and the reporter had retired to a quiet corner of the house, Johnson rolled a cigarette and asked him how he had been able to find him there, in one of the loneliest spots in Scotland. He also wanted to know the reason for the unexpected visit. Adams said: 'I imagine this is not the first time you have been interviewed by journalists?'

The remark reminded Johnson of my visit ten years earlier, in the company of the chief editor of a well-known German periodical. The ex-spy took off his glasses for a moment and his eyelids narrowed as if he had been suddenly blinded.

'That matter was settled at the time,' he said. 'That German journalist was forbidden to publish my story ... What those two men did not realize then was that our conversation was recorded on tape. Anything they published and which was not true could have been refuted by me ...

They offered me twenty thousand pounds at the time.' Mr Johnson laughed. 'The story I could tell would certainly be sensational. But I cannot talk about it. It would affect too many people in high positions.'

Harry Johnson, sitting facing Len Adams, in elegant tweed jacket and neatly pressed trousers, could not be persuaded to say any more. He only hinted once at the historic significance of his story when he said: 'What I did saved millions of lives. I saved them from death.'

That was all the sensation that my British colleague brought back from his journey to the Highlands. Mr Johnson had told him no more. Now Len Adams also had the first lead that would enable him to unravel the story it had taken me fifteen years to investigate.

Remembering the words that Mr Johnson had spoken as they said goodbye at the door of the cottage – 'I need only ring a certain number and the most senior departments would act on my behalf' – I am certain that Len Adams has also given up the attempt to pry into his past.

Before the British reporter returned to London Johnson had told him another reason why his past must still remain a mystery: half whispering, he said to Adams, who was sitting in the driver's seat with the side window down: 'It is because of the Russians. There is too much at stake, even now.'

The man whom Canaris called 3725 and whom the British called Tate stood still for a moment in the darkness. Then he went back into the house, back to his friends who had been his enemies when he dropped by parachute to prepare for the invasion of England in the distant past of 1940.

Bibliography

Andrews, Allen, *Proud Fortress*, London, 1956.

Brown, Anthony Cave, *Bodyguard of Lies*, New York, 1975.

Burdick, Charles B., *Germany's Military Strategy and Spain in World War II*, New York, 1968.

Churchill, Winston S., *The Second World War*, London, 1948–54.

Colvin, Ian, *Chief of Intelligence*, London, 1951.

Cookridge, E. H., *Inside S.O.E.*, London, 1966.

Delmer, Sefton, *Geisterarmee*, Munich-Vienna-Zurich, 1972

Donaldson, Frances, *Edward VIII*, London, 1974.

Dulles, Allen, *The Craft of Intelligence*, London, 1963.

Farago, Ladislas, *The Game of the Foxes*, London, 1972.

Hyde, H. Montgomery, *The Quiet Canadian*, London, 1962.

Ingersoll, Ralph, *Top Secret*, London, 1946.

Irving, David, *The Mare's Nest*, London, 1964.

Irving, David, *Hitler und seine Feldherren*, Berlin, 1975.

Look, Editors of, *The Story of the FBI*, New York, 1947.

Lovell, Stanley P., *Of Spies and Stratagems*, Englewood Cliffs, N. Y., 1963.

Mader, Julius, *Hitlers Spionagegenerale sagen aus*, Berlin, 1970.

Masterman, J. C., *The Double-Cross System in the War of 1939–45*, London, 1972.

Montagu, Ewen, *The Man Who Never Was*, London, 1953.

Muggeridge, Malcolm, *The Infernal Grove*, Glasgow, 1973.

Newman, Bernard, *The World of Espionage*, London, 1962.

Page, B., with D. Leitch and P. Knightly, *Philby*, London, 1968.

Pawle, Gerald, *The Secret War 1939–45*, London, 1956

Peis, Günter, *Robby gegen alle*, Hamburg, 1958.

— *The Man Who Started the War*, London, 1960.

— *Der Leutnant, der zu früh marschierte*, Hamburg, 1964.

Perrault, Gilles, *The Secrets of D-Day*, London, 1965.

Popov, Dusko, *Spy/Counterspy*, London, 1974.

Ritter, Nikolaus, *Deckname Dr. Rantzau*, Hamburg, 1972.

Robertson, Terence, *Dieppe – The Shame and the Glory*, London, 1963.
Ryan, Cornelius, *The Longest Day*, London, 1960.
Schellenberg, Walter, *The Schellenberg Memoirs*, London, 1956.
Schreieder, Josef, *Das war das Englandspiel*, Munich, 1950.
Stephan, Enno, *Spies in Ireland*, 1963.
Studnitz, Hans-Georg von, *While Berlin Burns*, London, 1964.
Thorwald, J., with Günter Peis, *Der Fall Pastorius*, Stuttgart, 1953.
— *Die unsichtbare Front*, Hamburg, 1953.
Wighton, C., with Günter Peis, *Hitler's Spies and Saboteurs*, New York, 1958.
— *They Spied on England*, London, 1958.
Wilmot, Chester, *The Struggle for Europe*, London, 1952.

Index